MODERN BLACK AMERICAN POETS AND DRAMATISTS

Writers of English: Lives and Works

MODERN BLACK AMERICAN POETS AND DRAMATISTS

Edited and with an Introduction by

Harold Bloom

CHELSEA HOUSE PUBLISHERS

New York   Philadelphia

Jacket illustration: Jacob Lawrence, *The Library* (1960) (courtesy of the National Museum of Art, Washington, D.C./Art Resource).

CHELSEA HOUSE PUBLISHERS

Editorial Director Richard Rennert
Executive Managing Editor Karyn Gullen Browne
Picture Editor Adrian G. Allen
Copy Chief Robin James
Art Director Robert Mitchell
Manufacturing Director Gerald Levine
Assistant Art Director Joan Ferrigno

Writers of English: Lives and Works

Senior Editor S. T. Joshi
Senior Designer Rae Grant

3 4633 00042 1998

Staff for MODERN BLACK AMERICAN POETS AND DRAMATISTS

Assistant Editor Mary Sisson
Research Robert Green
Picture Researcher Pat Burns

First Printing

1 3 5 7 9 8 6 4 2

Library of Congress Cataloging-in-Publication Data

Modern Black American poets and dramatists / edited and with an introduction by Harold Bloom.
      p.   cm.—(Writers of English)
   Includes bibliographical references. (p.).
   ISBN 0-7910-2221-8.—ISBN 0-7910-2246-3 (pbk.)
  1. American literature—Afro-American authors—History and criticism. 2. American literature—Afro-American authors—Bio-bibliography. 3. Afro-Americans in literature. I. Bloom, Harold. II. Series.
PS153.N5M63 1994
810.9′896073—dc20   94-5902
[B]   CIP

▣ Contents

◈ User's Guide

THIS VOLUME PROVIDES biographical, critical, and bibliographical information on the twelve most significant modern black American poets and dramatists. Each chapter consists of three parts: a biography of the author; a selection of brief critical extracts about the author; and a bibliography of the author's published books.

The biography supplies a detailed outline of the important events in the author's life, including his or her major writings. The critical extracts are taken from a wide array of books and periodicals, from the author's lifetime to the present, and range in content from biographical to critical to historical. The extracts are arranged in chronological order by date of writing or publication, and a full bibliographical citation is provided at the end of each extract. Editorial additions or deletions are indicated within carets.

The author bibliographies list every separate publication—including books, pamphlets, broadsides, collaborations, and works edited or translated by the author—for works published in the author's lifetime; selected important posthumous publications are also listed. Titles are those of the first edition; variant titles are supplied within carets. In selected instances dates of revised editions are given where these are significant. Pseudonymous works are listed, but not the pseudonyms under which these works were published. Periodicals edited by the author are listed only when the author has written most or all of the contents. Titles enclosed in square brackets are of doubtful authenticity. All works by the author, whether in English or in other languages, have been listed; English translations of foreign-language works are not listed unless the author has done the translation.

The Life of the Author

Harold Bloom

NIETZSCHE, WITH EXULTANT ANGUISH, famously proclaimed that God was dead. Whatever the consequences of this for the ethical life, its ultimate literary effect certainly would have surprised the author Nietzsche. His French disciples, Foucault most prominent among them, developed the Nietzschean proclamation into the dogma that all authors, God included, were dead. The death of the author, which is no more than a Parisian trope, another metaphor for fashion's setting of skirt-lengths, is now accepted as literal truth by most of our current apostles of what should be called French Nietzsche, to distinguish it from the merely original Nietzsche. We also have French Freud or Lacan, which has little to do with the actual thought of Sigmund Freud, and even French Joyce, which interprets *Finnegans Wake* as the major work of Jacques Derrida. But all this is as nothing compared to the final triumph of the doctrine of the death of the author: French Shakespeare. That delicious absurdity is given us by the New Historicism, which blends Foucault and California fruit juice to give us the Word that Renaissance "social energies," and not William Shakespeare, composed *Hamlet* and *King Lear*. It seems a proper moment to murmur "enough" and to return to a study of the life of the author.

Sometimes it troubles me that there are so few masterpieces in the vast ocean of literary biography that stretches between James Boswell's great *Life* of Dr. Samuel Johnson and the late Richard Ellmann's wonderful *Oscar Wilde*. Literary biography is a crucial genre, and clearly a difficult one in which to excel. The actual nature of the lives of the poets seems to have little effect upon the quality of their biographies. Everything happened to Lord Byron and nothing at all to Wallace Stevens, and yet their biographers seem equally daunted by them. But even inadequate biographies of strong writers, or of weak ones, are of immense use. I have never read a literary biography from which I have not profited, a statement I cannot make about any other genre whatsoever. And when it comes to figures who are central to us—Dante, Shakespeare, Cervantes, Montaigne, Goethe, Whitman, Tolstoi, Freud, Joyce, Kafka among them—we reach out eagerly for every scrap that the biographers have gleaned. Concerning Dante and Shakespeare we know much too little, yet when we come to Goethe and Freud, where we seem to know more than everything, we still want to know more. The death of the author, despite our current resentniks, clearly was only a momentary fad. Something vital in every authentic lover of literature responds to Emerson's battle-cry sentence: "There is no history, only biography." Beyond that there is a deeper truth, difficult to come at and requiring a lifetime to understand, which is that there is no literature, only autobiography, however mediated, however veiled, however transformed. The events of Shakespeare's life included the composition of *Hamlet,* and that act of writing was itself a crucial act of living, though we do not yet know altogether how to read so doubled an act. When an author takes up a more overtly autobiographical stance, as so many do in their youth, again we still do not know precisely how to accommodate the vexed relation between life and work. T. S. Eliot, meditating upon James Joyce, made a classic statement as to such accommodation:

> We want to know who are the originals of his characters, and what were
> the origins of his episodes, so that we may unravel the web of memory
> and invention and discover how far and in what ways the crude material
> has been transformed.

When a writer is not even covertly autobiographical, the web of memory and invention is still there, but so subtly woven that we may never unravel it. And yet we want deeply never to stop trying, and not merely because we are curious, but because each of us is caught in her own network of memory and invention. We do not always recall our inventions, and long before we age we cease to be certain of the extent to which we have invented our memories. Perhaps one motive for reading is our need to unravel our own webs. If our masters could make, from their lives, what we read, then we can be moved by them to ask: What have we made or lived in relation to what we have read? The answers may be sad, or confused, but the question is likely, implicitly, to go on being asked as long as we read. In Freudian terms, we are asking: What is it that we have repressed? What have we forgotten, unconsciously but purposively: What is it that we flee? Art, literature necessarily included, is regression in the service of the ego, according to a famous Freudian formula. I doubt the Freudian wisdom here, but indubitably it is profoundly suggestive. When we read, something in us keeps asking the equivalent of the Freudian questions: From what or whom is the author in flight, and to what earlier stages in her life is she returning, and why?

Reading, whether as an art or a pastime, has been damaged by the visual media, television in particular, and might be in some danger of extinction in the age of the computer, except that the psychic need for it continues to endure, presumably because it alone can assuage a central loneliness in elitist society. Despite all sophisticated or resentful denials, the reading of imaginative literature remains a quest to overcome the isolation of the individual consciousness. We can read for information, or entertainment, or for love of the language, but in the end we seek, in the author, the person whom we have not found, whether in ourselves or in others. In that quest, there always are elements at once aggressive and defensive, so that reading, even in childhood, is rarely free of hidden anxieties. And yet it remains one of the few activities not contaminated by an entropy of spirit. We read in hope, because we lack companionship, and the author can become the object of the most idealistic elements in our search for the wit and inventiveness we so desperately require. We read biography, not as a supplement to reading the author, but as a second, fresh attempt to understand what always seems to evade us in the work, our drive towards a kind of identity with the author.

This will-to-identity, though recently much deprecated, is a prime basis for the experience of sublimity in reading. *Hamlet* retains its unique position in the Western canon not because most readers and playgoers identify themselves with the prince, who clearly is beyond them, but rather because they find themselves again in the power of the language that represents him with such immediacy and force. Yet we know that neither language nor social energy created Hamlet. Our curiosity about Shakespeare is endless, and never will be appeased. That curiosity itself is a value, and cannot be separated from the value of *Hamlet* the tragedy, or Hamlet the literary character. It provokes us that Shakespeare the man seems so unknowable, at once everyone and no one as Borges shrewdly observes. Critics keep telling us otherwise, yet something valid in us keeps believing that we would know Hamlet better if Shakespeare's life were as fully known as the lives of Goethe and Freud, Byron and Oscar Wilde, or best of all, Dr. Samuel Johnson. Shakespeare never will have his Boswell, and Dante never will have his Richard Ellmann. How much one would give for a detailed and candid *Life of Dante* by Petrarch, or an outspoken memoir of Shakespeare by Ben Jonson! Or, in the age just past, how superb would be rival studies of one another by Hemingway and Scott Fitzgerald! But the list is endless: think of *Oscar Wilde* by Lord Alfred Douglas, or a joint biography of Shelley by Mary Godwin, Emilia Viviani, and Jane Williams. More than our insatiable desire for scandal would be satisfied. The literary rivals and the lovers of the great writers possessed perspectives we will never enjoy, and without those perspectives we dwell in some poverty in regard to the writers with whom we ourselves never can be done.

There is a sense in which imaginative literature *is* perspectivism, so that the reader is likely to be overwhelmed by the work's difficulty unless its multiple perspectives are mastered. Literary biography matters most because it is a storehouse of perspectives, frequently far surpassing any that are grasped by the particular biographer. There are relations between authors' lives and their works of kinds we have yet to discover, because our analytical instruments are not yet advanced enough to perform the necessary labor. Perhaps a novel, poem, or play is not so much a regression in the service of the ego, as it is an amalgam of *all* the Freudian mechanisms of defense, all working together for the apotheosis of the ego. Freud valued art highly, but thought that the aesthetic enterprise was no rival for psychoanalysis, unlike religion and philosophy. Clearly Freud was mistaken; his own anxieties about his indebtedness to Shakespeare helped produce the weirdness of his joining in the lunacy that argued for the Earl of Oxford as the author of Shakespeare's plays. It was Shakespeare, and not "the poets," who was there before Freud arrived at his depth psychology, and it is Shakespeare who is there still, well out ahead of psychoanalysis. We see what Freud would not see, that psychoanalysis is Shakespeare prosified and systematized. Freud is part of literature, not of "science," and the biography of Freud has the same relations to psychoanalysis as the biography of Shakespeare has to *Hamlet* and *King Lear*, if only we knew more of the life of Shakespeare.

Western literature, particularly since Shakespeare, is marked by the representation of internalized change in its characters. A literature of the ever-growing inner self is in itself a large form of biography, even though this is the biography of imaginary beings, from Hamlet to the sometimes nameless protagonists of Kafka and Beckett. Skeptics might want to argue that all literary biography concerns imaginary beings, since authors make themselves up, and every biographer gives us a creation curiously different from the same author as seen by the writer of a rival *Life*. Boswell's Johnson is not quite anyone else's Johnson, though it is now very difficult for us to disentangle the great Doctor from his gifted Scottish friend and follower. The life of the author is not merely a metaphor or a fiction, as is "the Death of the Author," but it always does contain metaphorical or fictive elements. Those elements are a part of the value of literary biography, but not the largest or the crucial part, which is the separation of the mask from the man or woman who hid behind it. James Joyce and Samuel Beckett, master and sometime disciple, were both of them enigmatic personalities, and their biographers have not, as yet, fully expounded the mystery of these contrasting natures. Beckett seems very nearly to have been a secular saint: personally disinterested, heroic in the French Resistance, as humane a person ever to have composed major fictions and dramas. Joyce, self-obsessed even as Beckett was preternaturally selfless, was the Milton of the twentieth century. Beckett was perhaps the least egoistic post-Joycean, post-Proustian, post-Kafkan of writers. Does that illuminate the problematical nature of his work, or does it simply constitute another problem? Whatever the cause, the question matters. The only death of the author that is other than literal, and that matters, is the fate only of weak writers. The strong, who become canonical, never die, which is what the canon truly is about. To be read forever is the Life of the Author.

✦ Introduction

IT IS A MELANCHOLY IRONY that the greatest African-American poet is one of the least read, because of the cognitive and imaginative difficulty that is essential to his best work. Jay Wright is a culmination of many strains in poetic tradition: Dogon mythology, Southwestern American and Mexican legend, Hölderlin, T. S. Eliot, Hart Crane, Robert Hayden, Paul Celan, amidst much else. He is an immensely learned poet, both in African culture and in European literature and philosophy. And yet he is frequently direct and passionate, the master of an invocatory strain that partly derives from Crane's *The Bridge* and Hayden's "Middle Passage." Wright's work is heroic in scope and intensity, so that in this brief introduction I will limit myself to the group of five grand odes that conclude *Elaine's Book* (1988), my favorite among his volumes to date. Taking their starting points from Hölderlin, Celan, and Aztec poetry, these odes establish themselves as permanent achievements in several traditions, yet return always to "an Ethiopian will that contends / with light's flaring cloth / in a logic that clothes the self with another self."

The sequence begins with "The Anatomy of Resonance," a series of variations upon a great metaphor of Hölderlin's: "And the bird of the night whirs / Down, so close that you shield your eyes." Wright's emphasis is upon that shielding away from poetic vision: "and the way we have come to terms / with our failure / to see anything but the blue point of desire / that leads us home." This subtle evasion is surmounted by "Journey to the Place of Ghosts," where a descent to the dead involves a rekindling of the soul, at considerable psychic expense. "Saltos" follows, in a majestic recuperation of the poetic self, a movement that is enhanced in "The Power of Reeds," an ode of "retrieved connections," the most crucial coming when: "Out of Africa, / the song's loom draws the maiden / into a new legend." All this prepares for the transcendent fifth ode, "Desire's Persistence," one of the finest contemporary American poems. The title itself derives from Aztec poetry, as does the marvelous line that organizes the ode: "I lift the red flower of winter into the wind." Following a structural pattern that he established in "The Anatomy of Resonance," Wright divides his poem into an invocation and six sections, each of which takes a work of the epigraph as title: *I, Lift, Red, Flower, Winter, Wind*. The lyric speaker (rather, a chanter) appears to be Desire itself, in the ambivalent guise

xi

of "a fishing-net, a maze, / 'a deadly wealth of robe,' " that last presumably an allusion to the shirt of Nessus that burned up Heracles. As the ode proceeds, this dangerous desire, "power's form in motion," is transfigured from a destructive force to a transcending charisma:

> I am the arcane body,
> raised at the ninth hour,
> to be welcomed by the moonlight
>   of such spirited air.
> I am the Dane of degrees
> who realizes how the spirit grows
>   even as it descends

At once astral body and a resurrected Hamlet, the chanter then undergoes a shamanistic metamorphosis, becoming a woman, turned south toward the fire of desire's persistence. An "aroma of power," different in kind from the deathly maze of the earlier, male vision, concludes the ode, which appears to carry an implicit prophecy related to some crucial enigmas of the African-American self, poised perpetually in its intricate cross-cultural predicaments, never more eloquently expressed than in the poetry of Jay Wright.

—H. B.

Maya Angelou
b. 1928

MAYA ANGELOU was born Marguerite Johnson in St. Louis, Missouri, on April 4, 1928. Her life has been both remarkably varied and occasionally grim (she was raped at the age of eight by her mother's boyfriend), and she has won greater critical acclaim for her several autobiographical volumes than for her poetry and drama. She attended public schools in Arkansas and California, studied music privately, and studied dance with Martha Graham. In 1954–55 she was a member of the cast of *Porgy and Bess*, which went on a twenty-two-nation world tour sponsored by the U.S. Department of State. Some of her songs were recorded on the album *Miss Calypso* (1957). Later she acted in several off-Broadway plays, including one, the musical *Cabaret for Freedom* (1960), that she wrote with Godfrey Cambridge.

In addition to these artistic pursuits, Angelou held a variety of odd jobs in her late teens and early twenties, including streetcar conductor, Creole cook, nightclub waitress, prostitute, and madam. She has been married twice: first, around 1950, to a white man, Tosh Angelos (whose surname she adapted when she became a dancer), and then, from 1973 to 1981, to Paul Du Feu. She bore a son, Guy, at the age of sixteen.

When she was thirty Angelou moved to Brooklyn. There she met John Oliver Killens, James Baldwin, and other writers who encouraged her to write. While practicing her craft, however, she became involved in the civil rights movement. She met Martin Luther King, Jr., was appointed the northern coordinator of the Southern Christian Leadership Conference, and organized demonstrations at the United Nations. She fell in love with the South African freedom fighter Vusumzi Make, and they left for Egypt, where in 1961–62 Angelou worked as associate editor of the *Arab Observer*, an English-language newspaper in Cairo. She broke up with Make when he criticized her independence and lack of subservience to him.

In 1963 Angelou went to Ghana to be assistant administrator of the School of Music and Drama at the University of Ghana's Institute of African Studies. In the three years she was there she acted in several additional

1

plays, served as feature editor of the *African Review*, and was a contributor to the Ghanaian Broadcasting Corporation. Returning to the United States, she was a lecturer at the University of California at Los Angeles and has subsequently been a visiting professor or writer in residence at several other universities.

Angelou's first published book was *I Know Why the Caged Bird Sings* (1969), an autobiography of the first sixteen years of her life; a tremendous critical and popular success, it was nominated for a National Book Award and was later adapted for television. Two more autobiographical volumes appeared in the 1970s, *Gather Together in My Name* (1974) and *Singin' and Swingin' and Gettin' Merry Like Christmas* (1976), along with three volumes of poetry: *Just Give Me a Cool Drink of Water 'Fore I Diiie* (1971), *Oh Pray My Wings Are Gonna Fit Me Well* (1975), and *And Still I Rise* (1978). She wrote several more dramas, including the unpublished *And Still I Rise!*, a medley of black poetry and music that was successfully staged in 1976; two screenplays (directing one of them and writing the musical scores for both); and several television plays, including a series of ten one-hour programs entitled *Blacks, Blues, Black*. She also continued to pursue her acting career and was nominated for a Tony Award in 1973 for her Broadway debut, *Look Away*. She was appointed a member of the American Revolution Bicentennial Council by President Gerald R. Ford in 1975.

In the last fifteen years Angelou has solidified her reputation with two more autobiographies, *The Heart of a Woman* (1981) and *All God's Children Need Traveling Shoes* (1986), along with two more volumes of poetry, *Shaker, Why Don't You Sing?* (1983) and *I Shall Not Be Moved* (1990). The peak of her fame was perhaps achieved when in 1993 she composed a poem, "On the Pulse of Morning," for the inauguration of President Bill Clinton. Angelou's latest prose work, *Wouldn't Take Nothing for My Journey Now*, a collection of essays and sketches, also appeared that year and, like most of its predecessors, was a best-seller.

Maya Angelou, who has received honorary degrees from Smith College, Mills College, and Lawrence University, currently resides in Sonoma, California.

◈ *Critical Extracts*

CHAD WALSH   Maya Angelou has had a versatile career—at various times an actor in *Porgy and Bess*, dance teacher in Rome and Tel Aviv, northern coordinator for the Southern Christian Leadership Conference—and at all times, a poet whose work is a moving blend of lyricism and harsh social observation.

Just Give Me a Cool Drink of Water 'Fore I Diiie is divided into two parts. The first is the more personal and tender, such as "To a Man"—

> My name is
> Black Golden Amber
> Changing.
> Warm mouths of Brandy Fine
> Cautious sunlight on patterned rug
> Coughing laughter, rocked on a whorl of French tobacco

Many of these poems have been set to music. The second part, "Just Before the World Ends," has more bite—the anguished and often sardonic expression of a black in a white-dominated world. "Riot: 60's" presents an angle of vision not shared by most suburbanites:

> Lightning: a hundred Watts
> Detroit, Newark and New York
> Screeching nerves, exploding minds
> lives tied to
> a policeman's whistle
> a welfare worker's doorbell
> finger.

Chad Walsh, "A Fact about Recent Poetry: Women First," *Washington Post Book World*, 9 April 1972, p. 12

UNSIGNED   The 36 poems in this book ⟨*Oh Pray My Wings Are Gonna Fit Me Well*⟩ are grouped, arbitrarily it seems, into five parts, the first four of which contain pieces that are all surface. The themes, chiefly lost or wronged love or frustrated desire, and their treatments are akin to country-western music. It is in the treatment that the superficiality is most obvious: motives not explored, little depth or interpretation of feelings, no sense of time or change, no allusion or any rich ambiguity, little melody.

Some are merely cute. Most could be as effectively stated in declarative sentences. A few poems capture some sense of loneliness, but without conveying any insight or universal values. The twelve poems in part five are generally better, containing some developed images, a degree of music, while also finding deeper meanings in man's actions or inactions.

> Unsigned, "Notes on Current Books," *Virginia Quarterly Review* 52, No. 3 (Summer 1976): 82

SANDRA M. GILBERT   I can't help feeling that Maya Angelou's career has suffered from the interest her publishers have in mythologizing her. *Oh Pray My Wings Are Gonna Fit Me Well* is such a painfully untalented collection of poems that I can't think of any reason, other than the Maya Myth, for it to be in print: it's impossible, indeed, to separate the book's flap copy, with its glossy celebration of "Maya Angelou . . . one of the world's most exciting women . . . Maya, the eternal female" from the book itself. All this is especially depressing because Angelou, "eternal female" or not, is a stunningly talented prose writer, whose marvelous *I Know Why the Caged Bird Sings* has quite properly become a contemporary classic. Why should it be necessary, then, for her to represent herself publicly as the author of such an embarrassing tangle as

> I'd touched your features inchly
>   heard love and dared the cost.
> The scented spiel reeled me unreal
>   and found my senses lost.

And why, instead of encouraging Angelou, didn't some friendly editor Block (as *The New Yorker* would say) the following Metaphor:

> A day
> drunk with the nectar of
> nowness
> weaves its way between
> the years
> to find itself at the flophouse
> of night. . . .

To be fair, not all the verse in *Oh Pray . . .* is quite as bad as these two examples. A few of the colloquial pieces—"Pickin Em Up and Layin Em Down" or "Come. And Be My Baby"—have the slangy, unpretentious vitality of good ballads. "The Pusher" ("He bad / O he bad"), with its echoes of Brooks's "We real cool", achieves genuine scariness. And "John J." might be a portrait in verse of Bailey, the handsome brother Angelou renders so beautifully in *I Know Why*. . . . But these are only four or five poems out of the thirty-six in this collection. And most of the others, when they're not awkward or stilted, are simply corny. The writer whose unsentimental wit and passionate accuracy gave us such a fresh account of growing up black and female really doesn't need to publish "No one knows / my lonely heart / when we're apart" or "No lady cookinger than my Mommy / smell that pie / see I don't lie / No lady cookinger than my Mommy" (from "Little Girl Speakings"). Angelou can hardly be accused of self-parody: for one thing, most of the poetry here is too unself-conscious, too thoughtless, to be in any sense parodic. But, for whatever reason, the wings of song certainly don't seem to fit her very well right now.

Sandra M. Gilbert, "A Platoon of Poets," *Poetry* 128, No. 5 (August 1976): 296–97

EUGENE REDMOND   A multi-tiered ballet-symphony conceived and directed by writer-director Maya Angelou, *And Still I Rise!* was exuberantly received by full houses during four August weekends at the Oakland Ensemble Theatre. ⟨. . .⟩

Black-based, with dramatic tentacles and sub-themes that are global (indeed, galaxial!), *And Still I Rise!* is an admirable adaptation of subtle, poignant and humorous verse-songs from a rich cross-spread of Afro-American poets. Household names such as Paul Laurence Dunbar, Gwendolyn Brooks, Langston Hughes and Nikki Giovanni, are mixed with an ample sprinkling of lesser known bards—Frank Horne, Richard A. Long, Joyce Carol Thomas and Ray Garfiend Dandridge. Spices from the "traditional" song-book (those "black and unknown bards") and Miss Angelou's own volumes make up the remainder of this tasty drama. These items form a histrionic bridge between Africa and the New World via six sub-themes (Childhood, Youth, Love, Work, Religion, and The Old Souls) that evoke nostalgia, fear, humor and pride. ⟨. . .⟩

As a dramatic exploration of black survival and endurance, *And Still I Rise!* is coincidentally an enormous praise-song, a totemic tribute to those gone souls and a challenge to those living and unborn. Maya Angelou has brought years of formidable experience, research and travel to bear on her serious interest in the black cultural legacy. *And Still I Rise!* congeals a substantial body of her own portfolio as writer-actress-dancer-singer-director into relentless drama. And we are all the better for it.

Eugene Redmond, [Review of *And Still I Rise!*], *Black Scholar* 8, No. 1 (September 1976): 50–51

UNSIGNED   *Black Scholar:* Can you comment a bit on the importance of endurance in black writers?

Maya Angelou: Endurance is one thing. I think endurance with output, endurance with productivity is the issue. If one has the fortune, good or bad, to stay alive one endures, but to continue to write the books and get them out—that's the productivity and I think that is important to link with the endurance.

I find myself taking issue with the term minor poet, minor writer of the 18th century, minor writer of the 19th century; but I do understand what people mean by that. Generally they mean that the writer, the poet who only wrote one book of poetry or one novel, or two, is considered a minor poet or a minor writer because of his or her output, its scarcity. I can't argue with that. I do believe that it is important to get work done, seen, read, published, and *given* to an audience. One has enjoyed oneself, one has done what one has been put here to do, to write. Another thing is that one has given a legacy of some quantity to generations to come. Whether they like it or not, whether the writer values the next generation, or values the work or not, at least there is something, there is a body of work to examine and to respond to, to react to.

I know a number of people who do work very slowly but I don't believe, although I have friends who write slowly, in taking five years to write one book. Now I think they have psyched themselves into believing they cannot work more quickly, that hence because they work slowly their work is of more value. They also believe—they have bought that American baloney, the masterpiece theory—everything you write must be a masterpiece, each painting you paint must be a masterpiece.

Black Scholar: I want to talk to you more about that. I think any artist in this society is inhibited in many ways because it is not an aesthetic society.

Maya Angelou: Materialistic.

Black Scholar: I think the black writer has even more difficulty because his vision is antagonistic, it's a racist society, his whole stuff is different. Do you think that the masterpiece syndrome further inhibits the output of black writers?

Maya Angelou: To me that inhibits *all* artists. Every artist in this society is affected by it. I don't say he or she is inhibited, he or she might work against it and make that work for them, as I hope I do, but we are affected by it.

It is in reaction to that dictate from a larger society that spurs my output, makes me do all sorts of things, write movies and direct them, write plays, write music and write articles. That's because I don't believe in the inhibition of my work; I am obliged, I am compulsive, I will work against it. If necessary I will go to work on a dictionary, you understand, just to prove that that is a lot of bullshit.

So every artist in the society has to deal with that dictate. Some are crippled by it, others, I believe, are made more healthy. Because they are made more strong, and become more ready to struggle against it.

Black Scholar: More vigilant.

Maya Angelou: Absolutely. But the black writer or black artist—I include every type, from graphics to entertainment—has generally further to come from than his or her white counterpart unless the artist is an entertainer. Often this black artist is the first in his family and possibly in his environment to strive to write a book, to strive to paint a painting, to sculpt, to make being an artist a life work. So the black writer, the black artist probably has to convince family and friends that what he or she is about is worthwhile.

Now that is damned difficult when one comes from a family, an environment, a neighborhood or group of friends who have never met a writer, who have only heard of writers, maybe read some poetry in school.

But try to explain to a middle-aged black that the life of art one wants to lead is a worthwhile one and can hopefully improve life, the quality of life for all people, that's already a chore.

Because, like most people anywhere, the middle-aged black American that comes from a poor background for the most part wants to see concrete evidence of success. So they want things. If you are really going to be a success go and become a nurse, be a doctor, be a mortician, but a *writer?* So there are obstacles to overcome, to be either done or else just given up on.

Unsigned, "The *Black Scholar* Interviews: Maya Angelou," *Black Scholar* 8, No. 4 (January 1977): 44–45

ANTAR SUDAN KATARA MBERI   Well, she's back and smoking with another bombshell under her belt. Maya Angelou, the author of five highly acclaimed works of lasting literary quality, has done it again. She sings with the evocative and sometimes provocative cadence of the blues master. In her world, language serves content. Characteristic depth of meaning blossoms and pollinates her work. She is a vintage craftswoman plying her artistic tools with polished economy and confidence.

Like the blues player she is, her lyrics bubble and brim over. She paces us through her snapshots of the Afro-American community, its women and their problems, which become ours as well; through love and its triumphs and defeats; and through shared personal experiences and outlooks that draw you further out of yourself and into her world. This is the power and the magic of *And Still I Rise*. ⟨. . .⟩

It is a book of instructiveness, love, joy, pain, but always *shared* optimism. And in a country with so many anti-human, self-negating values, it is like a cool glass of water finally received, to read Ms. Angelou's work. After doing so, we know one thing for sure—we are not going to "Diiie" of thirst. Do yourself a favor, and quench your thirst. Buy it.

Antar Sudan Katara Mberi, "Like a Cool Glass of Water," *Freedomways* 19, No. 2 (Second Quarter 1979): 109–10

ROBERT B. STEPTO   *And Still I Rise* is Angelou's third volume of verse, and most of its thirty-two poems are as slight as those which dominated the pages of the first two books. Stanzas such as this one,

> In every town and village,
> In every city square,
> In crowded places
> I search the faces
> Hoping to find
> Someone to care.

or the following,

> Then you rose into my life,
> Like a promised sunrise.
> Brightening my days with the light in your eyes.
> I've never been so strong,
> Now I'm where I belong.

cannot but make lesser-known talents grieve all the more about how this thin stuff finds its way to the rosters of a major New York house while their stronger, more inventive lines seem to be relegated to low-budget (or no-budget) journals and presses. On the other hand, a good Angelou poem has what we call "possibilities." One soon discovers that she is on her surest ground when she "borrows" various folk idioms and forms and thereby buttresses her poems by evoking aspects of a culture's written and unwritten heritage. "One More Round," for example, gains most of its energy from "work songs" and "protest songs" that have come before. In this eight-stanza poem, the even-number stanzas constitute a refrain—obviously, a "work song" refrain:

> One more round
> And let's heave it down.
> One more round
> And let's heave it down.

At the heart of the odd-number stanzas are variations upon the familiar "protest" couplet "But before I'll be a slave / I'll be buried in my grave," such as the following: "I was born to work up to my grave / But I was not born / To be a slave." The idea of somehow binding "work" and "protest" forms to create a new art is absolutely first rate, but the mere alternation of "work" and "protest" stanzas does not, in this instance, carry the idea very far. ⟨. . .⟩

Up to a point, "Still I Rise," Angelou's title poem, reminds us of Brown's famous "Strong Men," and it is the discovery of that point which helps us define Angelou's particular presence and success in contemporary letters and, if we may say so, in publishing. The poetic and visual rhythms created by the repetition of "Still I rise" and its variants clearly revoice that of Brown's "strong men . . . strong men gittin' stronger." But the "I" of Angelou's refrain is obviously female and, in this instance, a woman forthright about the sexual nuances of personal and social struggle:

> Does my sexiness upset you?
> Does it come as a surprise
> That I dance like I've got diamonds
> At the meeting of my thighs?

Needless to say, the woman "rising" from these lines is largely unaccounted for in the earlier verse of men and women poets alike. Most certainly, this "phenomenal woman," as she terms herself in another poem, is not likely to appear, except perhaps in a negative way, in the feminist verse of our time. Where she *does* appear is in Angelou's own marvelous autobiographies, *I Know Why the Caged Bird Sings* and *Gather Together in My Name*. In short, Angelou's poems are often woefully thin as poems but they nevertheless work their way into contemporary literary history. In their celebration of a particularly defined "phenomenal woman," they serve as ancillary, supporting texts for Angelou's more adeptly rendered self-portraits, and even guide the reader to (or back to) the autobiographies. With this achieved, Angelou's "phenomenal woman," as persona *and* self-portrait, assumes a posture in our literature that would not be available if she were the product of Angelou's prose or verse alone.

Robert B. Stepto, "The Phenomenal Woman and the Severed Daughter," *Parnassus: Poetry in Review* 8, No. 1 (Fall–Winter, 1979): 313–15

CAROLYN KIZER   It is as if Maya Angelou was born knowing how to write, and how to do a great many other things well, with seeming effortlessness: act, compose, direct, edit, make a film or a baby, and much much more. She rhymes with ease and assurance and there's the rub. If writing poems is easy, it's apt to seem that way to the reader as well. It can collapse into near-doggerel, like the following:

> Life is too busy, wearying me.
> Questions and answers and heavy thought.
> I've subtracted and added and multiplied,
> and all my figuring has come to naught.
> Today I'll give up living.

Her verse is not all like this, though too often it is. ⟨. . .⟩ there is a wonderful ballad, of just 10 lines, that Auden, if he were here, might memorize, recite and anthologize, "Contemporary Announcement":

> Ring the big bells,
> cook the cow,
> put on your silver locket.
> The landlord is knocking at the door
> and I've got the rent in my pocket.
>
> Douse the lights
> Hold your breath,
> take my heart in your hand.

I lost my job two weeks ago
and rent day's here again.

More like these, please, Ms. Angelou! But if you don't have time, we will
understand.

Carolyn Kizer, [Review of *Shaker, Why Don't You Sing?*], *Washington Post Book World*,
26 June 1983, p. 8

CANDELARIA SILVA   Maya Angelou's poetry is easily accessible,
relying often on rhythm for its success. The poems are pared down with a
sculptor's precision to simple yet elegant lines. She writes about love, beauty,
the South, the human struggle for freedom and the incredible dignity black
people have maintained against all odds. Her perceptive vision is emphatic
and clear. Angelou is best in her poems which rhyme, like "Weekend
Glory" and "Impeccable Conception." Her rhymes never seem awkwardly
constructed or contrived. (She is less successful when she uses other methods
for they don't seem to come from her natural voice.) Her sense of music
in language, her heritage from her Southern black roots, is not utilized as
much as in other volumes, notably *And Still I Rise;* however, Angelou writes
poems which are very appropriate for junior high and high-school students.

Candelaria Silva, [Review of *Shaker, Why Don't You Sing?*], *School Library Journal* 30,
No. 1 (September 1983): 143

CAROL E. NEUBAUER   Within four years of the publication of
Just Give Me a Cool Drink 'Fore I Diiie, Maya Angelou completed a second
volume of poetry, *Oh Pray My Wings Are Gonna Fit Me Well* (1975). By
the time of its release, her reputation as a poet who transforms much of
the pain and disappointment of life into lively verse had been established.
During the 1970s, her reading public grew accustomed to seeing her poems
printed in *Cosmopolitan.* Angelou had become recognized not only as a
spokesperson for blacks and women, but also for all people who are committed
to raising the moral standards of living in the United States. The poems
collected in *My Wings,* indeed, appear at the end of the Vietnam era and
in some important ways exceed the scope of her first volume. Many question
traditional American values and urge people to make an honest appraisal

of the demoralizing rift between the ideal and the real. Along with poems about love and the oppression of black people, the poet adds several that directly challenge Americans to reexamine their lives and to strive to reach the potential richness that has been compromised by self-interest since the beginnings of the country.

One of the most moving poems in *My Wings* is entitled "Alone," in which carefully measured verses describe the general alienation of people in the twentieth century. "Alone" is not directed at any one particular sector of society but rather is focused on the human condition in general. No one, the poet cautions, can live in this world alone. This message punctuates the end of the three major stanzas and also serves as a separate refrain between each and at the close of the poem:

> Alone, all alone
> Nobody, but nobody
> Can make it out here alone.

Angelou begins by looking within herself and discovering that her soul is without a home. Moving from an inward glimpse to an outward sweep, she recognizes that even millionaires suffer from this modern malaise and live lonely lives with "hearts of stone." Finally, she warns her readers to listen carefully and change the direction of their lives:

> Storm clouds are gathering
> The wind is gonna blow
> The race of man is suffering.

For its own survival, the human race must break down barriers and rescue one from loneliness. The only cure, the poet predicts, is to acknowledge common interests and work toward common goals. ⟨. . .⟩

In one poem, "Southern Arkansia," the poet shifts her attention from the general condition of humanity to the plight of black people in America. The setting of this tightly structured poem is the locale where Angelou spent most of her childhood. At the end of the three stanzas, she poses a question concerning the responsibility and guilt involved in the exploitation of the slaves. Presumably, the white men most immediately involved have never answered for their inhumane treatment of "bartered flesh and broken bones." The poet doubts that they have ever even paused to "ponder" or "wonder" about their proclivity to value profit more than human life.

Carol E. Neubauer, "Maya Angelou: Self and Song of Freedom in the Southern Tradition," *Southern Women Writers: The New Generation,* ed. Tonette Bond Inge (Tuscaloosa: University of Alabama Press, 1990), pp. 134–35

GLORIA T. HULL   *I Shall Not Be Moved* is Maya Angelou's fifth book of poetry. Because of who she is as actress, activist, woman of letters, and acclaimed autobiographer (*I Know Why the Caged Bird Sings* and succeeding volumes), she is able to command our ear. As I listen, what I hear in her open, colloquial poems is racial wit and earthy wisdom, honest black female pain and strength, humor, passion, and rhetorical force. What I miss— probably because of my academic training and my own predilections as reader and practicing poet—is verbal ingenuity, honed craft, intellectual surprise, and flawless rhythms. Each of her books has at least one striking poem that stands as a centerpiece. Here, it is the title-inspiring work, "Our Grandmothers," which begins:

> She lay, skin down on the moist dirt,
> the canebrake rustling
> with the whispers of leaves, and
> loud longing of hounds and
> the ransack of hunters crackling the near branches.
>
> She muttered, lifting her head a nod toward freedom,
> I shall not, I
> shall not be
> moved.

With slavery figuring so prominently in recent African American women's writings, it is not surprising that this keystone poem of Angelou's mines that tenacious reality.

Gloria T. Hull, "Covering Ground," *Belles Lettres* 6, No. 3 (Spring 1991): 1–2

◈ *Bibliography*

I Know Why the Caged Bird Sings. 1969.

Just Give Me a Cool Drink of Water 'Fore I Diiie: The Poetry of Maya Angelou.
        1971, 1988 (with *Oh Pray My Wings Are Gonna Fit Me Well*).

Gather Together in My Name. 1974, 1985.

Oh Pray My Wings Are Gonna Fit Me Well. 1975.

Singin' and Swingin' and Gettin' Merry Like Christmas. 1976.

And Still I Rise. 1978.

Weekend Glory. 198-.

The Heart of a Woman. 1981.

Poems. 1981, 1986.

Shaker, Why Don't You Sing? 1983.

All God's Children Need Traveling Shoes. 1986.

Now Sheba Sings the Songs. 1986.

Conversations with Maya Angelou. Ed. Jeffrey M. Elliot. 1989.

I Shall Not Be Moved. 1990.

Maya Angelou Omnibus. 1991.

On the Pulse of Morning. 1993.

Soul Looks Back in Wonder. 1993.

Lessons in Living. 1993.

Life Doesn't Frighten Me. 1993.

Wouldn't Take Nothing for My Journey Now. 1993.

I Love the Look of Words. 1993.

And My Best Friend Is Chicken. 1994.

Imamu Amiri Baraka
b. 1934

IMAMU AMIRI BARAKA was born Everett LeRoy Jones on October 7, 1934, in Newark, New Jersey. Although his original intention was to join the ministry, upon graduating from high school in 1951 he attended Rutgers University on a science scholarship, at which time he changed his name to LeRoi Jones. He transferred to Howard University in 1952, but found the conservative political atmosphere at this black school stifling and left after two years.

Between 1954 and 1957, Jones served in the air force's Strategic Air Command, spending much of this time stationed in Puerto Rico. It was in the air force that he began his first attempts at writing poetry. His experiences in the military, however, increased his suspicion of the white power structure, and his failure to conform to military discipline led to a dishonorable discharge in 1957. The next year he moved to Greenwich Village and began working as a jazz critic for such magazines as *Jazz Review*, *Downbeat*, and *Metronome*. It was in the Village that Jones became associated with Beat poets such as Allen Ginsberg and Charles Olson. Also in 1958 he married a Jewish woman, Hettie Cohen, with whom he had two children. With her, he founded the avant-garde poetry magazine *Yugen*, which lasted from 1958 to 1973. She has recently written a book about her marriage with Baraka, *How I Became Hettie Jones* (1990).

Baraka's first major book was a collection of poetry, *Preface to a Twenty Volume Suicide Note* (1961). He continued to be very active in the New York literary scene, editing an anthology of new writing, *The Moderns* (1963), and a study of black music, *Blues People* (1963). He also taught courses in contemporary poetry and creative writing at the New School for Social Research and Columbia University, where he completed his M.A. in literature in 1964.

That same year his plays *Dutchman* and *The Slave* were produced, the former winning an Obie Award as best play of the season. In 1965 he had published a novel, *The System of Dante's Hell*, and received a Guggenheim

Fellowship. However, Jones became increasingly discontented and later withdrew from the Village, divorced his wife, and moved to Harlem.

It was also at this time that he changed his name to Imamu Amiri Baraka. The names generally signify the following: Imamu, a Muslim philosopher/ poet/priest; Amiri, an African warrior/prince; and Baraka, spiritual conversion from Christianity to Islam as well as elimination of the slave name Jones. The new name was indicative of a more politically and socially committed point of view: in the late 1960s Baraka worked as a writer and activist for black unity both in Harlem and in his hometown of Newark, with the United Brothers of Newark and the Black Community Development and Defense Organization.

Baraka's poetry and plays began to incorporate both an increasingly radical political orientation (inspired in part by his visit to Cuba in 1960) and an increasing use of specifically black forms of speech. Such plays as *The Motion of History* and *S-1* are openly Marxist, and Baraka created a sensation with such collections as *Four Black Revolutionary Plays* (1969) and *The Motion of History and Other Plays* (1978). Such poetry collections as *The Dead Lecturer* (1964) and *Black Magic* (1969) also reflected his political concerns. Baraka became personally involved in the struggle for civil rights when he was arrested in 1967 during the Newark riots; at his trial he was convicted of a misdemeanor, but the verdict was later overturned on appeal.

Baraka has continued to be a prolific poet (*Hard Facts*, 1975; *Selected Poetry*, 1979), essayist (*Raise Race Rays Raze*, 1971; *Daggers and Javelins*, 1984), and anthologist (*Confirmation: An Anthology of AfricanAmerican Women*, 1983). Since 1979 he has been a member of the African Studies department of the State University of New York at Stony Brook. He married Amina Baraka (originally Sylvia Robinson) in 1966; they have five children. In 1984 he published his autobiography.

Critical Extracts

DENISE LEVERTOV   His special gift is an emotive music that might have made him predominantly a "lyric poet," but his deeply felt preoccupation with more than personal issues enlarges the scope of his poems beyond what the term is often taken to mean.

> . . . Lighter, white man
> talk. They shy away. My won
> dead souls, my, so called
> people. Africa
> is a foreign place. You are
> as any other sad man here
> american.

I feel that sometimes his work is muddled, and after the event he convinces himself that it had to be that way; in other words, his conception of when a poem is ready to be printed differs from mine. But while he is not the craftsman ⟨Gilbert⟩ Sorrentino is, he is developing swiftly and has a rich potential. Certain poems—especially "The Clearing," "The Turncoat," "Notes for a Speech"—show what he can do. They are beautiful poems, and others that are less complete have passages of equal beauty.

Since beauty is one of the least precise words in the language I had better define what I mean by it in this instance: the beauty in Jones's poems is sensuous and incantatory, in contrast to the beauty in Sorrentino's which is a sensation of exactitude, a hitting of nails on the head with a ringing sound. In his contribution to the notes on poetics at the back of the Grove Press anthology, *The New American Poetry*, Jones speaks of García Lorca as one of the poets he has read intensely; and what is incantatory (magical) in his work, while it is natural to him, may well have been first brought to the surface by the discovery of an affinity in the magic of Lorca.   ·

Denise Levertov, "Poets of the Given Ground," *Nation*, 14 October 1961, p. 252

M. L. ROSENTHAL   LeRoi Jones ⟨. . .⟩ has the natural gift for quick, vivid imagery and spontaneous humor, and his poems are filled with sardonic or sensuous or slangily knowledgeable passages. His first book, *Preface to a Twenty Volume Suicide Note* (1960), was interesting—as much of our newer poetry is—for the structural similarity of some of its pieces to jazz improvisation. Thus, the ending of what is perhaps the best poem in the volume, 'Way Out West':

> . . . Insidious weight
> of cankered dreams. Tiresias'
> weathered cock.

> Walking into the sea, shells
> caught in the hair. Coarse
> waves tearing the tongue.
>
> Closing the eyes. As
> simply an act. You float

The spiraling, dreaming movement of associations, spurts of energetic pursuit of melody and motifs, and driftings away of Jones's poems seem very much an expression of a new way of looking at things, and of a highly contemporary aesthetic, of a very promising sort. The perspectives include traditional directions and symbols, yet are not dominated by them. Jones, a Negro intellectual and playwright, at first seemed to be finding a tangential way of making use of Negro experience and its artistic and psychological aspects in such a way as to enable himself, at the same time, to develop within the normal context of American poetry of this period. As he came into some prominence, however, and, for the time being at least, began to ally himself with the new tendencies toward intransigent hostility to the 'white' civilization, his poetry became more militant in its projection of that hostility.

M. L. Rosenthal, *The New Poets: American and British Poetry Since World War II* (New York: Oxford University Press, 1967), pp. 189–90

LARRY NEAL   Jones' particular power as a playwright does not rest solely on his revolutionary vision, but is instead derived from his deep lyricism and spiritual outlook. In many ways, he is fundamentally more a poet than a playwright. And it is his lyricism that gives body to his plays. Two important plays in this regard are *Black Mass* and *Slave Ship*. *Black Mass* is based on the Muslim myth of Yacub. According to this myth Yacub, a Black scientist, developed the means of grafting different colors of the Original Black Nation until a White Devil was created. In *Black Mass*, Yacub's experiments produce a raving White Beast who is condemned to the coldest regions of the North. The other magicians implore Yacub to cease his experiments. But he insists on claiming the primacy of scientific knowledge over spiritual knowledge. The sensibility of the White Devil is alien, informed by lust and sensuality. The Beast is the consummate embodiment of evil, the beginning of the historical subjugation of the spiritual world.

Black Mass takes place in some prehistorical time. In fact, the concept of time, we learn, is the creation of an alien sensibility, that of the Beast. This is deeply weighted play, a colloquy on the nature of man, and the relationship between legitimate spiritual knowledge and scientific knowledge. It is LeRoi Jones' most important play mainly because it is informed by a mythology that is wholly the creation of the Afro-American sensibility. ⟨. . .⟩

Slave Ship presents a more immediate confrontation with history. In a series of expressionistic tableaux it depicts the horrors and the madness of the Middle Passage. It then moves through the period of slavery, early betrayal, and the final act of liberation. There is no definite plot (LeRoi calls it a pageant), just a continuous rush of sound, groans, screams, and souls wailing for freedom and relief from suffering. This work has special affinities with the New Music of Sun Ra, John Coltrane, Albert Ayler, and Ornette Coleman. Events are blurred, rising and falling in a stream of sound. Almost cinematically, the images flicker and fade against a heavy backdrop of rhythm. The language is spare, stripped to the essential. It is a play which almost totally eliminates the need for a text. It functions on the basis of movement and energy—the dramatic equivalent of the New Music.

Larry Neal, "The Black Arts Movement," *Drama Review* 12, No. 4 (Summer 1968): 36–37

THEODORE R. HUDSON   In a general way, Jones is a romantic in the sense that many literary historians and scholars consider the post-Romantic Period of symbolists, imagists, realists, naturalists, dadaists, impressionists, and other modern writers as latter day romantics or as part of a romantic continuum. He is a romantic in more specific ways as well. Like Emerson and certain other romantic writers, in a transcedentalistic way Jones places great faith in intuition, in feelings. As he applies this faith in an ethnocentric way, he would have blacks place faith in what he assumes to be their singular mystical impulses. He is antirational in the way that romantics of Western European literature were opposed to the "cold" rationality of neoclassicism. Moreover, in connection with this reliance upon innate urgings and promptings, Jones inescapably asserts, as Blake and other romantic mystics contended, that man is divine, although, as Baraka, Jones would argue that the white man has perverted his, the white man's, divinity.

Also, Jones is, like those romantics who would not conform to neoclassical religious dogma and traditions, romantic in that he is disdainful of the organized and orthodox religion of the majority and in that he has been himself a religous speculator and seeker. Next, Jones is romantic in his concern for the well-being, freedom, and dignity of the economically and politically weak, the dispossessed, the oppressed, and the downtrodden, as were the past century's romantic political and social libertarians and romantic champions of "humble" people. Further, Rousseau-like in his concern for the full development of man's potential, Jones sees his contemporary social, cultural, and political institutions as destructive of (black) man, so he would have man destroy, change, or control these institutions so that they, in his opinion, serve man rather than have man serve them. Further, Jones, like the Shelleys of the Romantic Period, is a visionary who sees creative artists as providers of philosophical and ideological bases of change. Next, in regard to technique, Jones, like many romantics of the past, will have little to do with conventional and prescribed forms and techniques, insists upon using the "language of the people," and constantly strives for new ways of writing, searching for what he calls a "post-American form." And it is obvious that Jones, as have countless romantics, uses his creative imagination to inform and shape his literary work.

Theodore R. Hudson, *From LeRoi Jones to Amiri Baraka* (Durham, NC: Duke University Press, 1973), pp. 179–80

CLYDE TAYLOR   The mark of LeRoi Jones' poetry is the mark of his personality on the printed page. He is the most personal so far of the Afro-American poets. For him poetry is the flow of being, the process of human electricity interacting with the weight of time, tapped and possibly trapped on paper. Feelings, impressions, moods, passions move unedited through a structure of shifting images. Quick poems, light on their feet, like a fancy middle-weight. Mostly, his poems carry no argument, no extractable, paraphraseable statement. They operate prior to the pros and cons of rational, persuasive, politic discourse. Even after several readings, one is likely to remember mainly a flavor, a distinct attutude of spirit, an insistent, very personal voice.

His poetry is written out of a heavy anti-rationalist, anti-didactic bias. Its obligation is to the intentions of its own feelings. Its posture is in defiance of criticism. The critic is for him the sycophant and would-be legislator of official (white) reality, an implacable enemy, the best symbol of the spiritually dead pseudo-intellectuality of the West. (Lula in *Dutchman* is a white *critic*, if you watch closely.) Against the strictures and constipations of this official reality, his poetry is an imposition upon the reader of the actuality, the majesty even (hence, Le*Roi*) of his subjectivity. The personalism of his earlier poetry, particularly, is a challenge to the ready-to-wear definitions of the sociologically defined "Negro writer" lying in wait for him.

The arrogance of *Preface to a Twenty Volume Suicide Note* and *The Dead Lecturer* is in this personalism and intimacy, not in any pretensions of impeccability of character. The poetry alternately invites the reader to jam his face into his own shit or to love or condemn the poet. It is the work of a spiritual gambler who wants to think of himself as waging heavy stakes. A reflection of this spirituality is its absoluteness. All his poems give the notion of being end-of-the-line thoughts, where attempts to reach an understanding dance on the edge of ambiguity. They are the works of an apprentice guru, "stuntin' for disciples," he later decided.

A major source of this creative orientation came from the streets. The hipsterism that nourished his poetry has to be regarded respectfully since whatever its limitations hipsterism was the germ of several cultural and social revolutions still turning in the world today. Hipsterism was a counter-assertion to brand-name, white values and the conformism of middle America, a serio-comic celebration of energies and forms unaccounted for, a mysticism (with some odd resemblances to Zen and other spiritual disciplines) of rhythms and tempos inside of and beyond metronomic, bureaucratic time, reflective of the polyrhythmic time of black music (particularly bebop) and of the fluid, open time-space sensation of a pot high. Hipsterism was a new, Afro-American ontology, a style of knowing the world and acknowledging in the parody of one's own posture the craziness of a materialistic, hyper-rationalist, racist, self-contradictory square world on the one hand and the absurdity of a universe that mocked human values in its variousness and arbitrariness on the other.

Clyde Taylor, "Baraka as Poet," *Modern Black Poets: A Collection of Critical Essays,* ed. Donald B. Gibson (Englewood Cliffs, NJ: Prentice-Hall, 1973), pp. 127–28

KIMBERLY W. BENSTON   Baraka's literary career, more than that of any other Afro-American writer, has illustrated the ethic/aesthetic of "change." The impulse to harness the energy of black life's chaos is consonant with the desire for political and cultural transformation. Thus "the revolution = change," and Malcolm X, the exemplar of cultural revolution, "was killed, for saying, / and feeling, and being / change" (from "Poem for Black Hearts"). At the core of Baraka's art is the insistence upon the formlessness of life-giving energy and the energetic or fluid nature of all form. It is no wonder that events in his work are violent, his images often alarmingly brutal. The only fruition or finality honored is that of death, which produces a sudden enlargement of vision—the realization that personality, or the "deadweight" of any fixed idea or being, is inevitably annihilated by history's progress: "The only constant is change."

In the purgatorial domain of his "ever-blacker" life, the artist learns to submit to his people's pure energy. He must surrender the shape of his own life, freeing his soul to flow into the black nation. The most extreme form of such identity-loss is the ceremonial dismemberment of the poet, so that he is no longer a man but instead becomes his singing, fateful words and purest deeds, a man reduced to the barest of essences:

> When I die, the consciousness I carry I will to
> black people. May they pick me apart and take the
> useful parts, the sweet meat of my feelings. And leave
> the bitter bullshit white parts
> alone.
>
> [from "leroy"]

This poem had begun in a pastoral dimension, a realm of accomplished forms and stilled gestures, a realm suffused with sadness:

> I wanted to know my mother when she sat
> looking sad across the campus in the late 20's
> into the future of the soul.

The violent ending is a stunning reversal of the poem's opening: the history of black consciousness is a generation-by-generation stripping of "sweet meat" from "bitter bullshit white parts." Here, Baraka sustains the hope that a static resolution of black experience can be avoided by willing the collective purification of his specific personality: "leroy" dies and Imamu is born.

Kimberly W. Benston, *Baraka: The Renegade and the Mask* (New Haven: Yale University Press, 1976), pp. 261–62

WERNER SOLLORS   Despite Baraka's insistence that he was concerned with Black culture as Black people live it, his cultural nationalism never allowed much room for Black culture and Black consciousness as it actually existed; instead, he tended to view Black culture as something Black people could *learn*, or even as something that might have to be forced on people by intellectuals who had renounced their own backgrounds. Thus, being "Black" in the sense of Baraka's nationalism may mean being immersed in a disciplined acceptance of certain codes, may mean being "modernized." It seems doubtful that people generally, or Black people in particular, have to be de-brainwashed against "l'art pour l'art" or "New Criticism." Baraka's strategies often reveal that he is really thinking of his own past when he attempts to exorcise absurd drama, or that he silently equates people's consciousness with popular culture, which convinces him that de-brainwashing is necessary. While rhetorically people-oriented, tradition-conscious, and folk-directed, Baraka may be a modernizer who attempts to impose new synthetic religious-cultural constructions which he calls Black. Thus it is at least paradoxical that Karenga propagated a Napoleonic military organization as very Black, while denouncing the blues as "invalid," since they teach resignation. And it is equally puzzling that many writers of the Black Arts Movement were formally Western avant-gardists, although they expressed strong ethnic exhortation. The demand for a "collective" art was often a camouflage for individualistic, modernizing artists who feigned collectivity. Despite all the invocation of "the people," despite the claims that alienation has been transcended in Black cultural nationalism, there remains a struggle between the elitist writer and the people who are to learn the right Black consciousness from him. Writing "for the people" may mask a deep-seated opposition to the people. In this context, the elements of opposition to other groups of people—women, Jews, homosexuals—are indicative of a larger opposition between artist and people.

Werner Sollors, *Amiri Baraka/LeRoi Jones: The Quest for a "Populist Modernism"* (New York: Columbia University Press, 1978), pp. 193–94

LLOYD W. BROWN   *Slave Ship* predates Baraka's major socialist dramas by several years. But the play's historical themes, and historically defined structure, make it a direct forerunner of *The Motion of History* (1976) and *S-1* (1976). And this remains true despite the fact that *Slave Ship* is not committed to socialist ideology. The perception of history in all three plays is intrinsic to Baraka's emphasis on the theater as a teaching device. In black nationalist drama like *Slave Ship* the reenactment of history fulfills a major assumption of black nationalism: the full understanding of black history is crucial to a vital sense of black identity because the crippling of black pride in the past has been partly the result of white distortions of black history. Moreover, the very process of reenactment becomes a form of celebration, the celebration of that black ethnicity which emerges from the exploration of the past.

On the whole this approach to the play as teaching device and as celebration is similar to the fundamental premise of Baraka's socialist drama, although in the latter there is a far more explicit self-consciousness about the teaching role. The norms of "scientific socialism" reflect a certain commitment to education: the inevitability of the socialist revolution is partly the consequence of politically enlightening the masses. Art, especially dramatic art, facilitates the revolutionizing process by depicting the past and its impact on the present. While the black nationalist's historical sense enhances the discovery and celebration of a distinctive black culture, the historical perspectives of scientific socialism encourage the social awareness that will hasten revolution across racial lines. As Baraka himself describes *The Motion of History* and *S-1*, "both plays are vehicles for a simple message, viz., the only solution to our problems . . . is revolution! And that revolution is inevitable. *The Motion of History* brings it back through the years, focusing principally on the conscious separation created between black and white workers who are both exploited by the same enemy."

Both plays also reflect a continuing weakness in Baraka's committed art. In this socialist phase, as in the black nationalist period, he suffers from a tendency to indulge in ideological wish-fulfillment at the expense of social realities. Hence the earlier habit of exaggerating the depth and breadth of black nationalism in America has been replaced by unconvincing images of one great socialist rebellion in all the countries of the world (*The Motion of History*) and by the highly unlikely spectacle of the American labor union movement as an anticapitalist, prorevolutionary force. Of course these "weaknesses" are less troublesome if we are inclined to accept the underlying purpose of such plays: they are concerned less with strict social realism as such, and more with the advocacy of social change. ⟨. . .⟩

This kind of drama does have its built-in limitations, of course. The characters are rudimentary types conceived in very broad terms, so broad indeed that the revolutionary figures of *S-1* are indistinguishable not only from each other but from their counterparts in *The Motion of History*. Scenes in which ideological conflicts are presented are severely underdeveloped, largely because the extreme sketchiness of the characterization limits the possibilities of the very confrontations that are supposed to dramatize the clash of ideas. And as a result of all this the audience is left with a theater of rhetoric in which potentially interesting situations and personalities are inundated with a flood of repetitive statements from all sides of the political landscape. Ironically enough Baraka's lack of emotional control in his ideological statements and his increasing indifference to characterization have resulted in a thin, one-dimensional drama that contravenes his own ideal of dramatic art as one that fuses word, act, and idea. Instead what he has produced is largely a loosely connected series of scenes filled with shopworn clichés of reactionaries and revolutionaries alike. At its worst this method exemplifies the predominance of ideological word over dramatic art, the very kind of imbalance that Baraka himself abhors in theory.

Lloyd W. Brown, *Amiri Baraka* (Boston: Twayne, 1980), pp. 162–65

HENRY C. LACEY   Like the train of its setting, *Dutchman* moves with tremendous bursts of energy and periodic lulls. As the train pulls out of the station, the tension accelerates immediately with Lula's increasingly abusive treatment of Clay, who, by virtue of his apparent naivete, wins the sympathy of the audience. Midway through the play, however, this incessant goading threatens to completely exasperate the audience, to drain them all too hastily. The maturing dramatist effectively counters this by ending the first scene. By dividing the action into two scenes, he not only gives the audience a chance to regroup emotionally, he also manages to give the play a greater sense of depth. After those few seconds of darkness, the audience views the opening action of scene II with the distinct feeling that a great deal has happened, as well as the hope that Clay has started to better acquit himself with Lena. This hope is short-lived, however, for the dramatist starts anew the pattern of scene I as the train pulls out at the beginning of scene II. ⟨. . .⟩

Along with his masterful manipulation of suspense and tension, Baraka shows his growth in the ease with which he combines the mythic and the literal in *Dutchman*. We are prepared for his duality of meaning from the opening lines of the text. *Dutchman* takes place *"In the flying underbelly of the city. Steaming hot, and summer on top, outside. Underground. The subway heaped in modern myth."* The setting suggests that the play will delve into the troubling, but too often denied truths of race relations, American style. This setting, like the encounter between the exaggeratedly "real" characters, is, indeed, meant to represent a more elusive inner or psychic reality. As if he wanted to make sure no one mistook this work for the overt naturalism of, say, *The Toilet*, Baraka gives important alternative directions: *"Dimlights and darkness whistling by against the glass. (Or paste the lights, as admitted props right on the subway windows.)"* He seeks to synthesize the naturalistic and expressionistic modes, to take the best each has to offer. This is evidenced not only in his approach to setting, but also in the characterization of *Dutchman*. Lula and Clay are simultaneously "real" persons and highly symbolic types. The powerful effect of the drama, derived from this synthesis of artistic modes, has been compared frequently to that of Albee's *The Zoo Story*, another lean, parable-like work concerned with the tragic consequences of failure to communicate.

The play's title and setting have prompted many commentators to explore its mythic implications. Hugh Nelson asserts, rather convincingly, that Baraka converts the legend of "the Flying Dutchman" into modern myth. Seeing Lula as the doomed Dutchman and Clay as the pure lover who could release her from her deathly existence, Nelson notes striking similarities in the legendary ship and Baraka's train. The cold, impersonal train, like the doomed ship, seems to operate "according to some diabolical plan. It goes nowhere, never emerges from its darkness; reaching one terminus, it reverses itself and speeds back towards the other with brief pauses at identical stations. . . ." Like the crew of the "Dutchman," Baraka's passengers exhibit the same spiritual torpor in acceding to the wishes of their "captain," Lula. Other commentators have noted the implication of the myth of Adam and Eve—and on occasion, Lilith—in the story of Clay and Lula. It is obvious that Baraka drew upon all these elements in the creation of *Dutchman*.

> Henry C. Lacey, *To Raise, Destroy, and Create: The Poetry, Drama, and Fiction of Imamu Amiri Baraka (LeRoi Jones)* (Troy, NY: Whitston Publishing Co., 1981), pp. 73–75

AMIRI BARAKA   I had come into poetry from a wide-open perspective—anti-academic because of my experience, my social history and predilections. Obviously, as an African American I had a cultural history that should give me certain aesthetic proclivities. In the US and the Western world generally, white supremacy can warp and muffle the full recognition of a black person of this history, especially an "intellectual" trained by a system of white supremacy. The dead bourgeois artifact I'd cringed before in *The New Yorker* was a material and spiritual product of a whole way of life and perception of reality that was hostile to me. I dug that even as a young boy weeping in San Juan. Coming out of Howard and getting trapped in the Air Force had pulled me away from the "good job" path which is also called The Yellow Brick Road. The Yalla heaven of the undead!

I'd come to the Village *looking*, trying to "check," being open to all flags. Allen Ginsberg's *Howl* was the first thing to open my nose, as opposed to, say, instructions I was given, directions, guidance. I dug *Howl* myself, in fact many of the people I'd known at the time warned me off it and thought the whole Beat phenomenon a passing fad of little relevance. I'd investigated further because I was looking for something. I was precisely open to its force as the statement of a new generation. As a line of demarcation from "the silent generation" and the man with the (yellow) grey flannel skin, half brother of the one with the grey flannel suit. I took up with the Beats because that's what I saw taking off and flying and somewhat resembling myself. The open and implied rebellion—of form and content. Aesthetic as well as social and political. But I saw most of it as Art, and the social statement as merely our lives as dropouts from the mainstream. I could see the young white boys and girls in their pronouncement of disillusion with and "removal" from society as being related to the black experience. That made us colleagues of the spirit. Yet I was no stomp-down bohemian. I had enough of the mainstream in me, of lower-middle-class craving after order and "respectability," not to get pulled all the way over to Wahooism. Yet as wild as some of my colleagues and as cool as I usually was, the connection could be made because I was black and that made me, as Wright's novel asserted, an *outsider*.

Amiri Baraka, *The Autobiography of LeRoi Jones* (New York: Freundlich Books, 1984), pp. 156–57

WILLIAM J. HARRIS   Baraka not only set the tone of the black poem in the 1960s—violent, defiant, and independent—in the 1980s he

has become the senior revolutionary voice of the black community. Graying hair notwithstanding, he is as fiery and militant as ever. Even though it is not as easy today to trace Baraka's influence, we can immediately see it in the work of Jayne Cortez, Ntozake Shange, and Lorenzo Thomas as well as its continuance in the work of Sonia Sanchez and Askia Touré. The current generation of writers responds to Baraka as a symbol of the engaged and socially committed third-world artist, referring to him "as a major and as a world poet," to quote Quincy Troupe's introduction of Baraka at a black art poetry reading in April, 1984. Because for a long period at the beginning of his Marxist stage Baraka could not get his books published by major publishers, his continuing importance was glimpsed only at black meetings, where he was treated with great respect. Perhaps it is useful to see Baraka as the new W. E. B. Du Bois for the black community, the distinguished, learned, and committed dissenter. Perhaps a measure of his influence is the dedication of a forthcoming issue of the black journal *Steppingstones* to a celebration of his work.

At fifty-one, with over thirty books behind him, Baraka is still an enigma to the American literary establishment, which cannot come to terms with this difficult and brilliant maverick. Possibly the establishment's reluctance to recognize him as it finally recognized the other two great contemporary mavericks, Mailer and Ginsberg, rests on the real—as opposed to the metaphysical—threat he poses. At most, the ramifications of Ginsberg's and Mailer's arts threaten consciousness, while Baraka's art threatens property and the actual structure of society. Or, perhaps, Baraka simply has too big a mouth, too much readiness to say the wrong thing. Whatever the reason for Baraka's exclusion, the American literary scene would be enriched by his more obvious presence: we need him to expand the definition of the American poem and to show us how to demonstrate moral commitment. At the very least, we need him to show us that a major poet does not have to heed the rules the establishment has proclaimed to be "universal."

William J. Harris, *The Poetry and Poetics of Amiri Baraka: The Jazz Aesthetic* (Columbia: University of Missouri Press, 1985), pp. 138–39

ROBERT ELLIOT FOX   The revolutionary tradition of black Americans which Baraka and others speak of has always found its most vital and persistent expression in the arts, especially music. It advocates freedom, change, roots, and it is not materialistic in orientation. This may help us to explain why works like *A Black Mass* and *Slave Ship* are so much more powerful and effective as art than works like *The Motion of History*, when all three are so clearly polemical. The former dramas derive from the (pre-Baraka) early cultural-nationalist phase, the latter from the Marxist-Leninist-Maoist (M-L-M) phase, and this appears to provide the key, rather than any serious diminution of power or skill on Baraka's part. The Marxist work is intellectually determined, whereas the cultural-nationalist pieces are emotionally felt. For Baraka—indeed, for the majority of artists and intellectuals in America—the international capitalist/communist struggle must remain an abstraction in a way that it can never be for our counterparts in the Third World. Racism, on the other hand, is experienced far more concretely. *The Motion of History* and many of Baraka's recent poems display too overtly a materialist skeleton hung with the papier-mâché of ideology, while *Slave Ship,* contrastingly, is a ritual reenactment, an historical communion.

The strength of successful works of a socialist orientation derives not from the persuasiveness of their informing ideology but rather from their energy of opposition, the power of their portrayal of injustice—precisely those virtues which characterize many non-socialist protest writings. However, the studied polemic, the doctrinal script are always inferior to those works in which the political import is broadly fused with imaginative power—in which we are compelled by life, not lectures. A polemical and polarizing ideology can never lead us out of the "labyrinth of history" or navigate us safely around the "confusing land-masses of myth" (Wilson Harris).

In his cultural-nationalist period, Baraka sought to blacken the zero of white values and to make that hermeneutical circle, unrevealing of black experience, a rooted sphere through the added dimension of a "spirit reach." Excessively ritualized and mythologized, the black value system then espoused still had the virtue of organizing black energies in reconstructive channels. However, in Baraka's latest phase, designated by the alphabetical incantation M-L-M, the ceremonialized, celebrative sphere is flattened once more into an area of materialist conflict.

If one desires an antidote to Baraka's Marxist rhetoric derived from a black perspective, one could profitably turn to Richard Wright's *American Hunger* (1944). By making a significant individual contribution to the scope and presence of Afro-American literature, Wright did more to advance the cause of blackness than the Communist Party ever did, and the same is true of Baraka. There is nothing original in his present political commitment; all the positions he has held in the course of his career have been held before in Afro-American history. What is original and vital is his artistry. Chairman Baraka simply can't cut it, compared with LeRoi Jones/Amiri Baraka as tale-teller, as black word magician, as, in essence, one of the blues people.

Robert Elliot Fox, *Conscious Sorcerers: The Black Postmodernist Fiction of LeRoi Jones/ Amiri Baraka, Ishmael Reed, and Samuel R. Delany* (Westport, CT: Greenwood Press, 1987), pp. 31–32

JAMES DE JONGH   The existential intensity of the Harlems of Oliver Pitcher and William Browne is summarized in the opening statement of "Return of the Native," the only Harlem poem by Amiri Baraka/LeRoi Jones:

> Harlem is vicious
> modernism, BangClash.
> Vicious the way it's made.
> Can you stand such beauty.
> So violent and transforming.

Baraka makes much the same point in "City of Harlem," from his volume of essays entitled *Home:*

> The legitimate cultural tradition of the Negro in Harlem (and
> America) is one of wild happiness, usually at some black man's
> own invention—of speech, of dress, of gait, the sudden twist of a
> musical phrase, the warmness or hurt of someone's voice. But that
> culture is also one of hatred and despair. Harlem must contain all
> of this and be capable of producing all these emotions.

Harlem was a pivotal issue for Baraka as he made the transition from the antibourgeois individualism of his Greenwich Village bohemianism of the 1950s to the consciousness of a group identity in the black nationalism of the 1960s. In the earlier phase, Baraka's attitude toward the cultural signifi-cance of Harlem had been negative: "Harlem is today the veritable capital city of the Black Bourgeoisie. The Negro Bohemian's flight to Harlem is not a flight from the world of color but the flight of any would-be Bohemian from . . . 'the provinciality, philistinism and moral hypocrisy of American life.' By the late 1950s and early 1960s, though, Baraka's view of Harlem was changing:

> In a very real sense, Harlem is the capital of Black America. . . .
> But even the name Harlem, now, means simply Negroes (even
> though some other peoples live there too). The identification is
> international as well: even in Belize, the capital of predominantly
> Negro British Honduras, there are vendors who decorate their
> carts with flowers and the names and pictures of Negro culture
> heroes associated with Harlem like Sugar Ray Robinson. Some of
> the vendors even wear T-shirts that say "Harlem, U.S.A.," and
> they speak about it as a Black Paris.

This is the Harlem of "vicious modernism": "The place, and place / meant of black people. Their heavy Egypt. (Weird word!)." Harlem's value is a consciousness of self that is loving, hoping, celebratory, significant, and, therefore, joyful, for all its pain. With this Harlem the poet can identify without reservation:

> Their minds, mine.
> the black hope, mine. In Time,
> We slide along in pain or too
> happy. So much love
> for us. All over, so much of
>
> what we need.

James De Jongh, *Vicious Modernism: Black Harlem and the Literary Imagination* (Cambridge: Cambridge University Press, 1990), pp. 111–12

Bibliography

Jan. 1st 1959: Fidel Castro (editor). 1959.
April 13. 1959.
Spring & Soforth. 1960.
Cuba Libre. 1961.
The Disguise. 1961.
Preface to a Twenty Volume Suicide Note. 1961.
Blues People: Negro Music in White America. 1963.

The Moderns: An Anthology of New Writing in America (editor). 1963.

Dutchman and The Slave. 1964.

The Dead Lecturer. 1964.

The System of Dante's Hell. 1965.

In-formation (editor). 1965.

Home: Social Essays. 1966.

The Baptism. 1966.

Afro-American Festival of the Arts Magazine (editor). 1966, 1969 (as *Anthology of Our Black Selves*).

Black Art. 1966.

Slave Ship. 1967.

A Poem for Black Hearts. 1967.

A Traffic of Love. 1967.

Striptease. 1967.

The Baptism and The Toilet. 1967.

Arm Yourself, or Harm Yourself! A Message of Self-Defense to Black Men! 1967.

Tales. 1967.

Black Music. 1967.

Answers in Progress. c. 1967.

The Cricket: Black Music in Evolution (with Larry Neal and A. B. Spellman). 1968, 1969 (as *Trippin': A Need for Change*).

Black Fire: An Anthology of Afro-American Writing (editor; with Larry Neal). 1968.

Short Speech to My Friends. 1969.

Black Magic: Sabotage; Target Study; Black Art: Collected Poetry 1961–1967. 1969.

Four Black Revolutionary Plays: All Praise to the Black Man. 1969.

In World War 3 Even Your Muse Will Get Killed! 197-.

New Era in Our Politics: The Revolutionary Answer to Neo-colonialism in Newark Politics. 197-.

A Black Value System. 1970.

J-E-L-L-O. 1970.

It's Nation Time. 1970.

In Our Terribleness: Some Elements and Meaning in Black Style (with Fundi [Billy Abernathy]). 1970.

Raise Race Rays Raze: Essays Since 1965. 1971.

Strategy and Tactics of a Pan-African Nationalist Party. 1971.

Kawaida Studies: The New Nationalism. 1972.

Spirit Reach. 1972.

African Congress: A Documentary of the First Modern Pan-African Congress (editor). 1972.

Beginning of a National Movement. 1972.

Afrikan Revolution. 1973.

Crisis in Boston!!!! 1974.

Black People and Imperialism. 1974.

Toward Ideological Clarity. 1974.

The Meaning and Development of Revolutionary Kawaida. 1974.

Creating a Unified Consciousness. c. 1974.

Revolutionary Party: Revolutionary Ideology. c. 1974.

Hard Facts: Excerpts. 1975.

Three Books (The System of Dante's Hell, Tales, The Dead Lecturer). 1975.

The Motion of History and Other Plays. 1978.

Caution: A Disco Near You Wails Death Funk. 1978.

What Was the Relationship of the Lone Ranger to the Means of Production? 1978.

The Sidney Poet Heroical. 1979.

Spring Song. 1979.

AM/TRAK. 1979.

Selected Plays and Prose. 1979.

Selected Poetry. 1979.

Afro-American Literature and Class Struggle. 198-.

Important Sonnet. 1980.

In the Tradition: For Black Arthur Blythe. c. 1980.

Reggae or Not. 1981.

Confirmation: An Anthology of AfricanAmerican Women (editor; with Amina Baraka). 1983.

Daggers and Javelins: Essays 1974–1979. 1984.

The Autobiography of LeRoi Jones. 1984.

Three Articles. c. 1985.

The Music: Reflections on Jazz and Blues (with Amina Baraka). 1987.

An Amiri Baraka/LeRoi Jones Poetry Sampler. 1991.

The LeRoi Jones/Amiri Baraka Reader. Ed. William J. Harris and Amiri Baraka. 1991.

Thornton Dial: Image of the Tiger (with others). 1993.

Conversations with Amiri Baraka. Ed. Charlie Reilly. 1994.

Gwendolyn Brooks
b. 1917

GWENDOLYN ELIZABETH BROOKS was born on June 7, 1917, in Topeka, Kansas, but grew up in Chicago. At the age of seven she began to write poetry, and her first poem was published when she was thirteen. Some of these poems were sent to James Weldon Johnson and Langston Hughes, who encouraged her work. As Willard Motley had done before her, Brooks began a weekly column for the *Chicago Defender* when she was sixteen. After graduation in 1936 from Wilson Junior College, she worked as publicity director for the NAACP Youth Council in Chicago. Brooks married Henry Lowington Blakely II in 1939; they have two children.

Brooks's career was launched in 1945 with the publication of her first book of poems, *A Street in Bronzeville*. Its acclaim was immediate; Brooks received a grant from the National Institute of Arts and Letters the next year, as well as a Guggenheim Fellowship. Her next book, *Annie Allen* (1949), won her the Pulitzer Prize for poetry: she was the first black American ever to receive the Pulitzer Prize. More poems followed, as well a book of poems for children (*Bronzeville Boys and Girls*, 1956), frequent book reviews, and the novel *Maud Martha* (1953).

In 1967 Brooks attended the Second Fisk University Writers' Conference and as a result became increasingly concerned with black issues. She left Harper & Row, her longtime publisher, for the black-owned Broadside Press, submitted her poetry to black-edited journals only, edited the magazine *Black Position*, and wrote introductions to several anthologies of work by young black writers. In May 1967 she formed a poetry workshop in Chicago for teenage gang members, eventually encountering Don L. Lee (Haki R. Madhubuti) and Carolyn M. Rodgers, who would go on to become distinguished poets in their own right. Brooks's anthology, *Jump Bad* (1971), collects poems written at this workshop. In 1968 she was named Poet Laureate of the State of Illinois.

By the time she was fifty Gwendolyn Brooks had already become an institution. The Gwendolyn Brooks Cultural Center opened at Western

Illinois University (Macomb, Illinois) in 1970. The next year a large anthology, *The World of Gwendolyn Brooks*, appeared, collecting several of her previous books. Between 1969 and 1973 she was separated from her husband, but they reconciled and in 1974 traveled to Ghana, England, and France. In 1976 Brooks became the first black woman elected to the National Institute of Arts and Letters.

Honors continued to accrue during the 1980s. On January 3, 1980, she recited a poem at the White House. In 1981 the Gwendolyn Brooks Junior High School opened in Chicago. She became the first black woman to serve as Consultant in Poetry at the Library of Congress in 1985–86. Although health problems in the 1970s reduced her output, she continues to write poems, poetry manuals for children (*Young Poet's Primer*, 1980; *Very Young Poets*, 1983), and articles for major magazines. A second omnibus of her work, *Blacks*, appeared in 1987.

Brooks has taught at City College, the University of Wisconsin at Madison, Northeastern Illinois University, Elmhurst College, and Columbia College in Illinois. She has received honorary degrees from nearly fifty universities. The first volume of her autobiography, *Report from Part One*, appeared in 1972; a second volume is in progress. Gwendolyn Brooks presently lives in Chicago.

▣ *Critical Extracts*

STANLEY KUNITZ   If only a single poem could be saved out of this book ⟨*Annie Allen*⟩, I should speak up for the one entitled (from a witty line by Edward Young) "Pygmies Are Pygmies Still, Though Percht on Alps":

> But can see better there, and laughing there
> Pity the giants wallowing on the plain.
> Giants who bleat and chafe in their small grass,
> Seldom to spread the palm; to spit; come clean.
>
> Pygmies expand in cold impossible air,
> Cry fie on giantshine, poor glory which
> Pounds breast-bone punily, screeches, and has
> Reached no Alps: or knows no Alps to reach.

I should vote for this brief poem because of the exquisite rightness of its scale; because, knowing its own limits, it is cleanly and truly separated from the jungle of conception and sensibility that constitutes the not-poem; because the imagery is sharp, the rhythm supple, the word-choice and word-play agreeably inventive; because the small and sequent pleasures of the verse are continually linked and at the last resolved, made one, and magnified. The concluding line is obviously triumphant in its massive concentration; among the other details that please me are the effective manipulation of the off-rhyme, the wallowing and bleating of the giants, the teasing ambiguity of "come clean"; the magical connotations of "giantshine"; the explosive irony in context of the adverb "punily."

How right Gwendolyn Brooks can be, as in projecting the crystalline neatness of—"Pleasant custards sit behind / The white Venetian blind"; or in arriving at the studied casualness of—"Chicken, she chided early, should not wait / Under the cranberries in after-dinner state. / Who had been beaking about the yard of late"; or in producing on occasion the flat, slapping image—"stupid, like a street / That beats into a dead end"; or in distilling her irony into—"We never did learn how / To find white in the Bible"; or in raising her voice without shrillness to the pitch of—"What shall I give my children? who are poor, / Who are adjudged the leastwise of the land, / Who are my sweetest lepers . . ."; or in achieving the beautiful and passionate rhetoric of the lines that close her book—"Rise. / Let us combine. There are no magics or elves / Or timely godmothers to guide us. We are lost, must / Wizard a track through our own screaming weed."

These are as many kinds of rightness, scattered though they be, as are tentatively possessed by any poet of her generation. To make the possession absolute and unique is the task that remains.

Stanley Kunitz, "Bronze by Gold," *Poetry* 76, No. 1 (April 1950): 55–56

HUBERT CREEKMORE   "She was learning to love moments. To love moments for themselves." And this tale of Maud Martha Brown's youth, marriage and motherhood is made up of the moments she loved. With a few exceptions when straightforward narrative takes over, it is presented in flashes, almost gasps, of sensitive lightness—distillations of the significance of each incident—and reminds of Imagist poems or clusters of ideograms from which one recreates connected experience. Miss Brooks' prose style here embodies the finer qualities of insight and rhythm that were notable in her two earlier books of poetry (her *Annie Allen* received the Pulitzer Prize), and gives a freshness, a warm cheerfulness as well as depth of implication to her first novel. In technique and impression it stands virtually alone of its kind.

> Hubert Creekmore, "Daydreams in Flight," *New York Times Book Review*, 4 October 1953, p. 4

ARTHUR P. DAVIS   The range of color in the Negro community is fascinating; but, unfortunately, it tends to create a problem *within* the group similar to that between colored and white America. The *inside* color line has never been as definitely prescribed or as harshly drawn as the outside; nevertheless, the problem *has* existed, and it *has* caused friction, misunderstanding and on occasion heartache and tragedy. For obvious reasons, this color difference within the group has made things particularly difficult for the dark girl. ⟨. . .⟩

Miss Brooks uses again and again some variant of a black-and-tan symbol, often that of a dark girl in love with a tan boy who rejects her. But she is always aware of the larger implications of the theme. Her characters, we feel, are not just poor, lost black girls in an inhospitable world; they are poor, lost humans in a modern world of other rejections equally as foolish as those based on color.

Gwendolyn Brooks has published three works: *A Street in Bronzeville* (1945), a volume which ranks with ⟨Countee Cullen's⟩ *Color* and ⟨Langston Hughes's⟩ *The Weary Blues* as a significant first work; *Annie Allen* (1949), which won for her the Pulitzer Prize in Poetry; and the *Bean Eaters* (1960), her latest work. It is not my intention to deal with all of the poems in these works. I am concerned only with those which either directly or by implication involve the black-and-tan symbol. It is my belief that an understanding of Miss Brooks's use of this symbol will give added meaning and significance to all of her works.

The scene on which Miss Brooks places her characters is always "a street in Bronzeville," and Bronzeville is not just Southside Chicago. It is also Harlem, South Philadelphia, and every other black ghetto in the North. Life in these various Bronzeville streets is seldom gay or happy or satisfying. The Bronzeville world is a world of run-down tenements, or funeral homes, or beauty parlors, of old roomers growing older without graciousness, or "cool" young hoodlums headed for trouble, of young girls having abortions. Unlike the South, it is not a place of racial violence, but in other respects it is worse than the South. It is a drab, impersonalized "corner" of the metropolitan area into which the Negro—rootless and alone—has been pushed. A sombre cloud of futility lies over Bronzeville, and nowhere is its presence more tragically felt than in its black-and-tan situations. ⟨. . .⟩

From the time of Phillis Wheatley on down to the present, practically every Negro poet has protested the color proscription in America. Perhaps it is what every sensitive and honest Negro poet *has* to do if he is to retain his self-respect. Gwendolyn Brooks has followed the tradition, but she has written poetry and not polemic.

> Arthur P. Davis, "The Black-And-Tan Motif in the Poetry of Gwendolyn Brooks," *CLA Journal* 6, No. 2 (December 1962): 90–92, 97

DAVID LITTLEJOHN   What she seems to have done is to have chosen, as her handle on the "real" (often the horribly real), the other reality of craftsmanship, of technique. With this she has created a highly stylized screen of imagery and diction and sound—fastidiously exact images, crisp Mandarin diction, ice-perfect sound—to stand between the reader and the subject; to stand often so glittering and sure that all he can ever focus on is the screen. The "subjects"—racial discrimination, mother love, suffering—are dehumanized into *manerismo* figurines, dancing her meters. It is *her* intelligence, *her* imagination, *her* brilliant wit and wordplay that entrap the attention. Always, the subjects are held at arm's length away. Whoever the persona—and she is often forced to make the speakers fastidious, alienated creatures like herself—it is always her mind and her style we are dwelling in.

This can (to a reader still concerned with "subjects") run to excess, when all "idea" is honed away in overcontrol, when all that is left, it seems, is wordplay and allusion and technique: crisp, brisk phrases and images like the taps of steel spike heels, going nowhere. In many of her early poems (especially the *Annie Allen* poems) Mrs. Brooks appears only to pretend to talk of things and of people; her real love is words. The inlay work of words, the *précieux* sonics, the lapidary insets of jeweled images (like those of Gerard

Manley Hopkins) can, in excess, squeeze out life and impact altogether, and all but give the lie to the passions professed in the verbs.

The style itself cannot be described briefly. There is enough new-bought diction and shivery tonic phrasing and rhythmic play to fascinate a university seminar in modern poetics for months. She has learned her art superbly. The words, lines, and arrangements have been worked and worked again into poised exactness: the unexpected apt metaphor, the mock-colloquial asides amid jeweled phrases, the half-ironic repetitions—she knows it all. The stylistic critic could only, at his most keen, fault the rare missed stitch of accent, the off-semitone of allusion.

> David Littlejohn, *Black on White: A Critical Survey of Writing by American Negroes* (New York: Grossman Publishers, 1966), pp. 90–91

MARGARET T. G. BURROUGHS   Will she be remembered because of a limited vocabulary filled with sensational and titillating four letter words used and excused on the basis of relevancy? I think not.

Will she be remembered because her poetry is filled with rage, hate and violence, that hate which is the antithesis of creativity, that hate which corrupts, destroys, and thwarts creativity? I think not.

Will she be remembered because she has mastered the dexterity to embroider cute designs on the page with a typewriter? I think not.

Miss Brooks and her poetry will be remembered and will speak to generations yet to come because in the first instance she is a creative human being who is concerned with all humanity. She will be remembered because she speaks from the deep wellsprings of her own black experience which shares common universals with all downtrodden and oppressed peoples, black, brown, red, white and yellow.

However above all, there is this fact which should be of great import to all younger poets who would seek to emulate Miss Brooks; Miss Brooks is a student and scholar of poetry and writing. She has done and continues to do her homework, that meticulous dedication which is necessary to produce a meaningful and lasting work of art. Miss Brooks has thoroughly mastered her craft. She knows it inside and out and in all of its aspects. She does not resort to fads, tricks or gimmicks of the moment.

> Margaret T. G. Burroughs, " 'She'll Speak to Generations Yet to Come,' " *To Gwen with Love: An Anthology Dedicated to Gwendolyn Brooks*, ed. Patricia L. Brown, Don L. Lee, and Francis Ward (Chicago: Johnson Publishing Co., 1971), pp. 129–30

TONI CADE BAMBARA   Like the younger black poets, Gwen
Brooks since the late Sixties has been struggling for a cadence, style, idiom
and content that will politicize and mobilize. Like the young black poets,
her recent work is moving more toward gesture, sound, intonation, attitude
and other characteristics that depend on oral presentation rather than private
eyeballing. It is important to have the poet herself assess these moves in
her own way so as to establish the ground for future critical biographies.
But "change" and "shift" may be too heavy-handed, somewhat misleading;
for in rereading the bulk of her work, which *Report ⟨from Part One⟩* does
prompt one to do, we see a continuum.

Gwen Brooks's works have also been very much of their times. Prior to
the late Sixties, black writers invariably brought up the rear, so to speak,
having to prove competence in techniques already laid down by mainstream
critics. Jim Crow esthetics decreed that writing "negro" was not enough,
not valid—not universal. In these times, however, black writers and critics
are the vanguard. Black works of the Thirties and Forties reflect the "social
consciousness" of the times. There was a drastic reduction in race themes
as compared with the Twenties and an adoption of a "global" perspective;
concern about European War II or whatever. The works of the Forties and
Fifties gave credence to the shaky premise on which "protest" literature
rests—that the oppressor simply needed information about grievances to
awaken the dormant conscience. The works of these times, on the other
hand, reflect quite another sensibility.

As Gwen Brooks says, "I knew there were injustices, and I wrote about
them, but I didn't know what was behind them. I didn't know what kind
of society we live in. I didn't know it was all organized." Or, assessing her
appeal-to-the-Christian-heart period: "But then, I wasn't reading the books
I should have read when I was young. If I'd been reading W. E. B. Du Bois,
I would have known." Or, "I thought I was happy, and I saw myself going
on like that for the rest of my days, I thought it was the way to live. I wrote
. . . But it was white writing, the different trends among whites. Today I
am conscious of the fact that my people are black people: it is to them that
I appeal for understanding."

> Toni Cade Bambara, [Review of *Report from Part One*], *New York Times Book Review*,
> 7 January 1973, p. 1

GLORIA T. HULL   Verbal economy ⟨. . .⟩ is accomplished more easily in an imperative or declarative mood. Consequently, these moods predominate in Miss Brooks's poetry and, combined with her short lines and generalizing statements, produce gnomic saws and aphorisms. The whole of her famous sonnet, "First fight. Then fiddle," is a classic instance of her speaking in this mode. She adopts the same tone in her later "Second Sermon on the Warpland," part two of which begins: "Salve salvage in the spin. / Endorse the splendor splashes" (*Mecca*). Her penchant for simple declaratives is illustrated by these Eliotic lines:

> The only sanity is a cup of tea.
> The music is in minors.
> (*Mecca*)

Her prediliction for raw statement often results in a string of one-word modifiers appended to a declaration she has just made:

> Peanut is
> Richard—a Ranger and a gentleman.
> A signature. A Herald. And a Span.

Such a juxtaposition of phrases without supplying the grammatical, logical, or emotional links leaves this rich but potentially-difficult creative task to the reader and holds her overt statement of her idea down to its minimum length.

This second set of qualities comprising the economical use of language almost totally characterizes Miss Brooks's *Annie Allen*, the book for which she won the Pulitzer Prize and which, ironically, is generally least liked— particularly by young blacks who reject it for reasons which directly relate to its rugged, intellectual style. Don L. Lee's reaction is typical:

> *Annie Allen* (1949), important? Yes. Read by blacks? No. *Annie Allen* more so than *A Street in Bronzeville* seems to have been written for whites. . . . This poem ("The Anniad") is probably earth-shaking to some, but leaves me completely dry.

Miss Brooks says that when she wrote "The Anniad," she "was fascinated by what words might do there in the poem," and calls it "labored, a poem that's very interested in the mysteries and magic of technique" (*Report from Part One*).

Finally, Miss Brooks has a characteristic way of handling three minor devices. First, her alliteration is often heavy and unsubtle—as a glance back through the quotations will show. Second, she uses rhyme and quick rhyme to integrate her free verse ("In the Mecca," for instance). And last, she sometimes personifies abstractions and non-human entities—a practice which may reflect her animistic beliefs, and certainly contributes to her quaint, colloquial tone. Examples occur plentifully in her poetry: "clawing the suffering dust," "the sick and influential stair," and "The ground springs up; / hits you with gnarls and rust."

In isolation, these peculiarities of style identified in Miss Brooks's poetry seem to be stilted and artificial. Yet it is obvious that she is able to make them work for her, with relatively few lapses or outright failures. She has taken definitive techniques of diction, verbal economy, and sound which are the shared tools of every poet and used them in an individual way to give herself a recognizably distinctive poetic voice.

> Gloria T. Hull, "A Note on the Poetic Technique of Gwendolyn Brooks," CLA *Journal* 19, No. 2 (December 1975): 283–85

HORTENSE J. SPILLERS   For over three decades now, Gwendo-lyn Brooks has been writing poetry which reflects a particular historical order, often close to the heart of the public event, but the dialectic that is engendered between the event and her reception of it is, perhaps, one of the more subtle confrontations of criticism. We cannot always say with grace or ease that there is a direct correspondence between the issues of her poetry and her race and sex, nor does she make the assertion necessary at every step of our reading. Black and female are basic and inherent in her poetry. The critical question is *how* they are said. Here is what the poet has to say about her own work:

> My aim, in my next future, is to write poems that will somehow
> successfully "call" all black people: black people in taverns, black
> people in alleys, black people in gutters, schools, offices, factories,
> prisons, the consulate; I wish to reach black people in mines, on
> farms, on thrones; *not* always to "teach"—I shall wish often to
> entertain, to illumine [emphasis Brooks]. My newish voice will
> not be an imitation of the contemporary young black voice,
> which I so admire, but an extending adaptation of today's G. B.
> voice.

Today's G. B. voice is one of the most complex on the American scene precisely because Brooks refuses to make easy judgments. In fact, her disposition to reserve judgment is directly mirrored in a poetry of cunning, laconic surprise. Any descriptive catalog can be stretched and strained in her case: I have tried "uncluttered," "clean," "robust," "ingenious," "unorthodox," and in each case a handful of poems will fit. This method of grading and cataloguing, however, is essentially busywork, and we are still left with the main business: What in this poetry is stunning and evasive?

To begin with, one of Brooks's most faithfully anthologized poems, "We Real Cool," illustrates the wealth of implication that the poet can achieve in a very spare poem:

> We real cool. We
> Left school. We
> Lurk late. We
> Strike straight. We
> Sing sin. We
> Thin gin. We
> Jazz June. We
> Die soon.

The simplicity of the poem is stark to the point of elaborateness. Less then lean, it is virtually coded. Made up entirely of monosyllables and end-stops, the poem is no non-sense at all. Gathered in eight units of three-beat lines, it does not necessarily invite inflection, but its persistent bump on "we" suggests waltz time to my ear. If the reader chooses to render the poem that way, she runs out of breath, or trips her tongue, but it seems that such "breathlessness" is exactly required of dudes hastening toward their death. Deliberately subverting the romance of sociological pathos, Brooks presents the pool players—"seven in the golden shovel"—in their own time. They make no excuse for themselves and apparently invite no one else to do so. The poem is their situation as *they* see it. In eight (could be nonstop) lines, here is their total destiny. Perhaps comic geniuses, they could well drink to this poem, making it a drinking/revelry song.

Hortense J. Spillers, "Gwendolyn the Terrible: Propositions on Eleven Poems," *Shakespeare's Sisters: Feminist Essays on Women Poets,* ed. Sandra M. Gilbert and Susan Gubar (Bloomington: University of Indiana Press, 1979), pp. 233–34

HARRY B. SHAW   Perhaps the most important technique that Miss Brooks uses in developing her social themes is her masterful control of artful ambiguity. Demanding a great deal of creative response from the reader, her poems are all the more an embodiment of the black experience because the technique of indirection which is vital to black survival is so prevalent in them. Using the black experience and the condition of oppression at the hands of the white man as the underlying social theme of virtually all her poetry, Miss Brooks records the black man's anguish, protest, pride, and hope in his thralldom with the artful ambiguity characteristic of black United States folk poetry. The general approach of her poetry to the life around her reflects the tradition of the black spirituals, black secular slave songs, and blues ballads with their double and triple meanings that hide the underlying and sometimes subliminal meaning that was a form of unoffensive, inconspicuous, or even invisible protest.

As an extension of the intuitive beauty of ambiguity in art used to vent the pent-up feelings of a people whose survival has demanded acquiescence, Miss Brooks's poetry often couches the predominant social themes in such ostensibly displayed conventional themes as death, religion, war, sexual and Platonic love, and peace, to name a few. She also uses many commonplace concrete subjects, such as movies, pool players, old age, apartment dwellings, and physical deformity, that are so innocent or asocial in appearance that they may beguile the unperceptive reader into a superficial reading and, therefore, perhaps a superficial appreciation, missing the heart of the poetry's black message.

Miss Brooks's ability to use the tangible to explain the intangible to reveal the tangible in its proper perspective along with her continuous complexity and subtlety are assets in the overall efficacy of her poetry in conveying social messages. Her poetry is aligned with the black tradition of artful ambiguity and indirection and therefore communicates with a subconscious sophistication that is not possible with expression made solely on the conscious level.

Harry B. Shaw, Gwendolyn Brooks (Boston: Twayne, 1980), pp. 182–83

R. BAXTER MILLER   The simple plot and structure of "In the Mecca" (the poem) present an urban setting. For convenience one can divide the narrative into three sections. Part I sets forth the return home from work of Mrs. Sallie Smith, mother of nine. The focus here is on the neighbors that she encounters and on the characterizations of her children. In the second part, the shortest, the woman notices that Pepita, one of her girls, is missing. This prompts the first search through the tenement and allows for further characterization and biblical parody. Part II also concerns the paradox of American myth. The longest section is Part III, which constitutes almost half of the verse. Here the police retrace the Smiths' search. Because of its themes and styles, Part III is probably the richest. The following contribute to its power: militant declarations, interracial lovemaking, rhetorical questions, and Christian myth. The poem ends with the discovery of Pepita's corpse under the bed of Jamaican Edward.

"In the Mecca" represents opposite strains of the Anglo-American tradition. One finds a naturalistic version of Walt Whitman, by way of the industrial age, and the redemptive, if frustrated, potential that characterizes the world of T. S. Eliot. But these influences work so that the peculiarities of the Black American experience transform them into a new and creative vision. By adapting to the social forces of the sixties, the poet uses a new milieu. Her canvas is a most demanding time in American history. For this and other times, Gwendolyn Brooks holds to light the soundness of body and mind against the decline of courage and assurance, a lapse which emerged with modernity and the shadow of the holocaust. She continues to believe that imaginative and verbal power challenge and balance finally the danger which posits the insignificance of human life and the indifference to human extinction. For her generation, the defining emblem is ultimately the whirlwind, the collapse of self-confidence, the failure to transform social ill once more into epic victory and to reclaim from the time before the holocaust, and the later accusation of "reverse discrimination" in the United States, the heroic and bluesesque will of Black hope. Whereas for Margaret Walker, cleansing has been the metaphor for the perspective which woman takes on historical and cosmic evil, the depth here every bit as great as Melville's "mystery of iniquity," for Brooks the sign is medication. The artistic process itself plays out the action of healing, while the poem serves as both epic quest and sacramental liberation.

> R. Baxter Miller, " 'Define . . . the Whirlwind': Gwendolyn Brooks' Epic Sign for a Generation," *Black American Poets Between Worlds, 1940–1960,* ed. R. Baxter Miller (Knoxville: University of Tennessee Press, 1986), pp. 162–63

D. H. MELHEM   "Bronzeville," Brooks remarks, was a name invented by the *Chicago Defender.* She described it to ⟨Elizabeth⟩ Lawrence as a South Side area of about forty blocks, running north and south from 29th to 69th Streets, and east and west about thirteen blocks from Cottage Grove to State Street (Sept. 28, 1944). An anatomy of Bronzeville appears in the important sociological study *Black Metropolis*, by St. Clair Drake and Horace R. Clayton. These authors analyze the nature and consequences of segregated black life and call for integration to combat its evils. In "Bronzeville 1961," a new chapter for the 1962 edition, Drake and Clayton find that their foci of investigation or "axes of life" remain what they had been in 1945 when the study was first made. The categories are " 'staying alive,' 'getting ahead,' 'having fun,' 'praising god,' and 'advancing the Race.' " In some respects these topics gloss *A Street in Bronzeville*, although skepticism tinges "praising god" and irony touches the "Race Hero" who is "advancing the Race."

A corollary aspect of "advancing the Race" by individual achievement or through social action is "the demand for solidarity" (Drake). This long-standing desire roots Brooks's later concern, most marked in *Beckonings* and "In Montgomery." It partly explains the early sources of her interest and the depth of her later chagrin at the erosion of unity.

Brooks initially planned *A Street in Bronzeville* to portray a personality, event, or idea representing each of thirty houses on a street in the vicinity. The sequence of twenty poems in the first section, "A Street in Bronzeville," is close in tone and milieu to the following five, grouped here as "Five Portraits." All the poems give humanistic and compassionate glimpses of black life. The first section focuses on common existence; the middle one, except for "Hattie Scott," offers longer poems that probe distinct and dramatic characters. The third and last section, "Gay Chaps at the Bar," comprises the sonnet sequence. Thematically, the volume is largely structured around two units: local/black and national/multiracial. Brooks exposes their interrelationships—personal, social, and national. The theme of entrapment, by community norms, socioeconomic forces, and personal psychology, underlies the whole.

D. H. Melhem, *Gwendolyn Brooks* (Lexington: University Press of Kentucky, 1987), pp. 19–20

GLADYS WILLIAMS   Brooks has been an innovative poet. She is also an artist in whom the forces of tradition and continuity have enriched her craft. She has written carefully disciplined and well-wrought sonnets in the tradition of Shakespeare. Metrical craft and poetic form have been as much a consideration for Brooks as they have been in her antecedents Yeats and Frost. The metaphysical wit of Eliot, Pound, Frost, and the younger Robert Lowell have exerted a significant influence on the poet. The basic and central free-verse tradition that comes to Brooks through Walt Whitman, James Weldon Johnson, Sterling Brown, William Carlos Williams, and her beloved Langston Hughes is especially strong. Certain features of her art originate in the black folk art forms—the blues, the ballads, the folk tales, the sermons Brooks grew up with—as well as in the works of Shakespeare, Frost, Dickinson, et al. The poet's penchant for understatement, her wry and ironic humor, her terseness, her skill in giving her poetry the sound of the human voice, and the ethnotropic metaphor she creates are brilliantly present in her ballads as they are in the folk ballad antecedents. The Brooks ballad reveals one stream of the multiple literary influences that flow through her poetry.

> Gladys Williams, "The Ballads of Gwendolyn Brooks," *A Life Distilled: Gwendolyn Brooks, Her Poetry and Fiction*, ed. Maria K. Mootry and Gary Smith (Urbana: University of Illinois Press, 1987), pp. 222–23

GEORGE E. KENT   Actually, *Annie Allen* challenges not so much by its particularism as by its craft and its universality—further developments of the resources and approaches present in *A Street in Bronzeville*. The poems in *A Street* offer a deceptively full realistic surface and make use of well-known devices from the conventions and techniques of poetic realism. There are abrupt beginnings in *A Street* and some elliptical syntax, which demand that the reader drop everything and attend closely, but neither is developed to the extent manifested in *Annie Allen*.

One major difference between the two works is that the reader of *Annie Allen* is more openly confronted with the necessity to read actively. Although people and their life stories appear in plots sharply outlined, presenting easily recognized issues from the daily round of existence, and move to definite climaxes and decisive conclusions, there are frequent signals of the presence of more than one perspective—additional comments upon the human condition available beneath the poems' realistic surface, representing engagement with the contradictoriness and complexity of experience.

The opening poems of the two works illustrate the difference. *A Street* opens with "the old-marrieds": "But in the crowding darkness not a word did they say. / Though the pretty-coated birds had piped so lightly all the day." Except for the abrupt beginning with "but," there is nothing to discomfit the reader. The syntax is regular except for punctuation of a clause as a full sentence in the second line—certainly no radical break with established practice.

Annie Allen, proper, on the other hand, opens with "the birth in a narrow room": "Weeps out of Western country something new. / Blurred and stupendous. Wanted and unplanned." Whereas in "the old-marrieds" the issue and perhaps the mystery of the story are almost immediately suggested, "the birth" requires careful and repeated readings to grasp the theme: the slow absorption of "reality" by infant life and the creative experiences awaiting the infant between the stages of unreflecting confrontation with existence and realization of its limitations. The poem demands greater reader participation and creativity: an acceptance of the elliptical syntax in the first stanza and grasp of images with mythic functions—not merely of day-to-day "reality." The infant's first movement into time is an almost passive survey of artifacts, with the last image foreshadowing something of the magic of the childhood world: "the milk-glass fruit bowl, iron pot, / The bashful china child tripping forever / Yellow apron and spilling pretty cherries." The second stanza mixes images of reality with expressions and gestures connoting the transforming power of early childhood imagination:

> But prances nevertheless with gods and fairies
> Blithely about the pump and then beneath
> The elms and grapevines, then in darling endeavor
> By privy foyer, where the screenings stand
> And where the bugs buzz by in private cars
> Across old peach cans and old jelly jars.

George E. Kent, *A Life of Gwendolyn Brooks* (Lexington: University Press of Kentucky, 1990), pp. 80–81

❖ Bibliography

A Street in Bronzeville. 1945.
Annie Allen. 1949.

Maud Martha. 1953.

Bronzeville Boys and Girls. 1956.

We Real Cool. 1959.

The Bean Eaters. 1960.

Selected Poems. 1963.

In the Time of Detachment, in the Time of Cold. 1965.

The Wall. 1967.

In the Mecca. 1968.

Martin Luther King, Jr. 1968.

For Illinois 1968: A Sesquicentennial Poem. 1968.

Riot. 1969.

Family Pictures. 1970.

Aloneness. 1971.

The World of Gwendolyn Brooks. 1971.

Elegy in a Rainbow: A Love Poem. 1971.

A Broadside Treasury 1965–1970 (editor). 1971.

Black Steel: Joe Frazier and Mohammad Ali. 1971.

Jump Bad: A New Chicago Anthology (editor). 1971.

Aurora. 1972.

Report from Part One. 1972.

The Tiger Who Wore White Gloves; or, What You Are You Are. 1974.

Beckonings. 1975.

A Capsule Course in Black Poetry Writing (with Keorapetse Kgositsile, Haki
    R. Madhubuti, and Dudley Randall). 1975.

Other Music. 1976.

The Mother. 1978.

Primer for Blacks. 1980.

Young Poet's Primer. 1980.

To Disembark. 1981.

Black Love. 1982.

The Progress. 1982.

Mayor Harold Washington and Chicago, the I Will City. 1983.

Very Young Poets. 1983.

The Near-Johannesburg Boy and Other Poems. 1986.

Blacks. 1987.

Winnie. 1988.

The Second Sermon on the Warpland. 1988.

Gottschalk and the Grande Tarantelle. 1988.

Jane Addams: September 6, 1860–May 21, 1935. 1990.
Children Coming Home. 1991.
Christmas Morning Comes Too Soon. 1992.

Alice Childress
1920–1994

ALICE CHILDRESS was born in Charleston, South Carolina, on October 12, 1920. She was raised in Harlem in New York City by her grandmother, Eliza Campbell. Although her education extended only to the fifth grade, Campbell was a great storyteller; according to Childress, however, "she was not fond of remembering her mother's account of slavery and the mockery of so-called freedom" in the Reconstruction South. Childress dropped out of high school after two years, but was a voracious reader and continued her education at the public library. She became interested in acting after hearing Laura Bowman recite scenes from Shakespeare and, in 1941, joined the American Negro Theatre in Harlem, going on to perform in some of ANT's biggest hits, such as *On Strivers' Row* and *Anna Lucasta*.

In 1949 Childress wrote her first play, a one-act piece entitled *Florence*. The play (purportedly written in one night) was a moderate success and proved typical of Childress's work in its exploration of contemporary racial issues. *Florence* was followed by *Just a Little Simple* (1950), an adaptation of Langston Hughes's novel *Simple Speaks His Mind,* and by *Gold through the Trees* (1952), a play about Harriet Tubman that was the first play by a black woman to be professionally produced in the United States. In 1955 Childress wrote *Trouble in Mind,* a critically and financially successful play about a group of black actors who, while rehearsing a lynching melodrama written and directed by whites entitled *Chaos in Belleville,* protest the offensive stereotyping of the play's black characters. Childress published the play in Lindsay Patterson's *Black Theatre* in 1971, deleting a final act in which the director agrees to a rewrite of *Chaos*. Plays following *Trouble in Mind* include *Wedding Band: A Love/Hate Story in Black and White* (produced 1966; published 1973), a play about an interracial couple in Charleston in 1918; *Wine in the Wilderness* (1969), a television play about the insensitivity of "revolutionary" black nationalists toward less educated, older, and less politically correct black Americans; the one-act *String* (produced 1969; published, with *Mojo,* 1971), an adaptation of Guy de Maupassant's short story "A Piece of String"; and most recently *Moms* (1989), a biographical drama about the black vaudeville comedienne Jackie "Moms" Mabley.

In addition to plays, Childress wrote a book based on her conversations with black domestic workers, *Like One of the Family* (1956). She wrote a variety of works, including theatricals and novels, for children. Her first young adult novel, *A Hero Ain't Nothin' But a Sandwich* (1973), about a fourteen-year-old heroin addict, was adapted by the author into a critically successful film produced in 1977. Other young adult novels include *A Short Walk* (1979), *Rainbow Jordan* (1981), and *Those Other People* (1989). She also published two plays for children, *When the Rattlesnake Sounds* (1975) and *Let's Hear It for the Queen* (1976).

Childress was married twice, but information on her first husband is unavailable; from this marriage she had one daughter. She married musician Nathan Woodard in 1957. Alice Childress died on August 14, 1994.

❖ Critical Extracts

A. G.   A fresh, lively and cutting satire called *Trouble in Mind* is being played downtown by an inter-racial group of Equity members. ⟨. . .⟩

Their play's setting is backstage at a Broadway theatre during the first rehearsal of a tawdry melodrama dealing with a Negro lynching in the South. The author of *Trouble in Mind* is Alice Childress, a writer with a quick eye for the foibles and crotches, the humor and pathos of backstage life in the type of Broadway production that utilizes a predominantly Negro cast.

Miss Childress, who was a member of the original company of *Anna Lucasta*, has some witty and penetrating things to say about the dearth of roles for Negro actors in the contemporary theatre, the cut-throat competition for these parts and the fact that Negro actors often find themselves playing stereotyped roles in which they cannot bring themselves to believe.

She also has some sharp comments to make about the jumpy state of nerves in the much-investigated entertainment media. But it is all done with good humor and, except for the last ten or fifteen minutes, manages to avoid any impassioned sermonizing.

> A. G., "Play in Village Is Well Worth the Trip," *New York Times*, 5 Novemeber 1955, p. 23

DORIS E. ABRAMSON   *Trouble in Mind* has interesting characters and dialogue, though both tend to ring false whenever they are saturated with sermonizing. The setting, the stage of a theatre during rehearsals, invites an audience to participate in a ritual usually forbidden them and therefore tantalizing. The plot amounts to very little—a group of actors rehearse a play, quarrel about interpretation, get the director to agree to ask the playwright to make changes in the script. What lends the play significance is that the cast is predominantly Negro. As attitudes in the company are modified, people's lives are affected, and this play about a rehearsal makes a comment on life itself.

And yet, too much of *Trouble in Mind* is willed—what the French call *voulu*. A reader of the script is very much aware of the author pulling strings, putting her own words into a number of mouths. This is not, however, to deny the theatrical effectiveness of the play in production. One critic's description of the audience participation suggests a very direct involvement:

> The satirical scenes rocked and moved the audience until it
> became part of the action on the stage. Many members of the
> audience were so moved that they vocally expressed dislike or
> approval of the actions and speeches of the characters on stage. I
> have not seen anything like it since I was a boy and sat in the
> gallery with other kids watching Wild West melodramas.

Brooks Atkinson found the play "well worth a trip downtown" and praised Miss Childress for writing a "fresh, lively and cutting satire" without sermonizing until the last ten or fifteen minutes.

To read the play is to be much more aware than these critics were—they were under the spell of what was reportedly a good production—of the extent to which Miss Childress loaded the play with Negro problems. True, she makes us understand her need to write about her people when she says:

> Many of us would rather be writers than Negro writers, and when
> I get that urge, I look about for the kind of white writer—which
> is what we mean when we say "just a writer"—that I would
> emulate. I come up with Sean O'Casey. Immediately, I am a
> problem writer. O'Casey writes about the people he knows best
> and I must.

It would be better if she did not assault race prejudice at every turn, for she sometimes sacrifices depth of character in the process.

What a critic once said of Mildred, the heroine of Miss Childress' collection of stories, *Like One of the Family*, could be said of characters in her play, especially of Wiletta:

> One longs for the shock (so often encountered in life) of an
> unexpected taste or point of view. One longs also to penetrate
> beyond the "typical" view we are given . . . to the private agony
> and unique courage of such a woman.

The characters need a humanizing complexity to keep them from ever becoming the stereotypes featured in *Chaos in Belleville*.

Doris E. Abramson, *Negro Playwrights in the American Theatre 1925–1959* (New York: Columbia University Press, 1967), pp. 203–4

ELBERT R. HILL   The important differences between novels and films become particularly apparent when the same author treats a story in both media, as Alice Childress did when she wrote the screenplay for *A Hero Ain't Nothin' But a Sandwich* (1978), based on a novel she had published five years earlier. ⟨. . .⟩

⟨. . .⟩ the movie ⟨*A Hero Ain't Nothin' But a Sandwich*⟩ never makes it sufficiently clear how or why Benjie becomes addicted to drugs. To show that Benjie is becoming hooked, the filmmaker resorts to the device of repetitive scenes showing him using the drugs and earning money for this habit by delivering drugs. In the movie, the whole time lapse from Benjie's first use of marijuana to when we know that he is, in fact, unable to quit heroin, seems altogether too brief and unrealistically sudden. And the question of *why* Benjie takes drugs remains quite puzzling. Though bothered by the fact that he does not know where his real father is, he appears to have no other problem. Because of the shift in setting and some other changes as well, Benjie's environment seems neither hostile nor threatening. At home, he is surrounded by people who care about him, even though they have their own needs and preoccupations too. And in school he even seems to be something of a star. There is a scene in Nigeria's class in which Benjie is able to amaze the whole class, teacher included, with his knowledge about a particular black leader. And in Bernard Cohen's class, he is asked to read aloud a composition for which he is publicly praised and given an "A".

The scene is apparently used to show two things: first, assigned to write about a member of his family, Benjie has selected his mother, thus revealing her importance to him as his only remaining parent. Second, when as part of his praise Cohen says, "Keep this up and some day you'll be somebody," Benjie replies, "I'm somebody now." We are confronted with a common adolescent problem: the feeling that adults don't give them credit for being someone *now*, and focus too much on what they *may* grow up to be. The scene thus fulfills some valid functions in the movie, but combined with the scene in Nigeria's class it also suggests that Benjie's school provides a generally supportive atmosphere. In the book, the praise Benjie receives for the paper about his mother is said to be something that happened years before the time of the book, and it is not typical of his school career. There is no equivalent in the book of the scene in Nigeria's class.

In addition, the Benjie of the novel tells us several times that one of his problems is that he feels betrayed by Nigeria Greene, who, along with Cohen, has turned him in for drug use. Though the movie does show the two teachers taking him out of class when he is obviously stoned, it does not emphasize for us the importance that this betrayal has for Benjie because it has not made sufficiently clear how he has idolized Nigeria.

A time shift that is even more troublesome ⟨. . .⟩ concerns the change in the relationship between Benjie and Butler. In the book, after Butler has saved his life, Benjie writes "Butler is my father" one hundred times. This indicates that Benjie finally realizes that Butler does indeed care for him, and suggests to the reader that the boy is accepting Butler's role in his life. ⟨. . .⟩ In the movie, Benjie writes "Butler is my father" much earlier, *before* Butler has saved his life—and so far as we know Butler never sees the piece of writing. Thus, the movie Benjie's motivation for trying to get off drugs—like his motivation for getting on them—is not fully clear ⟨. . .⟩

The ending of the movie is revealing of the overall differences between the two forms. In the movie, when Butler waits for Benjie at the Rehab Center, the boy actually appears; in the book Butler only waits and hopes. The movie ending is weaker in consequence ⟨. . .⟩ The reader was led to believe that Benjie will appear, because this would be the logical result of his realization of Butler's love for him and of his acceptance of the older man as his hero. But since moviegoers have not had this clear motivation for Benjie to change, they need to be shown that the boy does indeed intend to change.

Elbert R. Hill, "*A Hero* for the Movies," *Children's Novels and the Movies*, ed. Douglas Street (New York: Frederick Ungar, 1983), pp. 236, 240–42

ALICE CHILDRESS   I try to bend my writing form to most truth-fully express content; to move beyond the either/or of "artistic" and politi-cally imposed limitations. I never planned to become a writer. Early writing was done almost against my will. Grandmother Eliza gently urged, "Why not write that thought down on a piece of paper? It's worth keeping." Writing was jotting things down. The bits and pieces became stories. Writing was a way of reminding myself to go on with thoughts, to take the next step. Jottings became forms after I discovered the public library and attempted to read two books a day. Reading and evaluating form, I taught myself to know the difference of structure in plays, books, short stories, teleplays, motion picture scenarios, and so forth. Knowledge of such form and much content taught me to break rules and follow my own thought and structure patterns with failure and success. I acquired a measure of self-discipline, to make myself write against my will in the face of a limited market. ⟨. . .⟩

My books tend to read somewhat like plays because theater heavily influenced my writing. I think mainly in terms of visual, staged scenes and live actors in performance—even in a novel. The novel and film allow for more wandering and changing of "setting." The stage play, confined to one area, taxes the imagination more than other forms. It is the greatest challenge because it also depends heavily on the cooperation of many other individuals with several approaches to creative expression—the director, the producer, set, scene and lighting people, costumer etc. ⟨. . .⟩

While one is creating a character there are glad moments of divorce from one's own conscious theories and beliefs. We can be taken over by a charac-ter. I was tempted to remove "The Pusher" from *A Hero Ain't Nothin' But a Sandwich:* the villain was too persuasive, too good at self-defense, too winning in his sinning; however, he is the toughest form of street temptation, so I let him live. The book was banned from the Island Trees School Library, case still pending along with several others after going through two courts. It was also the first book banned from a Savannah, Georgia, school library since *Catcher in the Rye* was banned during the fifties. Writing is indeed exciting and the joy of creation, though tedious at times, is the highest form of compensation. Well, I can't find a thought to better this old one. . . .

Alice Childress, "A Candle in a Gale Wind," *Black Women Writers (1950–1980): A Critical Evaluation*, ed. Mari Evans (Garden City, NY: Anchor Press/Doubleday, 1984), pp. 114–16

SAMUEL A. HAY   In two ways, *Florence* is typical of Alice Childress's seventeen plays: (a) Childress in interested in a well-crafted situation about an essentially good person who is hurt by Blacks or whites because the person mistakes (false) signs for (true) symbols; and (b) Childress changes her dramatic structure according to whether a Black or a white person creates the hurt. The first typicality places Childress in the William Wells Brown tradition of writing well-structured plays which aim to show how things ought to be, or where they have gone wrong. ⟨. . .⟩

What sets Childress apart is the second typicality. Childress switches the protagonist-antagonist functions and creates several other revolutionary changes in order to support her political and ethical concerns. ⟨. . .⟩

Childress can be classified as a traditionalist in structure because she (a) treats her episodes as the building blocks of her play, (b) distinguishes one episode from another by the appearance of a new character or by a principal character's leaving the scene or retiring from participation in the action, and (c) avoids improvisational and experimental structural devices altogether. Nevertheless, Childress designs her episodes for quite different purposes than the usual psychological characterization popularized by Eugene O'Neill during the forties and fifties, and adopted by such newcomers in the fifties as Tennessee Williams and Arthur Miller. Instead, Childress keeps the traditional beginning, middle, and end, and she substitutes theme for character. The substitution strains the traditional structure because Childress does not reveal the theme through characterization but through argumentation. Therefore, each episode develops not only the usually slim Childress story but, more importantly, the Main Idea. Because the constituent ideas simply repeat the Main Idea, the purpose of each episode, then, is to represent another "circumstantial detail" of the Main Idea. Elder Olson explains:

> If I remark that the news of the day includes a murder, a robbery, a fire, a suicide, a bank failure, and a divorce, you respond with simple ideas of these; but if I go into circumstantial detail, you frame very complex ones. By "circumstances," I mean the doer of the action, the act, the purpose, the instrument with which it was done, the manner in which it was done, the person or object to which it was done, the result, the time, the place, and all similar matters.

To understand fully the substitutions of the idea for character and of circum-stantial detail for the Main Idea development, the concerns must be to identify which circumstantial detail develops which constituent idea of the

Main Idea. For example, the Main Idea in *Florence* is: "Black people—not white liberals—must struggle if there is to be real political and economic equality."

Samuel A. Hay, "Alice Childress's Dramatic Structure," *Black Women Writers (1950–1980): A Critical Evaluation*, ed. Mari Evans (Garden City, NY: Anchor Press/Doubleday, 1984), pp. 118–19

GAYLE AUSTIN   ⟨Childress's⟩ plays themselves ⟨. . .⟩ break down ⟨. . .⟩ binary oppositions. Stage one deals with the images of women composed by men, with woman as object. Stage two deals with women as artists, with women as subjects, actively telling their own stories. Stage three is still somewhat undefined but deals more with women as critics, with textual conventions and the ways women tell their stories.

Many of the characters and ideas in *Trouble in Mind* are as fresh as and perhaps more generally recognizable than they were thirty years ago. Both the character, Wiletta, and author Childress are actively protesting the few and false images of black women written by white men with "blind spots." ⟨. . .⟩ Childress, in writing the roles of Wiletta and Millie, has provided some alternative images of black women, three dimensional characters with weaknesses and strengths.

In terms of the second stage, Wiletta becomes a critic/artist of the play she is performing, changing from passive object to active subject in front of our eyes ⟨. . .⟩ Wiletta's argument against the character she is trying to "act" builds in act two ⟨. . .⟩ She asks, "Why we sendin' him out into the teeth of a lynch mob? I'm his mother and I'm sendin' him to his death. This is a lie. . . . The writer wants the damn white man to be the hero— and I'm the villain." ⟨. . .⟩ Wiletta's criticism reshapes some other cast members' ideas of the play, and her challenge to Manners that he is a racist rewrites Wiletta's career story, making her an unemployed subject rather than employable object. That situation will only change when the entire system changes, the difficulty of which is put into the mouth of the director during his tirade:

> MANNERS: . . . Get wise, there's damned few of us interested in putting on a colored show at all, much less one that's going to say anything. . . . Do you think I can stick my neck out by telling the truth about you? There are billions of things that *can't be said.* . . .

> Where the hell do you think I can raise a hundred thousand
> dollars to tell the unvarnished truth? (*Picks up the script and waves
> it.*) So maybe it's a lie . . . but it's one of the finest lies you'll
> come across for a damned long time! . . . The American public is
> not ready to see you the way you want to be seen because, one,
> they don't believe it, two, they don't want to believe it, and
> three, they're convinced they're superior—and that, my friend, is
> why Carrie and Renard [white characters] have to carry the ball!
> Get it? Now you wise up and aim for the soft spot in that
> American heart, let 'em pity you, make 'em weep buckets, be
> helpless, make 'em feel so damned sorry for you that they'll lend a
> hand in easing up the pressure.

That is a most concise and accurate statement of the dynamic of both black
and female cultural images in this country, and it comes from a white male
character who both knows the score and helps perpetuate the game. But
he does not get the final word in this play, and Wiletta's continuing presence
on stage is something new and potentially powerful. ⟨. . .⟩

Inserting women's *presence* into a story is an even more powerful weapon
⟨. . .⟩ and that is the one chosen by Childress in this play. She also uses
some theatrical devices in ways that help to write women into the script.
Her play-within-a-play structure allows her to demonstrate the way male
images portray black women and show both the actor's true and false feelings
about those images. ⟨. . .⟩ She also uses Wiletta's singing of a song in *Chaos
in Belleville*, first in a manner of "despair" and then in "strength and anger"
to show Wiletta's growing rebellion, Manners' dissatisfaction with the latter
interpretation, and the double-edged weapon art can become. Overlapping
dialogue more than once conveys chaos in both the rehearsal situation and
Wiletta's mind. In bending conventional tools to her use as well as "speaking
the unspoken" Childress helped fill the absence of role models for black
women playwrights (this was four years before Lorraine Hansberry wrote *A
Raisin in the Sun*) and the lack of substantial roles for black actresses.

Gayle Austin, "Alice Childress: Black Woman Playwright as Feminist Critic," *Southern Quarterly* 25, No. 30 (Spring 1987): 56–59

SANDRA Y. GOVAN   ⟨. . .⟩ moving readers, and demonstrating
that her characters are indeed human and not mere symbols, statistics,

images, or stones, is clearly a part of Childress's multi-layered strategy, part of the function of her art.

And when we examine ⟨Rainbow Jordan . . .⟩ we see Childress being attentive not only to function but to the other considerations of the Black Aesthetic as well. If, for instance, the function of Black art is to accent racial identity—who we are and where we are going; or if it is to make myths and render the ordinary extraordinary—Childress achieves this "function" and yet accomplishes this in her own singular fashion. Unlike a Mildred Taylor or a Toni Cade Bambara, writers known for their creation of sassy or tough young female protagonists, in Rainbow Jordan Childress makes her heroine, and each of her other characters, walk the high wire in a solo balancing act, alone and unsteady until they learn first to reach inward for self-validation and strength, then outward to touch others who themselves are authentic and thus willing to reach out.

The usual or traditional community support structures typically illustrative of Afro-American life and culture play virtually no role in Rainbow. The Black church, a staple symbol in much Afro-American literature, is notable by its absence. In fact, Josephine's Quaker neighbor teaches Rainbow the Quaker concept of "centering down" rather than prayer to help face a problem. The strong nurturing community with neighbor helping neighbor, a recurring motif in much Afro-American literature, especially that set in the South, is also absent. Rather, Childress unabashedly depicts the divisive, splintered, often antagonistic communities which are, regretfully, a truism of contemporary urban living.

Rainbow's awkward family situation stands as ironic counterpoint to the dominant Afro-American literary tradition that paints a strong cohesive family, either nuclear or extended, as central element in the formation of character. Here we have a portrait of family disintegration, again an all too frequent truism of modern urban life. Authentic female bonding among peers, such as that which occurs in Toni Morrison's Sula (1973) or Paule Marshall's Brown Girl, Brownstones (1959), is also missing. Of course, Rainbow and Josephine "bond" but 14 and 57 is hardly the same peer group. Instead, Rainbow painfully learns the wisdom of that deathless folk pronouncement, "Everybody who say they your friend, ain't." Intriguingly, the one remaining traditional symbol or cultural ritual which Childress permits is a very subtle bow to the blues. Both Rainbow and Josephine suffer from heartache; and heartaches are, as every mature reader knows, a staple of the blues. Even Kathie has heartaches, but she is essentially a "good time girl," another kind of staple blues figure. Heartaches, of course, don't last always and by novel's end, Rainbow and Josephine have hardened their will, left the "low-down" men in their lives behind, and walked away. They suffer still, but they've experienced the catharsis the blues afford.

Because of the skill with which they are invoked, both Rainbow (and certainly the name is weighted with obvious symbolic intent) and Josephine become, despite any intent to the contrary, symbols of survival. They are also powerful images of what it can mean to "hold fast" to one's dreams, as Langston Hughes has said, and to live with integrity and dignity. Childress's commitment to depicting the lives of people within the working class and middle class Black communities provides us with, as Trudier Harris says, a "sensitive readable book which entertains quietly and teaches without being overly didactic."

Sandra Y. Govan, "Alice Childress's *Rainbow Jordan:* The Black Aesthetic Returns Dressed in Adolescent Fiction," *Children's Literary Association Quarterly* 13, No. 1 (Summer 1988): 73

CATHERINE WILEY   Julia's problem throughout the play ⟨Wedding Band⟩ is less her white lover than her reluctance to see herself as a member of the black community. Although a mostly white theater audience would see her as a different sort of heroine because of race, her black neighbors perceive her as different from them for issues more complex than skin color. She assumes that her racial transgression with Herman will make her unwelcome among the women she wishes to confide in, but her aloofness from their day-to-day interests also serves as a protective shield. In this, Julia is similar to Lutie Johnson in Ann Petry's *The Street,* written in 1946. Both characters are ostensibly defined by their unequal relations with men, but their potential for salvation lies in the larger community that depends on the stability of its women. ⟨. . .⟩ Neither poor nor uneducated, Julia finds herself defying the black community by asserting her right to love a white man, but this self-assertion is, in a larger sense, a more dangerous defiance of the white community. She wants her love story to be one of individual commitment and sacrifice, but it is that only in part. Julia's refinement in manners, education, and financial independence, which are middle-class, traditionally white attributes, make her and Herman available to each other.

But theirs is, as the subtitle insists, a "love/hate" story, in which interracial love cannot be divorced from centuries of racial hate. ⟨. . .⟩

The first white character to appear in the play is the Bell Man, a foil to Herman, who pedals dime-store merchandise in the poor neighborhood using the insidious installment system, "fifty cent a week and one long, sweet year to pay." Recognizing Julia from another neighborhood, he comments sardonically that she moves a lot, invites himself into her bedroom, and bounces on the bed. "But seriously, what is race and color?" he asks. "Put a paper bag over your head and who'd know the difference." When Julia chases him out with a wooden hanger, he calls her a "sick-minded bitch" because she refuses to play the historical role of the master's sexual toy, already bought and paid for on the slave market. Like the landlady, who also has pushed herself unwanted into Julia's rented room, the Bell Man objectifies Julia into a representative of her race. If for Fanny the proper black woman is to be asexual, for the salesman she is to be a body with a paper bag over her head, hiding not only her race but her existence as an individual with a face and a name. Fanny's attitude constitutes one legitimate response to centuries of white men's sexual abuse of black women. Julia's relationship with Herman should not leave her open to the insults of a traveling salesman, but in his eyes, and perhaps in Fanny's, that relationship makes her another black woman who "prefers" white men.

This scene points to the inseparability of racism and sexism, an issue that cannot be isolated from the historical relationship of the civil rights and women's movements. ⟨. . .⟩ The signal white women's liberationists ⟨of the 1960s⟩ sent to black women echoed the one suffragists had sent to their abolitionist sisters a century earlier: your race matters less than your gender. ⟨. . .⟩ If a black woman is to be a feminist, it appears she must cease to be black. Julia's treatment by Fanny and the salesman effects the opposite but equally insidious contradiction: she can be a member of the black race, but as such she cannot be an individual woman.

Catherine Wiley, "Whose Name, Whose Protection: Reading Alice Childress's *Wedding Band*," *Modern American Drama: The Female Canon*, ed. June Schlueter (Rutherford, NJ: Fairleigh Dickinson University Press, 1990), pp. 188–90

▨ *Bibliography*

Like One of the Family: Conversations from a Domestic's Life. 1956.

Wine in the Wilderness: A Comedy-Drama. 1969.

Black Scenes (editor). 1971.

Mojo and String. 1971.

A Hero Ain't Nothin' But a Sandwich. 1973.

Wedding Band: A Love/Hate Story in Black and White. 1973.

When the Rattlesnake Sounds. 1975.

Let's Hear It for the Queen. 1976.

A Short Walk. 1979.

Rainbow Jordan. 1981.

Many Closets. 1987.

Those Other People. 1989.

Lucille Clifton
b. 1936

LUCILLE CLIFTON was born Thelma Lucille Sayles on June 27, 1936, in Depew, New York. She was named Lucille after her great-grandmother, who was the first black woman legally hanged in Virginia (she shot and killed the white man who impregnated her, but her mother's standing in the community was such that she was not lynched). Lucille Sayles's parents were estranged and her family quite poor; nevertheless, she grew up in a nurturing and supportive environment filled with stories of her family's history, all of which she missed a great deal when she attended Howard University in Washington, D.C., from 1953 to 1955. After two years at Howard, she attended Fredonia State Teachers College (now State University of New York College at Fredonia) for a year. She married educator, writer, and artist Fred James Clifton in 1958; they would eventually have six children. Her family figures prominently in Clifton's work.

Clifton's first job was as a claims clerk for the New York State Division of Employment in Buffalo, New York. After working there for two years (1958–60), she gave up her career to stay home and raise her children. She took to writing only in her early thirties, by which time she also resumed employment, this time in the academic community: she was a literature assistant for the Central Atlantic Regional Educational Laboratory from 1969 to 1971 and poet in residence at Coppin State College in Baltimore from 1971 to 1974.

Clifton's first book of poetry, *Good Times*, was published in 1969 to critical acclaim, being cited as one of the year's ten best books by the *New York Times*. This volume was followed by several other books of poetry: *Good News about the Earth: New Poems* (1972), *An Ordinary Woman* (1974), *Two-Headed Woman* (1980), the retrospective *Good Woman: Poems and a Memoir 1969–1980* (1987), *Next: New Poems* (1987), and *Quilting: Poems 1987–1990* (1991). Clifton's poems discuss racial issues, celebrate her blackness and her womanhood, and explore her spiritual experiences. Clifton also has examined her family's history in America in the prose volume *Generations: A Memoir* (1976) as well as in her poetry.

In addition to her adult books, Clifton has been a prolific writer of children's books specifically aimed at black juvenile readers. These take the form of highly accessible poems accompanied by illustrations. Her children's books include *The Black BC's* (1970), *The Boy Who Didn't Belive in Spring* (1973), and the Everett Anderson stories, which revolve around the life and adventures of a young urban black boy.

Clifton has in recent years been a visiting writer at a number of colleges and universities, including Columbia and George Washington. She made her family home in Baltimore, becoming Poet Laureate of the State of Maryland in 1979, a position she held until 1982. Clifton was widowed in 1984 and moved to Santa Cruz, where since 1985 she has been professor of literature and creative writing at the University of California at Santa Cruz.

Critical Extracts

JANE O'REILLY   *Everett Anderson's Christmas Coming* is for modern urban celebrators. Everett Anderson, black and boyish, is glimpsed, rather than explained through poems about him, written by Lucille Clifton. White middle-class parents will want answers to certain questions. For example, on Dec. 22 Everett thinks about "If Daddy was here," but where Daddy is, is never explained. It doesn't really have to be and city children know that. The joys of living in Apt. 14A are perfectly clear, and I really liked Dec. 15:

> Boys with lots
> of boxes
> smiles Everett Anderson
> spend all day Christmas
> opening
> and never have much fun.

which appears with a picture of Everett holding the world's most splendid guinea pig, labeled "Merry Christmas."

Jane O'Reilly, "For Young Readers: 'Tis the Season," *New York Times Book Review*, 5 December 1971, p. 90

LUCILLE CLIFTON   I write the way I write because I am the kind of person that I am. My styles and my content stem from my experience. I grew up a well-loved child in a loving family and so I have always known that being very poor, which we were, had nothing to do with lovingness or familyness or character or any of that. ⟨. . .⟩ We were/are quite sure that we were/are among the best of people and not having any money had nothing to do with that. Other people's opinions didn't influence us about that. We were quite sure. When I write, especially for children, I try to get that across, that being poor or whatever your circumstance, you are capable of being the best of people and that best, as a human, does not come from the outside in, it comes from the inside out.

I use a simple language. I have never believed that for anything to be valid or true or intellectual or "deep" it had to first be complex. I deliberately use the language that I use. Sometimes people have asked me when I was going to try something hard or difficult, as if my work sprang from my ignorance. I like to think that I write from my knowledge not my lack, from my strength and not my weakness. I am not interested if anyone knows whether or not I am familiar with big words, I am interested in being understood not admired. I wish to celebrate and not be celebrated (though a little celebration is a lot of fun).

I am a woman and I write from that experience. I am a Black woman and I write from that experience. I do not feel inhibited or bound by what I am. That does not mean that I have never had bad scenes relating to being Black and/or a woman, it means that other people's craziness has not managed to make me crazy. At least not in their way because I try very hard not to close my eye to my own craziness nor to my family's, my sex's, nor my race's. I don't believe that I should only talk about the beauty and strength and goodness of my people but I do believe that if we talk about our room for improvement we should do it privately. I don't believe in public family fights. But I do think sometimes a good fight is cleansing. We are not perfect people. There are no perfect people. ⟨. . .⟩

When my first book was published I was thirty-three years old and had six children under ten years old. I was too busy to take it terribly seriously. I was very happy and proud of course, but had plenty of other things to think about. It was published by Random House and that seemed to bother some of my friends. At first my feelings were a little hurt that anyone would even be concerned about it but I got over that. I decided that if something doesn't matter, it really doesn't matter. Sometimes I think that the most anger comes from ones who were late in discovering that when the world said nigger it meant them too. I grew up knowing that the world meant me too but that was the world's insanity and not mine. I have been treated in publishing very much like other poets are treated, that is, not really very well. I continue to write since my life as a human only includes my life as a poet, it doesn't depend on it. ⟨. . .⟩

My family tends to be a spiritual and even perhaps a mystical one. That certainly influences my life and my work. I write in the kitchen or wherever I happen to be though I do have a study. I write on a typewriter rather than in longhand. My children think of me as a moody person; I am shy and much less sunny than I am pictured. I draw my own conclusions and do not believe everything I am told. I am not easily fooled. I do the best I can. I try.

> Lucille Clifton, "A Simple Language," in *Black Women Writers (1950–1980): A Critical Evaluation*, ed. Mari Evans (Garden City, NY: Anchor Press/Doubleday, 1984), pp. 137–38

AUDREY T. McCLUSKEY   ⟨Clifton's⟩ children's books are her most prolific literary product, and no analysis of her work could ignore their overall importance. Her books for children introduce themes, ideas and points of view that may sometimes find their way into her poetry. It is important to note that she does not greatly alter her style as she moves from one genre to another. Her language remains direct, economical, and simply stated. She does not patronize the children for whom she writes. She gives them credit for being intelligent human beings who do not deserve to be treated differently because of their age. Being the mother of six children must certainly give her material for her books, but it is her respect for children as people and her finely tuned instincts about what is important to them—their fears, their joys—that make her a successful writer of children's literature. ⟨. . .⟩

Clifton is very cognizant of the fears that are ignited by a child's imagination. Her books are written to help give reassurance. She delicately treats both the pains and joys of childhood in order to help children accept both emotions as part of the unique experience of being who they are. In Clifton's books for children, self-love, and self-acceptance is the message. An example of this message is summarized in *The Black BC's*, a collection of rhymes depicting Black history and the Black experience.

> N is for natural
> or real or true
> the you of yourself
> and the self in you

In her poetry, Clifton continues to advocate that Black children be taught self-worth and encouraged to develop the mental and spiritual toughness that they will require to survive in a society that is hostile to their development. In the following poem, the children are called upon to make decisions for themselves and to begin to take control of their lives. They must become socially responsible—for they will someday lead.

> Come home from the movies
> Black girls and boys.
> The picture be over and the screen
> be cold as our neighborhood.
> Come home from the show,
> don't be the show . . .
> Show our fathers how to walk like men,
> they already know how to dance.

The movies serve as a metaphor for the fantasies and falseness in society that stunt our children's growth. She believes that what is important in life is found, not in the movies but in the values that are passed through generations.

> we have always love each other
> children   all ways
> Pass it on.

Clifton's view of herself as a writer is based, in part, upon her belief that "things don't fall apart. Things hold. Lines connect in ways that last and last and lives become generations made out of pictures and words just kept." She is interested in the continuity of experience and the writer's unique ability to connect generations of people and to remind them who they are and from whence they came.

Audrey T. McCluskey, "Tell the Good News: A View of the Works of Lucille Clifton," in *Black Women Writers (1950–1980): A Critical Evaluation*, ed. Mari Evans (Garden City, NY: Anchor Press/Doubleday, 1984), pp. 140–42

ANDREA BENTON RUSHING   Clifton's early verse clearly indicates the influence of the Black Arts movement. In accord with its dictates about how poetry should raise the cultural and political consciousness of "the Black community," Clifton dedicates *Good News about the Earth* to those killed in student uprisings at Orangeburg, South Carolina, and Jackson, Mississippi. 〈. . .〉 The volume also features verse to Angela Davis, Eldridge Cleaver, and Bobby Seale. In addition to treating these political subjects, Clifton mirrors the tenets of the Black Arts movement by directing herself to a general African-American audience using the grammar, vocabulary, and rhythm of idiomatic African-American speech. Interestingly, none of Clifton's verse on these vivid figures parallels so many of the tributes to them in relying on typographical quirks, like capitalized words and slashes, or haranguing either African-American or Euro-American readers.

In light of Clifton's later poetry, it is crucial to indicate the ways in which her early work diverges from the creations of her contemporaries. Many of the women poets who came to prominence during the sixties and seventies shocked readers. Despite their slight stature and (in a few cases) bourgeois upbringing, they mirrored the strident stance, profane language, and violent imagery of urban, male poetry. Part of my interest in Clifton's lyrical verse arises from my admiration for the acumen with which she found her own voice during a turbulent period when so many poets sounded the same chords of outrage and militancy. 〈. . .〉 Furthermore, while other poets have tended to focus on historical figures such as Harriet Tubman, Sojourner Truth, Frederick Douglass, and Malcolm X, Clifton anticipated Alex Haley's *Roots* in personalizing history and using her own natal family as a symbol of the anguish and triumph of the African-American experience. Moreover, in an era when many African-American nationalists were harshly critical of their accommodating "Uncle Tom" and "Aunt Jemima" elders, the "opiate" of African-American Christianity, and the Anglo-Saxon proper names which are a living legacy of chattel slavery and cultural assimilation, Clifton wrote in a different key. While others complained of their elders' failures, she celebrated her ancestors, while others converted to Islam, she wrote about the life-giving power of African-American religion; and, though others assumed African and Arabic names, Clifton justified her own.

> light
> on my mother's tongue
> breaks through her soft
> extravagant hip

into life.
Lucille
she calls the light,
which was the name
of the grandmother
who waited by the crossroads
in Virginia
and shot the whiteman off his horse,

. . . .

mine already is
an Afrikan name.

Beginning with an allusion to the origins of the name "Lucille" in the Latin
for "bright light," Clifton goes on to affirm a throbbing connection between
Africa, the slave experience, and her own twentieth-century life.

> Andrea Benton Rushing, "Lucille Clifton: A Changing Voice for Changing Times,"
> *Coming to Light: American Women Poets in the Twentieth Century,* ed. Diane Wood
> Middlebrook and Marilyn Yalom (Ann Arbor: University of Michigan Press, 1985),
> pp. 215–17

E. K. LAING   Clifton's poems have an internal brilliance ⟨. . .⟩
Chanting, droning, humming, her poems almost always work something
out.

With Clifton, nothing is reckless—neither her multifaceted use of "i,"
nor the absence of titles on most poems, nor the lack of punctuation. Each
poem appears as a meditation on power; what it means to control, withhold,
or relinquish power as an ultimate demonstration of mastery.

Unadorned, Clifton's gemlike forms are resplendent, refracting the
author's themes of family, the grace that can mean survival, the environment,
and perhaps most of all, individual responsibility for the future. ⟨. . .⟩

Black and white on the page, black and white in society, Clifton's poems
do not equivocate. If ever they are gray, it is because they are as exacting
as a steel blade cutting to central issues. They say a lot about black being
white in America. "I grieve my whiteful ways," she says. But this is not the
limit of her scope. She uses her experience as black, woman, mother, and
child to describe relationships more far-reaching than those labels would
admit. ⟨. . .⟩

Her words reveal not a victim, but a visionary. In the witness tradition of Brooks and Baldwin, Whitman and Wheatley, Clifton eagerly takes up arms in the struggle to salvage what grace in life remains.

E. K. Laing, "Lucille Clifton's Poetry: The Voice of a Visionary, Not a Victim," *Christian Science Monitor*, 5 February 1988, p. 83

DIANNE JOHNSON   Fortunately for the world of young people's literature, there are those authors who broaden our realms of experience by representing and exploring African-American culture. Lucille Clifton is one of the most prolific and accomplished of this number. In this context, her work is especially impressive when viewed as an entire oeuvre. Each book works in concert with the others to illuminate aspects of the communities, largely African-American, in which the characters live their lives. Everett Anderson's is one of the lives which is documented through a series of books. An examination of the Everett Anderson stories reveals the range and richness of this youngster's life and of the series book itself. This is especially true when examined within the context of the secondary function (intentional or not) of Clifton's telling of story: the exploration of Afro-American community and consciousness.

Everett Anderson is, in fact, the character most readily identified with Lucille Clifton. His story is both powerful and accessible precisely because of its inclusivity. It records not only memorable events such as births, but also the everyday. Everett Anderson can make any Wednesday afternoon into an adventure:

> Who's black
> and runs
> and loves to hop?
> Everett does.
>
> Who's black
> and was lost
> in the candy shop?
> Everett Anderson was.
>
> Who's black
> and noticed the
> peppermint flowers?
> Everett Anderson did.

> Who's black
> and was lost for
> hours and hours?
> Everett Anderson
>
> Hid!

Considered carefully, these verses from *Some of the Days of Everett Anderson* are not as simplistic as they might appear upon cursory examination. They are complicated—communicating more than a child's adventure—by the one recurring line, "Who's black."

A negative reaction to the line might include the argument that its prominent placement (not to mention its mere presence) is somewhat exclamatory and unjustifiable. What, after all, does being Black have to do with a trip to the candy store or playing hide and seek? This line of reasoning, however, obscures the more germane questions: Why is this particular detail included along with the unremarkable? One obvious answer is that this fact too should be unremarkable—unremarkable in the sense that it is so integral and organic a part of the character of Everett Anderson that it would be even more conspicuous in its absence.

Certainly the words "Who's black" are not called upon literally or bla-tantly in every episode that Clifton relates. But they are present in a spiritual and fundamental way. The point is that Everett is Black, as are many of his fellow characters. They are. And it is a condition of their being. This fact is simultaneously neither remarkable nor ignorable. It is for this reason that the boys share a brotherhood. When their blackness deserves or demands special attention, then it is accorded. When it deems no particular attention, it is left so. Everett's maturation process, like that of his peers, consists partly of learning how to mediate between the two levels of consciousness.

Dianne Johnson, "The Chronicling of an African-American Life and Consciousness: Lucille Clifton's Everett Anderson Series," *Children's Literary Association Quarterly* 14, No. 4 (Winter 1989): 174–75

HANK LAZER   As both her poetry and *All Us Come Cross the Water* illustrate, ownership is linked to language and to naming. Telling the story, choosing the dialect, and picking the name are acts of power with direct consequences in terms of dignity and autonomy. Clifton's acts of naming are *not* the transcendental "perfect fits" imagined by Ralph Waldo Emerson, whose Adam-poet gives the "true" and "original" names to the creatures of the earth. It seems to me that Emerson's ideal is imaginable *only* from a position of power and privilege, not from within a family and a race where names are imposed as a brand and an exercise of power by someone else. Clifton's position as namer gets written in "the making of poems":

> the reason why i do it
> though i fail and fail
> in the giving of true names
> is i am adam and his mother
> and these failures are my job.

But Lucille Clifton's failure is her success. That is, Clifton affirms most effectively when she fuses limitation and grace ⟨. . .⟩

In her newest poems, Clifton's revisionary history focuses more insistently on women. In one poem, she rewrites woman's power relationship to God, concluding "i am the good daughter who stays at home / singing and sewing. / when i whisper He strains to hear me and / He does whatever i say." Earlier in her writing, Clifton found herself "turning out of the / white cage, turning out of the / lady cage"; now, the poem she writes goes by the title "female" and affirms

> there is an amazon in us.
> she is the secret we do not
> have to learn.
> the strength that opens us
> beyond ourselves.
> birth is our birthright.
> we smile our mysterious smile.

Thus, her newest poems continue her work in defining and affirming "us."

The other equally effective affirmation in Clifton's poetry is akin to a power of the blues, what Houston Baker hears as the blues' "powers at the junctures of American experience—its power to wed quotidian rituals of everyday American experience to the lusters of a distinctively American expressive firmament." For Clifton, that wedding is accomplished in poems such as "homage to my hips," "homage to my hair," and "what the mirror said" ⟨. . .⟩

If, as many readers and writers of poetry are aware, a dominant feature of poetry in our time is its diversity, the absolute fragmentation of audience and the decentralization of its production and distribution, then many important consequences ensue from Ron Silliman's conclusion that "the result has been a decentralization in which any pretense, whether from the 'center' or elsewhere, or a coherent sense as to the nature of the whole of American poetry is now patently obvious as just so much aggressive fakery." It especially matters that white male readers, writers, and professors reach out and resist the drawing of xenophobic boundaries so that they can begin to live in the fullness of the present moment, so that we might have, as Gertrude Stein had wished, "all of our contemporaries for our contemporaries." In so doing, we can begin to undo one of the most damaging, lingering, and conservative goals of high modernist poetry. Instead of seeking to "purify the language of the tribe," we can begin to acknowledge with and through Lucille Clifton's writing, and the poetry of many other African-American poets, that "there are / too many languages for / one mortal tongue." What we need is not a purification of the language of the tribe, but an attentiveness to the languages of the many tribes constituting American expression.

Hank Lazer, "Blackness Blessed: The Writings of Lucille Clifton," *Southern Review* 25, No. 3 (Summer 1989): 768–70

JEAN ANAPORTE-EASTON   Last summer I gave a reading to a class of women in a prison for young drug offenders. I had read poems by a few other poets before I got to Clifton's "homage to my hips." The polite smiling audience sat up a little, looked at each other and grinned; there was even some noise. So I read "homage to my hair," and when I got to, "i'm talking about my nappy hair," the class burst into startled laughter. If big hips that are free and magical return to women some of our true identity, nappy hair was an even bigger shot of oxygen. There is no more political statement than saying to one deprived of self-esteem, "Take who you are and flaunt it."

"Nappy hair" is a point of contact between Clifton and her audience and also between Clifton and her truth-telling power. The touchstone for her truth-telling is the body and physical experience from a Black woman's perspective. Daily existence is the medium through which Clifton examines ethical and spiritual issues. The voice and rhythm emerge from the style of folk tales and the gutsy, here-and-now texture of Black vernacular. The imagery begins with brief, sometimes fragmentary observations about things ranging from hair and hips to the death of someone's son, and move inward where it is transformed by Clifton's particular brand of social and spiritual awareness.

Look at "homage to my hair." Not only the rhythm and sounds but the imagery is physical. The hair "jumps" and "dances" to suggest music. The pattern linking these images further energizes them:

> when i feel her jump up and dance
> i hear the music! my God
> i'm talking about my nappy hair!
> she is a challenge to your hand
> black man,
> she is as tasty on your tongue as good greens
> black man,
> she can touch your mind
> with her electric fingers and
> the grayer she do get, good God,
> the blacker she do be!

The spondee of "jump up" followed by the stressed "dance" at the end of the line creates a rising energy that lands on "hear" in the next line. The stresses in "nappy hair" are so close together as to have the impact of another spondee shooting electricity back to "jump up" and forward to "good greens." The spondees and the line breaks inject the rhythm with stops and flourishes so that the abstract "challenge" is given concrete meaning. Most of the lines contain three or two stresses. When extra stresses are added to lines one, six, and ten, those lines rush ahead with added impetus which is gathered and released deliberately in a slower beat in lines two and eleven—"i hear the music! my God" and "the blacker she do be!" The short two stress lines, "black man," hold up a rolling motion to deliver a challenge and give it time to sink in. The entire poem, in fact, is a challenge, an outrageous boast on the powers not only of dethroned nappy hair but grey hair.

Clifton's poetry specifically addresses Black people, but speaks to all who consider themselves ordinary. However, on Clifton's tongue, ordinary can be quite extraordinary so long as it is part of daily human experience. Since dailiness is global and cyclical, all varieties of human experience are admitted, including what is peculiar, excluded, or painful—womanhood, motherhood, Blackness, six-fingered hands, young boys dragging wagons to a riot. Acceptance is celebrations: Sing your nappy hair, your twelve fingers, your fear of being without a man, the cruelty and numbness of fear, the despair and violence in people's isolation. Sing these details of our lives until they become our mysteries and our magic, our means of transformation.

Jean Anaporte-Easton, " 'She Has Made Herself Again': The Maternal Impulse as Poetry," *13th Moon* 9, Nos. 1 & 2 (1991): 116–17

⬣ *Bibliography*

Good Times. 1969.

Some of the Days of Everett Anderson. 1969.

The Black BC's. 1970.

Everett Anderson's Christmas Coming. 1971.

Good News about the Earth: New Poems. 1972.

All Us Come Cross the Water. 1973.

Don't You Remember? 1973.

Good, Says Jerome. 1973.

The Boy Who Didn't Believe in Spring. 1973.

An Ordinary Woman. 1974.

Everett Anderson's Year. 1974.

All of Us Are All of Us. 1974.

The Times They Used to Be. 1974.

My Brother Fine with Me. 1975.

Three Wishes. 1976.

Everett Anderson's Friend. 1976.

Generations: A Memoir. 1976.

Amifika. 1977.

Everett Anderson's 1 2 3. 1977.

Everett Anderson's Nine Month Long. 1978.

The Lucky Stone. 1979.

My Friend Jacob (with Thomas DiGrazia). 1980.

Two-Headed Woman. 1980.

Sonora Beautiful. 1981.

Everett Anderson's Goodbye. 1983.

Good Woman: Poems and a Memoir 1969–1980. 1987.

Next: New Poems. 1987.

Why Some People Be Mad at Me Sometimes. 1988.

Ten Oxherding Pictures. c. 1988.
Quilting: Poems 1987–1990. 1991.
The Book of Light. 1993.

Owen Dodson
1914–1983

OWEN VINCENT DODSON was born on November 28, 1914, in Brooklyn, New York, the ninth child of Nathaniel Dodson, a journalist, and Sarah Elizabeth Goode Dodson. His father, who was director of the National Negro Press Association, introduced Dodson to such distinguished black American writers as W. E. B. Du Bois and James Weldon Johnson, while from his mother, a social worker and devout churchgoer, he gained a religious sensitivity that would infuse both his life and his work.

During his years at Thomas Jefferson High School in Brooklyn, Dodson began the study of poetry. He matriculated to Bates College in Lewiston, Maine, where he received a B.A. in 1936. For a large portion of his college years Dodson wrote one sonnet a week, and he had already published his poetry in *Phylon, Opportunity*, and other journals prior to his graduation.

Dodson received a fellowship to attend the Yale Drama School in 1936. Two years later his play *Divine Comedy* (published in 1974 in *Black Theatre, U.S.A.*, edited by James V. Hatch and Ted Shine) was staged there, later receiving the Maxwell Anderson Award for verse drama. Another play, *The Garden of Time*, is an adaptation of the Greek legend of Medea in which some of the action is set in South Carolina just after the Civil War.

Dodson received his M.F.A. from Yale in 1939. The previous year he had begun teaching speech and drama at Spelman College in Atlanta, where he remained until 1941. He then taught briefly at the Hampton Institute in Virginia before enlisting in the U.S. Navy in late 1942. Dodson was urged by his commander, Daniel Armstrong, to write plays on naval history for the benefit of black seamen; two of these were published in the prestigious journal *Theatre Arts*. One of Dodson's most successful dramatic productions was *New World A-Coming*, a pageant performed at Madison Square Garden in New York in 1944.

Dodson's first collection of poetry was *Powerful Long Ladder*, published in 1946. It was immediately hailed as a notable contribution to the black American poetic tradition, but Dodson turned his attention to drama,

78

joining the drama department of Howard University in Washington, D.C., where he would remain for the next twenty-three years. At Howard, Dodson acted in, directed, and wrote more than 300 plays; among his own most notable productions was *Bayou Legend* (1948; published in 1971 in *Black Drama in America*, edited by Darwin T. Turner), an adaptation of Ibsen's *Peer Gynt.*

Boy at the Window, Dodson's first novel, was published in 1951. This sensitive story of a young boy's experiences in a racially mixed section of Brooklyn was also received very favorably, and Dodson received a Guggenheim Fellowship in 1952 to write a sequel to it; but this novel—*Come Home Early, Child*, written in Ischia, Italy, in W. H. Auden's villa—was not published until 1977.

Dodson retired from Howard University in 1970 and moved to New York City. In that year he published *The Confession Stone: Song Cycles*, the title poem of which had appeared separately in 1960. This deeply religious series of poems features dramatic dialogues between Jesus, Mary, God, and other figures; Dodson considered it his masterpiece. In 1974 his opera, *Till Victory Is Won*, written to commemorate the centennial of Howard University, was performed at the Kennedy Opera House in Washington, D.C. In 1978 Dodson wrote a series of poems as captions to photographs by James Van Der Zee, published as *The Harlem Book of the Dead*. Dodson continued to write poetry in his later years, and he had written several chapters of a new novel before he died of a heart attack on June 21, 1983.

▨ *Critical Extracts*

JESSICA NELSON NORTH   As a poet, Dodson is versatile, original and simple. The book ⟨*Powerful Long Ladder*⟩ has a note of complete sincerity and lack of pose, accomplished chiefly by freedom of pattern and absence of inhibition. In the dialect poems this method is especially successful; it admits the reader directly into the simple heart of the speaker as when the "Black Mother Praying" says:

> My great God, You been a tenderness to me,
> Through the thick and through the thin;
> You been a pilla to my soul,

> You been a shinin light a mornin in the black dark,
> A elevator to my spirit.

In the more sophisticated sections of the book (the verse dramas, the topical poems), the same quality appears in a different form. The subconscious and primitive manage to get themselves into print unspoiled. ⟨. . .⟩ The collection is not entirely given over to protest nor to racial consciousness. There are plenty of evidences of the poet's realization that he is first of all a man in a free country, an informed, talented and privileged member of the human race. ⟨. . .⟩

The verse dramas are more conventional and sometimes have far-fetched and flamboyant speeches, such as "There's an acetylene torch / Tracing promises on my chest." They remind us again of the difficulties of combining drama with poetry. The Greeks did it with complete success, but try as we will, through thousands of years of Goethes, Shelleys, Maxwell Andersons and Little Theaters, we can't get back to the height from which we once tumbled. And it does not further the effort to have the chorus chanting in unison such empty abstract nouns as "Hypocrisy, terror, bigotry, lust, hatred." Even though the traditional Greek chorus cried *woe*.

Jessica Nelson North, "Somber and Real," Poetry 69, No. 3 (December 1946): 175–77

M. L. ROSENTHAL   In his first published volume of verse ⟨*Powerful Long Ladder*⟩, Owen Dodson joins that large group of modern "social" poets who seek to fuse ideological conviction with the personal emotion that is the traditional basis of lyric poetry. With this effort, in our time, have been associated such varied talents as, for instance, Auden, Kreymborg, Aragon; and, in other directions, Williams, Tate, Eliot, Pound. These are writers each of whom has, in his way, achieved a certain maturity and perfection. Dodson, however, aside from his persistent, and frequently successful, attempt to speak realistically and angrily for the American Negro, is still young enough to be looking for just the right vocabulary and viewpoint to suit his special abilities. He does many things excellently. In "Martha Graham," for example, he combines the Shelleyan note ("Seek, seek the dream") with lines approximating the movement of the modern dance, and makes the combination seem appropriate. He knows how to begin a poem with a shock: "Wake up, boy, and tell me how you died" is a little like Vaughan's "I saw eternity the other night" in its effect. ⟨. . .⟩

In all his poems there is—despite occasional carelessness—admirable proficiency. Dodson is trying out many forms, including the folk rhythms which Langston Hughes and such singers as White and Ledbetter have made familiar, in order to discover the best way to release a tremendous store of emotional and moral power.

That he has this power is undeniable. Sometimes the pages of *Powerful Long Ladder* fairly smoke with irony and indignation. The vocabulary becomes bitter with the conviction of betrayal and the self-mockery that so often goes with a real sense of suffering. A boy in *Divine Comedy*—a fragment from a symbolistic play which is the most interesting experiment in the book—says,

> I'm so black they call me nighttime.
> When I walk along every one looks for stars.

One can be sure he is not saying this to amuse a Mississippi Senator. ⟨. . .⟩

If there is an ultimate democratic optimism in this poem, it is a triumph of Mr. Dodson's will, for, like Richard Wright, he cannot pretend that stoical faith can suffice the Negro people today.

⟨. . .⟩ The positive achievements of *Powerful Long Ladder* are its vividness, its solid strength in picturing pain and disgust without losing the joy of life which marks the best artist, its ethical force. And if the choruses here given from *Divine Comedy* are any clew, perhaps Owen Dodson will make a real contribution to our poetic drama. It remains to be seen whether, in this medium and in his future work, he will display that mastery of structure and intellectual control in a really sustained work which are needed to fulfill the promise of the present volume.

M. L. Rosenthal, "Ideas Fused with Fire," *New York Herald Tribune Weekly Book Review*, 16 March 1947, p. 12

VANCE BOURJAILY   To the sparsely-populated playground for believable children in fiction, admit Coin Foreman. The nine-year-old Negro hero of Owen Dodson's *Boy at the Window* is a real boy.

Whatever the sociological problems of his race, Coin's awareness is mostly engaged by the same things which occupy all children: school; family—and his mother in particular; church, since the family is a religious one; the other kids in the neighborhood, a Jewish-Irish-Negro district in Brooklyn.

When Mrs. Carth, the next-door slattern, calls him a "dirty little nigger," Coin must ask his mother what the last word means. Uneasy and protective, the mother replies that the dictionary says a nigger is a "bad person."

"Then I'm no nigger," says Coin, completely reassured. It is a very good example of the restraint which makes Mr. Dodson's book successful that the author insists no further on the irony of this exchange. ⟨. . .⟩

The novel covers less than a year of Coin's life. The first important events of these months concern Coin's development of religious feeling, based principally on a touchingly literal belief that he will be able, by gaining faith, to pray effectively for his mother's health. When no miraculous cure occurs Coin is disillusioned, not only about the church but about all adult assurances. Interrupting games and school, come his mother's death and funeral; then Coin's departure, first for the home of an uncle and finally, running away, for unknowable far places.

At the end of the book, with a little "saved-up money" and a determination to give God another chance as his only assets, Coin is about to begin his lonely travels. Were he an adolescent, this might be a perfectly acceptable conclusion. But Coin is only nine years old, a Negro boy so inexperienced that he still isn't sure where babies come from, so innocent that he has decided to head South. We would hardly be human if we could accept this prospect without concern.

That we are concerned is, however, an indication of how well Mr. Dodson—a poet and dramatist of reputation—has done in his first novel. Our concern is for a child, a real one; neither artist—nor delinquent-to-be, for a change; and as appealing as any other likable nine-year-old you may happen to know.

Vance Bourjaily, "Changing Childhood World," *New York Herald Tribune Book Review*, 25 February 1951, p. 14

ROBERT A. BONE   Owen Dodson's *Boy at the Window* (1951) is a quiet novel, devoid of melodrama. It is the story of a boy's sudden maturation, precipitated by the death of his mother and the disruption of his childish world. The novel has a Wright School setting, but its focus is distinctly psychological, with emphasis on the boy's family constellation and early religious development. ⟨. . .⟩

Coin's relationship with his mother is the axis upon which the broader meaning of the novel turns. Who was his mother; what did she stand for; how can he keep her memory alive?—these are the questions which determine the direction of his growth. The catalytic agent is Ferris, a chance acquaintance of his own age who becomes a symbol of friendship, of sympathy and understanding, of imagination and love of beauty, of everything, in short, of which he has been deprived by his mother's death. It is Ferris who helps Coin to find his mother, by boasting that "My Mama's name is in the Bible." Not to be outdone, Coin searches for Naomi, and in the *Book of Ruth* he finds her, "saying the words of together." In the moving story of Naomi and Ruth, Coin finds guidance for his journey through the adult world.

Mr. Dodson's literary manner is essentially Joycean; he employs a highly disciplined stream-of-consciousness style within a loose narrative framework. The point of view is decidedly Coin's; we learn about him by sharing his thoughts, not by observing his actions. The time scheme is psychological rather than chronological; we are apprised of events not in the order of their occurrence but as they become important in Coin's consciousness. As in Joyce, fragments of church hymns, children's jingles, subway ads, and fourth-grade readers are introduced to establish psychological authenticity. The boyish diction and the bold metaphors, well within reach of an imaginative child, help further to validate the boy's consciousness.

A poet and a dramatist, Mr. Dodson does not wholly succeed in transposing his talent to the narrative mode. *Boy at the Window* contains both lyric and dramatic elements which have not been fully assimilated to the longer genre. In pursuit of lyric intensity, for example, the author slips occasionally into an extreme subjectivity bordering on Dada. Mr. Dodson's sense of form, moreover, is essentially dramaturgical; one can almost see the curtain coming down on certain scenes. Stylistic considerations aside, the novel is lacking in scope and significance. The burden of meaning intended by the author is simply too great for a child to bear. The problem of conveying an adult theme through the consciousness of a nine-year-old seems virtually insuperable, but Mr. Dodson has struggled with it valiantly. Perhaps in his next novel he will bring his virtuosity to bear on a less confining subject.

Robert A. Bone, *The Negro Novel in America* (New Haven: Yale University Press, 1958), pp. 185–87.

OWEN DODSON and JOHN O'BRIEN   INTERVIEWER: In your poetry and plays a recurrent theme is religion and history. You have an apocalyptic sense of both. Do you think this characterizes what your central concern is in your writing?

DODSON: I have written three books of poetry. The first was—I would say—somewhat propaganda, but the third was filled with stories, diaries, and remembrances of Jesus. They are really framed in diaries by Mary, Martha, Joseph, Judas, Jesus, and even God. This, I believe, is my most dedicated work. But I have also been interested in history. A record company asked me to write some kind of history of black people from slavery to their entrance into the United States and now. I did this in A Dream Awake. It is illustrated and spoken by James Earl Jones, Josephine Premice, Josh White, Jr., and others who are dedicated to the mainstream of making a world a wide world, a blessed world, a step-in world where all races hold hands and bless God. I have written and fought somehow in my writing, but I know now that the courage and forthrightness of writers and poets will change something a little in our dilapidation. ⟨. . .⟩

INTERVIEWER: I know that you were acquainted with many of the writers from the Harlem Renaissance. Did any of them have a direct influence upon your work?

DODSON: One writer is Langston Hughes. He presented the whole idea of Negro life. He said, "These are my people and I love them and I will live on 127th Street and I will grow flowers there." He wrote poems that had such thrust. Langston had a beautiful perception about people. In his will he wanted two things. He said, "Do nothing until you hear from me." And, of course, I've been writing and hearing from him. Second, he wanted a combo at his funeral. And he had a combo—ain't that nice? A combo. The combo was on a little stage. But when the combo came in, Langston had to get out because his coffin was too large for the combo. So they moved him out. Countee Cullen was another influence. He was black and lost because he made—or rather we did—his dedication to society. He wanted to be a lyric poet; that's what he wanted. He didn't want to write all these things about race, but he did. He was pushed into death. They say he died of some blood disease. No! That man was made to die, by himself and by us, because we did not recognize the universal quality of what he wanted to say. In one of his poems he wrote, "Wake up world, O world awake." That's what he wanted to write. He didn't want to write

about rioting in old Baltimore. He wanted to write about the lyrical quality
of life.

Owen Dodson and John O'Brien, "Owen Dodson," *Interviews with Black Writers*, ed.
John O'Brien (New York: Liveright, 1973), pp. 58–61

NOEL SCHRAUFNAGEL   The problems of a black youth in
adjusting to an unfriendly environment, a popular theme in the fifties, are
again depicted in Owen Dodson's *Boy at the Window* (1951). Originally
published under this title and later released as *When Trees Were Green*, the
novel is more objective than ⟨William Demby's⟩ *Battlecreek* in dealing with
the difficulties of a young Negro boy in facing an atmosphere of hostility.
Dodson's characters possess an element of freedom that is absent in Demby's
novel. While the protagonist's situation is basically the same as that of
Johnny Johnson, his life is not entirely predetermined by his environment.
It is limited, however, by the deprivations usually associated with a ghetto.

Coin Foreman spends his early years in New York, but when his mother,
Naomi, dies he is sent to Washington, D.C. to live with Uncle Troy, a
blind man who has more than enough troubles of his own. Without the
protection of Naomi, Coin discovers many of the unpleasant aspects of life,
including what it is to be a "nigger." The boy decides that he will not live
with his uncle after observing that the blind man is more concerned with
drinking and sex than in being a replacement for his mother. Fortified by
memories of Naomi and visions of biblical heroes, Coin prepares to leave
his new home as the short novel concludes. He is determined to find love
in a world that has suddenly deteriorated.

Dodson uses a stream-of-consciousness technique to reveal the thoughts
of the young protagonist. It is largely through the recording of the mental
responses of the boy to the things around him that the author is able to
convey his impressions of life in a ghetto. One of the revelations that makes
an impact on the protagonist is the indignity innately related to being black.
The impressions of Coin are revealed after he has traveled by train to
Washington.

> Coin knew something was wrong with the way everyone had
> acted but he didn't know where to place the blame. One thing he
> had learned: what nobody would tell him. He knew now what a
> nigger was. His mother really had been right. A bad person. What

confused him was that it meant much more than that. Maybe you
weren't a bad person but you were colored and they called you
nigger.

Coin's severest problems are more personal, though, than those stemming
from the color of his skin. He is primarily concerned with establishing a
companionship that can take the place of his mother's love and understanding. In his search for fulfillment, the boy discovers some of the handicaps
of being among the disadvantaged, but he refuses to become discouraged.
The scope of the novel is extremely limited, however, as Dodson tries to
channel his material through the consciousness of a ten-year-old boy. The
book is almost too short to explore fully some of the problems it presents,
but within these limitations it is an interesting portrait of the various aspects
of the maturation of a youth from a ghetto.

Noel Schraufnagel, *From Apology to Protest: The Black American Novel* (DeLand, FL:
Everett/Edwards, 1973), pp. 76–77

BERNARD L. PETERSON, JR.   In 1971, a tape-recorded interview of Dodson was made by James V. Hatch and his assistants at the City
College of New York, for inclusion in the Hatch-Billops Archives. (Copies
of these tapes are also in the Schomburg Center for Research, New York,
and in the Cohen Library of the City College of New York.)

In this interview, Dodson expressed one of his fundamental beliefs about
the uses of the theatre and the duties of the black playwright:

> In our time when there is so much talk of black power, and of
> black playwrights' throwing garbage in the faces of people, it
> should be the duty of black playwrights to show what theatre can
> and should be. We should present all classes of people as human
> beings.

This was an idea which Dodson had expressed in his numerous lectures
on "The Definition and Use of Drama," given on such campuses as Cornell,
Vassar, Kenyon and Iowa University. He also expressed the belief that black
playwrights should emulate the great masters and seek to pursue "the healing
and blessed presence of artistic values."

In an article, "Playwrights in Dark Glasses," he listed a number of these
values, the chief among which is *universality*. He wrote:

> So many of our Negro playwrights are so saturated with the
> idea of Negro oppression, which of course they should be, that
> they have left out the lasting power, the universality, of their art:
> "They just keep trampin'." They aren't trying to make heaven
> their home. They seem to prefer infernos to the blaze of light that
> can come in the future. Many of them have discipline . . . but
> they hardly have the daring or the flair to infuse high vision with
> our present angry condition. (*Negro Digest,* April, 1968.)

Although Dodson has always been concerned with the oppression of black people, he has tried to write about his people and his time "in terms we may all understand without losing the healing and blessed presence of artistic values."

Because he has not stooped to sordidness or sensationalism in his pursuit of universality, many of his ardent devotees feel that his work has not received the wide audience that it deserves. It was in this spirit that Glenda Dickerson, one of Dodson's colleagues in the Drama Department at Howard, and Mike Malone of the D.C. Black Repertory Company, collaborated in their efforts to create *Owen's Song,* a theatrical work in tribute to Dodson, which ran for six weeks at the Lost Colony Theatre in Washington, D.C., opening October 24, 1974.

The authors describe the production as "a collage, weaving together lines from his works, including *Divine Comedy, Powerful Long Ladder,* his many poems, and his full-length play *Bayou Legend.*" They also state that "The story line . . . is inspired by the magnificent theme that runs through all of his works: climbing a powerful long ladder to catch the bird of freedom. . . ."

Bernard L. Peterson, Jr., "The Legendary Owen Dodson of Howard University: His Contributions to the American Theatre," *Crisis* 86, No. 9 (November 1979): 378

C. JAMES TROTMAN   "Counterpoint" is the concluding section of *Powerful Long Ladder.* It contains strong poems on established social and psychological themes; and we do not tire of them because the imagery is sharpened by exquisite phrasing. In "Jonathan's Song," subtitled "A Negro Saw the Jewish Pageant, 'We Will Never Die,'" demonstrates Dodson's universal vision and his commitment to a spiritual view of humanity:

I am part of this
Memorial to suffering,
Militant strength:
I am a Jew.

Dodson's social consciousness, as Margaret Just Butcher has written, is also the subject of "Conversation on V" where race and war are Dodson's focus. But "Iphigenia," because of its allusion through the title to the Greek myth of social innocence and ritualized sacrifice, has special significance. Its use of myth reminds one of Dodson's broad view of the materials capable of rendering authentically the truth of humanity; in "The Watching" Dodson turns to the Biblical saga of Samson to once again use material from the broadest elements of western culture to depict modern anguish and human fear. ⟨. . .⟩

    As one might expect from a poet whose work engages reality and especially the dark side of experience, there are perspectives, sometimes even philosophies, and human truths to be found in this collection. Perhaps the largest among them is the necessary struggle of the human predicament to know that there is struggle and conflict, handicap and pain. It is sometimes brought on by war, racism, poverty, loneliness and misunderstanding; but it is painful. And that human pain, Dodson's poetry suggests, not only defines our common humanity but can lead to visions of independence and spiritual wealth, to sights and sounds of the impossible made possible by each of us. That statement on human potential is not going to be accepted by all, if that matters, but what is certain is the experience of responding to the verbal orchestration, the measured steps, that brought us to the point of making that decision for ourselves.

    C. James Trotman, "The Measured Steps of a Powerful Long Ladder: The Poetry of
    Owen Dodson," *Obsidian II* 1, Nos. 1 & 2 (Spring–Summer 1986): 104–7

LEO HAMALIAN and JAMES V. HATCH   By the end of the nineteenth century and the beginning of the twentieth century, several American poets had attempted verse plays—William Vaughn Moody and Edwin Arlington Robinson among them—but their stage verse ran close to rhetoric, and the craft of playwriting escaped them. Dramatists Eugene O'Neill and Maxwell Anderson mastered the art of theater, but when they attempted to soar in language, they had no wings. One of the very first to produce poetry rich in image and subtle in rhythm and voice for the theater, along with Edna St. Vincent Millay, was Owen Dodson. His verse drama *Divine Comedy*, produced at the Yale Drama School in 1938, stands as a pioneer American effort to have characters speak convincingly in dramatic verse.

In 1939, Dodson's second full-length play, *Garden of Time*, received mainstage production at the Drama School. This verse drama adapted the Medea story to the American South and was staged a second time by Dodson himself at the American Negro Theatre in 1945. *Bayou Legend*, his verse adaptation of *Peer Gynt* set in the Louisiana Cajun country, premiered at Howard University in 1948. Over the years, he wrote thirty-seven plays and operas. Twenty-seven have been produced, two at the Kennedy Center. In his career, Dodson wrote, directed, or acted in more than three hundred productions. Because of his influence in black drama, he became known as the dean of black theater.

Dodson's one-act *The Shining Town*, set during the Depression of the 1930s, dramatizes the domestic "slave market" in a subway station at 167th Street and Jerome Avenue in the Bronx. Here, to support their families, black women auctioned themselves to white women for day work. Under the knife of the Depression, the women underbid one another, often working for ten or fifteen cents an hour. Whether or not Dodson witnessed these auctions in person, he had heard black women speak of them, and he knew the bitterness of those who toiled in domestic service. His play was perhaps too damning of the white society in 1937 to receive a production at Yale.

Leo Hamalian and James V. Hatch, "Owen Vincent Dodson (1914–1983)," *The Roots of African American Drama: An Anthology of Early Plays 1858–1938*, ed. Leo Hamalian and James V. Hatch (Detroit: Wayne State University Press, 1991), pp. 328–29

JAMES V. HATCH   No project held Owen's heart as long or gripped it as tight as *The Confession Stone*. In 1960, for the opening of the Ira Aldridge Theatre, he had published eight monologues under the title *Sung by Mary about Jesus*. The poems covered the three days from Good Friday to Easter Sunday morning. For the next decade Owen played with his Easter litany, adding modern touches to a biblical cast—the telegram, the telephone. His verse, certainly the leanest he ever wrote, was as simple as a pine board; he called it "involved simplicity," and it attracted several composers who saw the poems as lieder, although none composed an oratorio for the whole cycle. Owen wrote Priscilla Heath, "The music will breathe through the pores and enrich, and, I believe, give astonishment of pain and wonder."

The collection's title, Owen claimed, came to him in Italy when he saw a peasant woman kneeling upon a stone: "There is a rock most people kneel upon and talk to God when trouble strikes, and wrestle there with soul agonies." The immediate impetus to write the poems came from Joyce Bryant, who told Owen she had given up her career as a cabaret singer, which she had begun at the age of fourteen, to join the Seventh Day Adventists—the life of working for Christ. ⟨. . .⟩

Never had Owen been so aggressively proud of a work as he was of this cycle; for him, the poems resolved the tiff between him and his father, between him and God, and at the same time laid Owen back into the arms of his mother for the pietà. By the year of his retirement, he had hammered out the razor edge of his response to God; it is Jesus who addresses the Father:

> Father, I know you're lonely:
> talk to me, talk to me,
> We need not speak of Calvary
> or the lakes of Galilee:
> as my Father, talk to me.
> Notify my soul where
> You will be,
> send some message:
> answer me.
> I sign me, your son,
> > Jesus.

Then God sends his response:

> Dear my Son
> my One, my constant One:
> . . . .
> Your Father has not deserted Thee
> to gardens of Gethsemane.
> The stars are the tears We weep,
> the sun is Our Mercy,
> the moon is Our slumber.
> Sleep, Jesus, sleep.
> Mary is come with a bowl of wine.

Sleep, Jesus, sleep.
Sleep, Jesus, sleep.
Your father first, then God!

So God and Owen tried to work it out: the son would not speak of Calvary; the father would not deny the son. But not without laughter. One day Owen admitted to a friend, "I have gotten more yardage out of Jesus and God than anyone you know."

James V. Hatch, *Sorrow Is the Only Faithful One: The Life of Owen Dodson* (Urbana: University of Illinois Press, 1993), pp. 246–49

◈ *Bibliography*

Epithalamion for Evelyn Boldes Young and Joseph Henry Jenkins. 1942.

Powerful Long Ladder. 1946.

Laughter Underneath the Rock. 1946.

Over the Mangy Cities . . . 1950.

Boy at the Window ⟨When Trees Were Green⟩. 1951.

The Confession Stone: A Song Cycle Sung by Mary about Jesus. 1960.

The Confession Stone: Song Cycles. 1970.

Come Home Early, Child. 1977.

The Harlem Book of the Dead (with James Van Der Zee and Camille Billops). 1978.

James A. Emanuel
b. 1921

JAMES ANDREW EMANUEL was born on January 15, 1921, in Alliance, Nebraska, the fifth of seven children of Alfred A. Emanuel, a farmer and railroad worker, and Cora Ann Mance Emanuel. From an early age he was exposed to the Bible as well as literature by black Americans and other writers. He was soon writing his own poetry; he was invited to read a Thanksgiving poem that he wrote to his high school class, of which he became valedictorian. After graduating from high school in 1939, Emanuel worked at odd jobs until 1942, when he became a confidental secretary in the U.S. War Department. Two years later he entered the army, serving with the 93rd Infantry Division in the Pacific.

After the war, Emanuel attended Howard University in Washington, D.C., from which he graduated summa cum laude. In 1950 he married Mattie Etha Johnson and began studying for a master's degree at Northwestern University in Evanston, Illinois, while working at the Army and Air Force Induction Station in Chicago. He continued his creative work, writing several poems as well as some chapters of a novel; one of these poems was published in *Phylon* in 1958.

Emanuel received an M.A. from Northwestern in 1953 and moved to New York City, where he enrolled in a Ph.D. program at Columbia University. In 1957 he began teaching at City College of the City of New York, on whose faculty he remained for the next twenty-five years. In 1959 he met Langston Hughes while working on a critical study of Hughes for his dissertation. The study was completed in 1962, when Emanuel received his Ph.D., and was published in 1967 as *Langston Hughes* as part of Twayne's United States Authors Series. Emanuel, becoming more aware of the lack of attention paid to black writers, increasingly contributed his own criticism and essays to magazines and journals. With Theodore L. Gross, he edited the landmark anthology *Dark Symphony: Negro Literature in America* (1968). From 1970 to 1975 he served as general editor of the Broadside Critics project, which issued monographs on important black writers.

Emanuel also continued to write poetry. *The Treehouse and Other Poems*, his first collection, was published in 1968. The theme and style vary from poem to poem, but many are concerned with racial problems. The collection was generally overlooked by reviewers and critics. The volume was followed two years later by *Panther Man*, which reflects Emanuel's increasing concern for problems of race. The seriousness in theme is matched by an appropriate starkness of style, producing powerfully compact verses.

From 1971 to 1973 Emanuel lived in Toulouse, France; he taught at the university there and wrote. *Black Man Abroad: The Toulouse Poems* (1978), records the personal struggles he suffered during this period. Returning to New York in 1973, he engaged in a bitter divorce suit with his wife and also suffered the theft of many of his literary papers. Emanuel spent a year teaching at the University of Warsaw in Poland (1975–76) and returned to the University of Toulouse from 1979 to 1981, although he also spent time in London and Paris. Emanuel retired from City College in 1983. In that year his one son, James A. Emanuel, Jr., committed suicide after being brutalized by police in San Diego.

Several more collections of Emanuel's poetry have appeared, including *A Chisel in the Dark* (1980), *The Broken Bowl* (1983), and *Whole Grain: Collected Poems 1958–1989* (1991). A manuscript autobiography, "Snowflakes and Steel: My Life as a Poet, 1971–80," is deposited in the Jay B. Hubbell Center for American Literary Historiography at Duke University.

▣ *Critical Extracts*

JAMES A. EMANUEL   Negro writers, as writers, share with white literary men one transcendent task: to discover truth personally and to render it aesthetically beautiful and powerful, speaking with honest clarity to the most human faculties of man. As Negroes, they uniquely offer literary evidence of that wracking miracle by which sustained psychic abuse at the hands of countrymen and in the name of freedom is steadily transformed into humane sensitivities and vigorous optimism. As Americans, they must cultivate a strong historical sense and absorb the factual past of their ancestors, becoming publicly available disseminators of long-neglected knowledge. Having thus authentically expanded their art, however, Negro writers (and critics) must disabuse their minds of the fancy that bigots will respond any more rationally or magnanimously to historical truth in characterization and theme than they do to the next-door realities of living Negroes. Convinced nevertheless that currently demonstrated individual pride and manly awareness of racial enormities are more pressing commandments than bygone respect for delinqent white opinion, Negro writers must supply corrective illumination to the darkness of their history. If moved to write "protest literature," they must work as unapologetically as a James Baldwin, a Thomas Paine, or a Samuel Adams, knowing that psychological liberation must precede artistic maturity. If moved occasionally to write without meaningful consciousness of race, they must remember that by birth and experience they are bonded to a field now watched by continents, long reaped by whites whose easier access to markets does not honorably supplant the obligations of Negro talent and heritage. To meet these obligations, Negro writers must discount even partial aid from whites, who, in the common task of developing a comprehensive national literature unmarred by racial distortions, must be trusted to discover their debt to a maligned race who nursed, strengthened, and fought for their nation in its youth. Negro writers, then, must speak courageously, knowledgeably, and artfully to their contemporaries, to the double end of fulfilling racial destiny and of helping to unfold the mystery of the literary mind evolving toward wholeness and excellence in both sympathetic and hostile surroundings.

James A. Emanuel, "The Task of the Negro Writer as Artist: A Symposium," *Negro Digest* 14, No. 6 (April 1965): 70, 73

KENETH KINNAMON   As a poet, ⟨Langston Hughes⟩ did not really improve. Of the twenty poems judged to be Hughes's best in James A. Emanuel's useful critical study, *Langston Hughes*—in which readers will find most of their favorites—all but six were written in the twenties. One could trace developments in Hughes's poetry—his movement from blues to bop rhythms, for example—but not artistic growth. Gertrude Stein's remark to Scott Fitzgerald: "One does not get better but different and older," could have been directed to Hughes as well.

Mr. Emanuel's thematic organization and cramped format do not permit him to trace this process in detail. But he does examine closely technique as well as theme in a number of representative poems and stories under such categories as "The Cult of the Negro" and "The Christ and the Killers." Occasionally one may feel that a particular Hughes piece is too slight to bear the weight of Mr. Emanuel's analysis, but generally his commentary is perceptive and sympathetic.

> Keneth Kinnamon, "The Man Who Created 'Simple,' " *Nation*, 4 December 1967, p. 600

JAMES CUNNINGHAM   The initial poem of *The Treehouse and Other Poems* describes a man awakened from a deep sleep into an actual nightmare in which he questions the dead; but not out of a mere frightened curiosity which asks, "Are you not dead?," but with the swift unconscious reflexes of a father who demands simply, "What *is* it?" The author, James A. Emanuel, follows this piece with two others, equally macabre, and just as strongly pervaded by a parent's feelings. The first one, "Emmett Till," begins:

> I hear a whistling
> Through the water.
> Won't be still.
> He keeps floating
> Round the darkness,
> Edging through
> The silent chill.

The concluding section of the poem invites the reader to furnish the story of a fairy "River Boy" who not only swims forever, but who also swims

> Deep in treasures,
> Necklaced in
> A coral toy.

The last of the two treats the same subject, youthful black victims of white violence, and if with far less matter-of-factness of tone, it still maintains an equally ironic attentiveness to grim, chilling detail:

> Where will their names go down,
> Our bloodied boys
> Sunk link by link—
> Socket, bone, and upright knee—
> Muscled down dead
> In the Tallahatchie, the Mississippi, and the Pearl?

The poet goes on to wonder:

> Will they rise again
> Except to velvet eyes
> And rainbow fins that pierce the deep?
> Except to flush in streams that knife the seas
> And rush their secrets through foundations of the world?

The next group of poems, beginning with "Negritude" and ending with "A View from the White Helmet," reveal the perceptions and sensibilities of a poet who conducts his thought and expression very much in the manner of an apparently unassuming gadfly—which is to say that in Emanuel we are to encounter yet another kind of Ellison whose individuality of viewpoint and smoothness of expression is bound to offend the more tribal-minded among the black conscious. Indeed, a poet is revealed whose singular toughness and keenness of mind and fancy is almost hidden by an apparent absence of any interest in the current fondness for, and preoccupation with, stunning spatial innovations that stress uniqueness in form and word arrangement. Indeed, in Emanuel, we encounter a poet who leans in the very unfashionable direction of not so very-long-ago traditional devices such as rhymed quatrains and regularity of line and stanza length. Yet, for all of this, we are faced with a formidable, deadly serious and technically assured, and even mischievous, talent. There is here a verbal dexterity and tightness not unworthy of a Brooks, and an emotional steadiness and resiliency underneath the light, humorous, gentle unassuming surface that will grip your fondest notions and make them SCREAM OUT as they are carried unceremoniously under.

To repeat, the ideas, the subjects dealt with, and the very strikingly bold and personal handling they all receive will hardly make this poet popular with those Super Blacks and Super Biggers whose common notion of revolutionary relevance and sense of urgency lead them to view with simple hostility any writing by any black man that is "good" by virtue of *precision* and *subtlety* of phrase rather than *simpleness* and consciously un/anti-literary *directness*. There is to be no stretching out with words that makes the least uncommon demand on "the people's" imagination. Allah, forbid!

James Cunningham, [Review of *The Treehouse and Other Poems*], *Negro Digest* 18, No. 3 (January 1969): 70–72

MICHAEL THELWELL   In *Dark Symphony* Professors Gross and Emanuel have supplied us with the most comprehensive anthology of black writing—fiction, poetry and the essay—since Sterling Brown and his associates published *The Negro Caravan* in 1941. No major writer is slighted and the editors have included such important but hardly available works as Alain Locke's "The New Negro" and Sterling Brown's classic dissection of white literary stereotypes, "Negro Characters as Seen by White Authors," which should be required reading in every course on American culture. Intended as an introduction to the finest achievements in Negro literature, the book succeeds splendidly. It is clearly meant for the classroom, where it will fill a real need for an all-inclusive basic text in which the "classics" of black literature—that is to say those works which lend themselves to criticism and understanding in terms of traditional critical assumptions about literature—can be found.

In the introduction the authors explain their criteria for selection, and mention that pre-literary material from the oral tradition and slave narratives had to be excluded for lack of space. This note suggests, and perusal of the volume confirms, that the editors were guided in their selections by traditionally formal critical assumptions, and the selections are those created by white critical definitions of literature. One can understand the impulse toward established and "respectable" literary criteria, but in a book of this kind they present real problems and limitations in understanding the cultural basis of the black experience.

An approach to black literature which ignores folklore, the oral tradition, and the musical-poetic aspects of folk-religion excludes the basic forms of creative expression of the black community. Thus, in the selection of poetry we get odes rather than blues lyrics or street poems (anonymous, usually ironic commentaries on contemporary history), or sonnets rather than field hollers or song sermons—those truly amazing examples of metaphorical dexterity and spontaneous poetic inspiration which, taken as a group, represent a vital, popular poetic tradition in the rural black community. On this point it is significant that while the aforementioned essay by Sterling Brown is included, his poetry is conspicuously absent. Yet Brown is one of the country's outstanding authorities on early jazz and the rural folk culture, and a fine poet whose work has inspired countless young black writers in this coutry and in the Third World. Crafted in the rhythms, sensibilities, and idiom of folk-speech, Brown's poetry provides, to my knowledge, some of the most instructive examples of the "literary" adaptation of black cultural materials and styles. The absence of this kind of material is regrettable, the more so because of what it indicates about the emphasis of the anthology.

Michael Thelwell, "Publishing the Black Experience," *Ramparts* 8, No. 4 (October 1969): 62

MARVIN HOLDT   A new book by one of the writers who has contributed most to what Stephen Henderson has called "the new conscious-ness of blackness" is a literary event of importance. *Black Man Abroad: The Toulouse Poems* (Detroit: Lotus Press, 1978) confirms James A. Emanuel's position as one of the most compelling black poets working today, one whose freshness of outlook makes each poem a discovery. Admirers of Emanuel's first two collections, *The Treehouse and Other Poems* (Detroit: Broadside Press, 1968) and *Panther Man* (Detroit: Broadside Press, 1970), will not be disappointed. *Black Man Abroad* is the work of an artist in full possession of remarkable creative faculties, which he uses here with greater subtlety and sureness of touch than ever to convey finer shades of meaning and greater complexities of purpose. The volume will disappoint only those who, like the "dude half down the aisle" in "After the Poetry Reading, Black," expect a black poet to be exclusively concerned with specifically black problems. The book contains fewer black-experience poems than *The Treehouse* or *Panther Man*. Yet the ones it does contain probe more deeply into the substance of that experience. The longest and most revealing of them, "After the Poetry Reading, Black," takes a nightmare plunge into an awareness of the lack of awareness of others and thereby plumbs the depths of an experience in the life of one black man. In this light, the black-experience poems of even *Panther Man* may appear anecdotal; although the eloquence of their dramatic impact offers broad human implications, they fall short of a complete vision. By delving more deeply into these implications in his new book, all the while playing down a strictly black point of view, Emanuel adds a new dimension to the scope of the black consciousness which informs the whole of his poetry, precisely by bringing into the sphere of human sensibility at large that kind of awareness which can only be contributed by one writing from a black perspective. ⟨. . .⟩

Black Man Abroad, as a collection, is less sharp in focus, more reflective in approach, and richer ⟨than *Panther Man*⟩. In it appear the author's first important love poems, together with evidence of further evolution and a new maturity. A multi-faced lyricism is once again the distinguishing feature of the book; more intensely intimate than ever, it is also freer and wider in range. In "Didn't Fall in Love," it is fleeting and bittersweet; the narrator's defenses are up, and he shies away from the involvement into which an irresistible attraction might lead him. But his refusal is bound up with a past, the hard reality of which excludes him from the present. Thus, in counterpoint to the rather tenuous argument itself, a theme is introduced which lends the latter unexpected substance, and which seems, incidentally, to hold increasing interest for the poet, that of interferences between past and present. In "Lovelook Back," one of the most moving love poems I know, the lyricism is, on the contrary, sensuous and full-blooded, even in nostalgia, for the past is the present and the future. What the author has called "a swelling of the memory" is taking place. There is in it the elation of remembered discovery and associations ever new, and there is a future of immense vistas of possibility opened up by the presence of one human being who has come to mean everything. There is, above all, wonder in an all-absorbing present that roots the lover in the eternity of his love as in some elemental vegetal reality, inextricably entwining his very fiber with the beloved. ⟨. . .⟩

⟨. . .⟩ in the final analysis, it would seem that the spiritual dimension in James Emanuel's poetry is the human dimension extended to its utmost limits. Even in bitterness, there is in this poet an identification with his fellow man and a sense of community which transcend resentment. When, in the preface to *Panther Man*, he speaks, with regard to American racism, of "the enormities of my countrymen," his awareness of his countrymen is fully as significant as is his consciousness of the injustice done. It is a sense of loss suffered at the hands of those who should be companions, not enemies, that gives rise to resentment. These, one's companions, are responsible; hence, Emanuel experiences an immense sadness. But the effort to create a community of free individuals made pure of such enormities must take prededence over resentment and sadness.

Marvin Holdt, "James A. Emanuel: Black Man Abroad," *Black American Literature Forum* 13, No. 3 (Fall 1979): 79–81, 84

JOE WEIXLMANN   *Black Man Abroad*, the most ambitious and polished of Emanuel's three published books of poetry, leaves no doubt that its creator is a true poet, for the reader ends the volume feeling more whole, more full as a result of having absorbed Emanuel's rich insights. While, in his new book, Emanuel has not abandoned the racial concerns that so dominate *The Treehouse and Other Poems* (Detroit: Broadside Press, 1968) and *Panther Man* (Detroit: Broadside Press, 1970), he has moved formally beyond both—chiefly through his use of word compounding and, to a limited extent, capitalization, indentation, and other experiments with the printed page—, and he's made more powerful use of non-racial subjects here than he'd been able to do in earlier volumes. ⟨. . .⟩

It is ⟨. . .⟩ in *Black Man Abroad*'s long first section "It Was Me Did These Things" that most of the book's real force resides. Each of the twenty-two selections in this part of the volume, like the four "Occasionals" which close the book, is finely honed. The almost invariable focus of each is love, and the setting, when not Toulouse, is usually another Western European city. Moods and attitudes shift from poem to poem, but the reader grows more accustomed to the sad than the happy. The poems' male protagonists are always reaching. Mentally, physically, they try, though fearful, to touch their longed-for female counterparts. If they fail more than they succeed, they never lose faith. ⟨. . .⟩

Black Man Abroad is an unsettling book, because it candidly confronts secret emotions and latent personality traits most of us would rather ignore than admit to—especially those associated with "manhood." ("We men knew what to do," he mocks in "Topless, Bottomless Bar, Manhattan": "we grinned / behind our puff of insight, / hidden still.") Emanuel weaves his tapestry from human frailties, from hidden places of pain and joy, prejudice and love. These new tones from an old voice should widen the poet's audience.

> Joe Weixlmann, "A Review of James A. Emanuel's *Black Man Abroad: The Toulouse Poems*," *Black American Literature Forum* 13, No. 3 (Fall 1979): 85–86

BETH BROWN   James A. Emanuel dedicates his volume of poetry ⟨*The Broken Bowl*⟩ to his son, James, "who in his purest light will long outlive three cowardly cops in San Diego." In his Preface, Emanuel justifies his inclusion of poems from an extended period of his creation. The factors of his development are pointed out gradually by the author himself, for example, when he changes the word "Negro" to "Black," the inclusion of rhyme, and the "chronological pattern" of his concern for love. His poetry repeats the autobiographical themes of "personal and racial injustice" in

Snowflakes and Steel (1968). Emanuel's own retrieval system makes possible the selection of poems which signify, in small ways, the attainment of larger meanings. He contrasts the black literary movements of the seventies— with their strength in images—with the emergence of the literature of the "history-making" eighties. ⟨. . .⟩

Through the direct influence of ⟨Langston⟩ Hughes and the proud and determined way his works stood up to American literary criticism, Emanuel has derived a notion that criticism is war. He has a traveled, international perspective which contributes to his broad approach to criticism. His poems are conservative and often traditional. "Primavera," "Gone," and "Tomorrow" were written between 1946 and 1949. These early poems are full of existential pain and anguish. Although Emanuel has been around the world, he is not boisterous or arrogant about his travels like Al Young, another internationally known poet. Emanuel is a reclusive voice attempting to withdraw even further from the world while weaving, in Debussyian phrase, the fabric of day's night. "The Circuit of Despair" represents his Beat stage, a period of the kind of soul-searching experienced by the protagonist of Richard Wright's *The Outsider*. Just not enough has been written about the potential of a poem's impact to approximate that of a novel. Emanuel is familiar with Russian poets Brodsky, Mandelstam, and Ahkmatova. There is a clarity of political vision which makes the poems biting in their messages.

Emanuel's poetry echoes the tone of Hughes' in the forties; however, it is the environment of war, rather than issues of technique, that have influenced Emanuel's style. In the early forties, Hughes put much of his creative energies into supporting the World War II effort. He wrote jingles, verses, and slogans for the Treasury Department's Defense Savings Staff in June, including a fifty-eight-line "Defense Bond Blues." He was employed by the Writers War Board and wrote articles on black soldiers, the Women's Army Corps, and Fort Huachuca's Station Hospital No. 1, the "World's Largest Negro Hospital." He also wrote musical lyrics, including the "Go and Get the Enemy Blues." Emanuel uses poetry in a political light, as do most Afro-American poets, and it is his disciplined approach that brings his poetry so close to social realities.

Beth Brown, "Five from Lotus," *CLA Journal* 28, No. 1 (September 1984): 103–5

MATTHEW C. BRENNAN   One of the blurbs on the dust jacket of James Emanuel's new collection of poems, *Whole Grain*, dramatically asserts that Emanuel ranks as "one of the two or three finest" poets. Nevertheless, the major anthologies of contemporary and modern poetry—such as those published by Norton, Longman, and Houghton Mifflin—all routinely exclude him as a representative Black voice in favor of Brooks, Harper, Hayden, Knight, Baraka, Clifton, Jordan, Dove, and others. 〈. . .〉 *Whole Grain: Collected Poems, 1958–89* should, however, help boost Emanuel's visibility and solidify his reputation, for it puts his entire career on view. 〈. . .〉

〈. . .〉 *Whole Grain* comprises many tight, imaginatively metaphoric, and interestingly rhymed haiku, all apparently written since 1986. They are a nice surprise. Besides an entire section of "Breakaway Haiku," Emanuel prefaces each thematic part of *Whole Grain* with a haiku. 〈. . .〉

〈. . .〉 nearly all the poems Emanuel is known by appear in the section "Afro-America, the Garden." While it is revealing to see these thematically related poems collected, *Whole Grain* perhaps best serves Emanuel by showcasing his love and sex poems. As Marvin Holdt has said, he is "better . . . at voicing tenderness than in giving vent to bitterness," and indeed Emanuel has stated that the poet "should turn his mind confidently inward upon himself, believing that the concrete details of his personal history connect him feelingly with all people." More so than any other group of poems, those about love reach Emanuel's goal of awakening "every reader to the private certainty that he is more spiritual than material." In "Topless, Bottomless Bar, Manhattan" (1978), Emanuel penetratingly uncovers the human yearning that transcends mere physical lust when the dancer

> . . . squatted squarely in the face of one
> who gawked at what she closely opened to his eyes
> . . . athrob to join-explore some warmly moving thing
> needful as flesh upon his bone.

〈. . .〉 Emanuel organizes *Whole Grain* by arbitrary categories of subject. Because the thematic groupings emphasize the depth and continuity with which he explores topics such as race, love, childhood, and writing, this scheme of organization helps both to undergird his reputation as a poet of Black experience and to remind critics and readers that his vision also encompasses more general concerns. 〈. . .〉 even if Emanuel is not "one of the two or three finest" poets, he *has* written several fine poems that deserve lasting attention. By collecting Emanuel's 215 poems, *Whole Grain* forms an important record of the poet's life as a writer.

Matthew C. Brennan, "Memories Affection Knows," *African American Review* 26, No. 2 (Summer 1992): 358–60

▧ *Bibliography*

Langston Hughes. 1967.

Dark Symphony: Negro Literature in America (editor; with Theodore L. Gross). 1968.

At Bay. 1968.

The Treehouse and Other Poems. 1968.

Panther Man. 1970.

How I Write/2 (with McKinlay Kantor and Lawrence Osgood). 1972.

Black Man Abroad: The Toulouse Poems. 1978.

A Chisel in the Dark: Poems, Selected and New. 1980.

A Poet's Mind. 1983.

The Broken Bowl: New and Uncollected Poems. 1983.

Deadly James and Other Poems. 1987.

Whole Grain: Collected Poems 1958–1989. 1991.

Lorraine Hansberry
1930–1965

LORRAINE VIVIAN HANSBERRY was born on May 19, 1930, in Chicago, Illinois, the youngest of four children of a well-to-do family. Her father, Carl Augustus Hansberry, the founder of his own real estate business, was a prominent figure in the black community in Chicago, and in her youth Hansberry encountered such distinguished figures as Paul Robeson and Duke Ellington. In 1938 her father bought a house in a white neighborhood and fought his case all the way to the Supreme Court for the right to live there. Even after his death in 1946, prominent black artists and politicians continued to be frequent guests to the Hansberry house.

Hansberry graduated from Englewood High School in Chicago in 1947. She studied art, English, and stage design at the University of Wisconsin but left in 1950 without taking a degree. Nevertheless, her urge to write was stimulated at Wisconsin, especially when she saw a production of Sean O'Casey's *Juno and the Paycock*. Moving to New York later that year, she began to write full-time for *Freedom* magazine, which was founded by Paul Robeson. Her articles on Africa and on civil rights issues affecting blacks, women, and the poor, and her speeches to civil rights and other groups, made her a prominent young spokeswoman for progressive causes. In 1952 she attended the Intercontinental Peace Congress in Montevideo, Uruguay, in place of Paul Robeson, whose passport had been removed by the U.S. government. After marrying Robert Barron Nemiroff, a Jewish man, in 1953, she devoted herself to writing while working at a variety of odd jobs, including a brief teaching stint at the Jefferson School of Social Science. The couple's financial worries were relieved when a song cowritten by Nemiroff became a hit, allowing Hansberry to quit her jobs and write full-time.

Hansberry's first play, *A Raisin in the Sun*, was begun in 1956 and completed in 1958. It is a starkly realistic play about the life of several generations of a black family on the South Side of Chicago, perhaps inspired in part by Arthur Miller's *Death of a Salesman*, although the title is taken from

Langston Hughes's celebrated poem "Harlem" ("What happens to a dream deferred . . . Does it dry up like a raisin in the sun . . . Or does it explode?"). It received tryouts in New Haven, Philadelphia, and Chicago before opening on Broadway in March 1959, starring Sidney Poitier, Ruby Dee, Lou Gossett, and others. The play received 530 performances in a nineteen-month run, and Hansberry became the first black American writer to win the New York Drama Critics Circle Award. In the screenplay she wrote for the film version, Hansberry added several scenes, but these were not filmed; nevertheless, the film was both a critical and popular success when it opened in 1961. Nemiroff's 1973 adaptation of *A Raisin in the Sun* as a musical won a Tony award. A made-for-television version of the play, which restored the omissions from the film version, aired in 1989. Hansberry's screenplay was published in 1992.

In 1960 Hansberry was commissioned by NBC to write a television play on slavery; the result was *The Drinking Gourd*, but NBC executives felt the play was too controversial and it was not produced. Her next play, *The Sign in Sidney Brustein's Window*, opened in October 1964, and in spite of mixed reviews was kept running by friends and admirers until the playwright's death of cancer at the age of thirty-four on January 12, 1965.

In spite of their divorce in 1964, Hansberry named Nemiroff her literary executor. His collection of excerpts from her plays, journals, speeches, and letters, *To Be Young, Gifted and Black: Lorraine Hansberry in Her Own Words*, was presented off-Broadway in 1969. He produced *Les Blancs*, a play set in Africa, in 1970. His edition of *Les Blancs: The Collected Last Plays of Lorraine Hansberry*, which includes *The Drinking Gourd* and *What Use Are Flowers?* as well as the title play, was published in 1972.

◈ *Critical Extracts*

HAROLD CLURMAN   *A Raisin in the Sun* is authentic: it is a portrait of the aspirations, anxieties, ambitions and contradictory pressures affecting humble Negro folk in an American big city—in this instance Chicago. It is not intended as an appeal to whites or as a preachment for Negroes. It is an honestly felt response to a situation that has been lived through, clearly understood and therefore simply and impressively stated.

Most important of all: having been written from a definite point of view (that of a participant) with no eye toward meretricious possibilities in showmanship and public relations, the play throws light on aspects of American life quite outside the area of race.

The importance of the production transcends its script. The play is organic theatre: cast, text, direction are homogeneous in social orientation and in quality of talent. Without the aid of an aesthetic program or bias of any kind but through cultural and emotional consanguinity—a kind of spontaneous combustion which occurs when individuals who share a common need find each other under the proper circumstances—a genuine ensemble has been achieved.

Harold Clurman, "Theatre," *Nation*, 4 April 1959, pp. 301–2

GERALD WEALES   Despite an incredible number of imperfections, *Raisin* is a good play. Its basic strength lies in the character and the problem of Walter Lee, which transcends his being a Negro. If the play were only the Negro-white conflict that crops up when the family's proposed move is about to take place, it would be an editorial, momentarily effective, and nothing more. Walter Lee's difficulty, however, is that he has accepted the American myth of success at its face value, that he is trapped, as Willy Loman was trapped, by a false dream. In planting so indigenous an American image at the center of her play, Miss Hansberry has come as close as possible to what she intended—a play about Negroes which is not simply a Negro play.

The play has other virtues. There are genuinely funny and touching scenes throughout. Many of these catch believably the chatter of a family— the resentments and the shared jokes—and the words have the ring of truth that one found in Odets or Chayefsky before they began to sound like parodies of themselves. In print, I suspect, the defects of *Raisin* will show up more sharply, but on stage—where, after all, a play is supposed to be— the impressive performances of the three leads (Poitier, Ruby Dee, and Claudia McNeil) draw attention to the play's virtues.

Gerald Weales, "Thoughts on *A Raisin in the Sun*: A Critical Review," *Commentary* 27, No. 6 (June 1959): 529

ARNA BONTEMPS   Lorraine Hansberry, the exciting author of *Raisin in the Sun*, is in some very fundamental literary ways related to the sturdy author of *Native Son, Black Boy* and *Uncle Tom's Children.*

Even the Hansberry-Wright link, however, which is by no means limited to the way in which they have drawn upon their common Chicago background for subject matter, is marked by notable differences. Miss Hansberry's star came up unheralded. Nothing from her typewriter had been published or produced prior to *Raisin in the Sun.* The critical and popular approval which followed this event made her famous, and the rejoicing this occasioned can only be compared to the kudos which followed Richard Wright's sunburst a little more than a decade earlier. But her recognition was based on a play. *Native Son* was a novel, *Black Boy* an autobiography, *Uncle Tom's Children* a collection of stories. And the two authors, though they had both spent crucial years of their lives in the Chicago jungle, if that's the word for the South Side of those days, were separated by more than just a span of time in their development.

Richard Wright's young manhood in Chicago was poverty ridden. Lorraine Hansberry's family was well-to-do by South Side standards. Her father was in the real estate business. He could, in a manner of speaking, have owned or managed the rental property in which Bigger Thomas killed the rat with the frying pan. How his perceptive daughter came to see the human turmoil in those substandard quarters through eyes of sympathy and deep understanding has not been told. Miss Hansberry's subsequent writing has consisted mainly of articles in periodicals. It has not tended toward autobiography.

A lesser writer, one imagines, particularly a lesser Negro writer in the United States, might have been in a hurry, given her talents and background, to give the world a picture of debutants' balls and gracious living to compensate for the ugliness Richard Wright had forced before the eyes of millions of readers, to the embarrassment of our favored few. She also avoided the equally unwise assumption that more of the same material that Wright had presented would prove to be equally arresting when presented by her, equally instructive. But it doesn't work that way without the addition of new elements, and the new Hansberry ingredient was *technique.*

In the theatre, a medium that demands a maximum of know-how, usually attained only after long and painful apprenticeship, years of heartbreaking trial and error, she showed up at first bow with complete control of her tools and her craft. This was little short of startling. Self-educated Richard

Wright had been a toiling, sometimes almost awkward manipulator of the devices of composition. He had won over this disadvantage by sheer power. In Lorraine Hansberry's case this particular shoe seemed to be on the other foot.

Arna Bontemps, "New Black Renaissance," *Negro Digest* 11, No. 1 (November 1961): 53–54

HAROLD CRUSE   *A Raisin in the Sun* demonstrated that the Negro playwright has lost the intellectual and, therefore, technical and creative, ability to deal with his own special ethnic group materials in dramatic form. The most glaring manifestation of this conceptual weakness is the constant slurring over, the blurring, and evasion of the internal facts of Negro ethnic life in terms of class and social caste divisions, institutional and psychological variations, political divisions, acculturation variables, clique variations, religious divisious, and so forth. Negro playwrights have never gone past their own subjectivity to explore the severe stress and strain of class conflict within the Negro group. Such class and clique rivalries and prejudices can be just as damaging, demoralizing and retarding as white prejudice. Negro playwrights have sedulously avoided dealing with the Negro middle class in all its varieties of social expression, basically because the Negro playwright has adopted the Negro middle-class morality. Therefore, art itself, especially the art of playwriting, has become a stepping stone to middle-class social status. As long as the morality of the Negro middle class must be upheld, defended, and emulated in social life *outside* the theater it can never be portrayed or criticized *inside* the theater à la Ibsen, or satirized à la Shaw. In this regard it becomes the better part of social and creative valor to do what Hansberry did—"Let us portay only the good, simple ordinary folk because this is what the audiences want, especially the white audiences; but let us give the whites the Negro middle-class ball to carry towards the goal of integration. Beyond that very functional use of the Negro in the theater, of what other value is this thing, the so-called Negro play? None at all, so let us banish it along with that other parochial idea 'The Negro Theater.' We don't like this 'Negro play' category in the American theater anyhow, and we don't like to be told that we must write it, but we'll *use* it (as a starter) and then we'll go on to better things; that is, we'll become what they call human and universal, which in the white folks' lexicon and cultural philosophy means 'universally white.' "

⟨. . .⟩ A *Raisin in the Sun* expressed through the medium of theatrical art that current, forced symbiosis in American interracial affairs wherein the Negro working class has been roped in and tied to the chariot of racial integration driven by the Negro middle class. In this drive for integration the Negro working class is being told in a thousand ways that it must give up its ethnicity and become human, universal, full-fledged American. Within the context of this forced alliance of class aims there is no room for Negro art (except when it pays off) or Negro art institutions (We middle-class Negroes ain't about to pay for that!), because all of this is self-segregation which hangs up "our" drive for integration. From all of this it can be seen how right E. Franklin Frazier was when he observed: "The new Negro middle class that has none of the spirit of service . . . attempts to dissociate itself as much as possible from identification with the Negro masses. . . . The lip service which they give to solidarity with the masses very often disguises their exploitation of the masses."

Harold Cruse, *The Crisis of the Negro Intellectual* (New York: William Morrow, 1967), pp. 281–83

JAMES BALDWIN   We really met ⟨. . .⟩ in Philadelphia, in 1959, when *A Raisin in the Sun* was at the beginning of its amazing career. Much has been written about this play; I personally feel that it will demand a far less guilty and constricted people than the present-day Americans to be able to assess it at all; as an historical achievement, anyway, no one can gainsay its importance. What is relevant here is that I had never in my life seen so many black people in the theatre. And the reason was that never in the history of the American theatre had so much of the truth of black people's lives been seen on the stage. Black people ignored the theatre because the theatre had always ignored them.

But, in *Raisin*, black people recognized that house and all the people in it— the mother, the son, the daughter and the daughter-in-law—and supplied the play with an interpretative element which could not be present in the minds of white people: a kind of claustrophobic terror, created not only by their knowledge of the house but by their knowledge of the streets. And when the curtain came down, Lorraine and I found ourselves in the backstage alley, where she was immediately mobbed. I produced a pen and Lorraine handed me her handbag and began signing autographs. "It only happens once," she said. I stood there and watched. I watched the people, who loved Lorraine for what she had brought to them; and watched Lorraine, who loved the people for what they brought to *her*. It was not, for her, a matter of being admired. She was being corroborated and confirmed. She was wise enough and honest enough to recognize that black American artists are in a very special case. One is not merely an artist and one is not judged merely as an artist: the black people crowding around Lorraine, whether or not they considered her an artist, assuredly considered her a witness. This country's concept of art and artists has the effect, scarcely worth mentioning by now, of isolating the artist from the people. One can see the effect of this in the irrelevance of so much of the work produced by celebrated white artists; but the effect of this isolation on a black artist is absolutely fatal. He *is*, already, as a black American citizen, isolated from most of his white countrymen. At the crucial hour, he can hardly look to his artistic peers for help, for they do not know enough about him to be able to correct him. To continue to grow, to remain in touch with himself, he needs the support of that community from which, however, all of the pressures of American life incessantly conspire to remove him. And when he is effectively removed, he falls silent—and the people have lost another hope.

Much of the strain under which Lorraine worked was produced by her knowledge of this reality, and her determined refusal to be destroyed by it.

James Baldwin, "Sweet Lorraine," *Esquire* 72, No. 5 (November 1969): 139

LLOYD W. BROWN   Ever since the sixties the reputation and significance of several established Black American writers have become issues in the running ethnopolitical debates on Black American literature. James Baldwin, Ralph Ellison, and LeRoi Jones, for example, have been at the center of confrontations between "militants" and "moderates," Black "extremists" and white "liberals," integrationists and Black nationalists, and so on. And it is increasingly evident that Lorraine Hansberry has joined this list of controversial writers, especially on the basis of her first play, *A Raisin in the Sun* (1959). On the anti-integrationist side, Harold Cruse ⟨in *The Crisis of the Negro Intellectual*, 1967⟩ deplores *Raisin* as "the artistic, aesthetic and class-inspired culmination of the efforts of the Harlem leftwing literary and cultural in-group to achieve integration of the Negro in the arts." In other words, it is a "most cleverly written piece of glorified soap opera," a "second-rate" play about working-class Blacks who "mouth middle class ideology." Moreover, the alleged shortcomings of Lorraine Hansberry's integrationist philosophy are linked, somehow, with her supposed inferiority as a dramatic artist: "A *Raisin in the Sun* demonstrated that the Negro playwright has lost the intellectual and, therefore, technical and creative, ability to deal with his own special ethnic group materials in dramatic form."

On the other side of the debate, both C. W. E. Bigsby ⟨in *Confrontation and Commitment: A Study of Contemporary American Drama 1959–1966*, 1967⟩ and Richard A. Duprey ⟨in "Today's Dramatists," *American Theatre*, 1967⟩ have praised Hansberry precisely because, in their view, she transcends those "special ethnic group materials." Thus, according to Duprey, *Raisin* is full of human insights that transcend any racial "concerns," and Bigsby praises her compassion and her understanding of the need to "transcend" history. In short, Hansberry's work has been caught up in the continuing conflict between the ethnic criteria of social protesters and the pro-integrationist's ethos of love and reconciliation. And when a critic such as Jordan Miller ⟨in "Lorraine Hansberry," *The Black American Writer*, Vol. 2, ed. C. W. E. Bigsby, 1971⟩ is confronted with this kind of debate he responds with the art-for-art's-sake thesis. He refuses to discuss Hansberry's work "on the basis of any form of racial consciousness" or "in any niche of social significance," and insists instead on the critic's "obligation" to judge the dramatist's work as "dramatic literature quite apart from other factors."

These three representative viewpoints need to be emphasized here because, taken together, they demonstrate a continuing problem in the study of Black literature: the tendency, for one reason or another, to isolate questions of structure or technique from those of social, or racial, significance.

Lloyd W. Brown, "Lorraine Hansberry as Ironist," *Journal of Black Studies* 4, No. 3 (March 1974): 237–38

ELLEN SCHIFF   A notably sensitive concept of the Jewish experience as archetypal furnishes the subtext of Lorraine Hansberry's *The Sign in Sidney Brustein's Window* (1965), at the same time illuminating one of the most successful characterizations of the Jew on the post-1945 stage. Brustein is the literary heir to the lineage established by Galsworthy's Ferdinand de Levis (*Loyalties*, 1922). He is the Jew who has found his niche in society and occupies it with the same aplomb with which he wears his identity.

In making Brustein the axis of her play and the magnet that attracts its other outsiders, Hansberry draws on the historical experience of the Jew. Her protagonist personifies an alien factor that has earned a degree of acceptance in society. Having accomplished that, he tends to regard race, creed and previous conditions of servitude largely as bothersome clichés and to devote himself to other pressing concerns. Hence Sidney, not unkindly, dismisses his black friend Alton's preoccupation with making a cause of his blackness: "Be a Martian if you wanna." He admonishes the homosexual David:

> If somebody insults you—sock 'em in the jaw. If you don't like
> the sex laws, attack 'em. I think they're silly. You wanna get up a
> petition? I'll sign one. Love little fishes if you want. *But*, David,
> please get over the notion that your particular sexuality is
> something that only the deepest, saddest, the most nobly tortured
> can know about. It ain't . . . it's just one kind of sex—that's all.
> And in my opinion . . . the universe turns regardless.

There is no question of Sidney Brustein's *becoming* assimilated. Married to "the only Greco-Gaelic-Indian hillbilly in captivity," preferring his bohemian life in Greenwich Village to the conventional security of his brother Manny's uptown office, removed enough to laugh with genuine amusement at his mother's carping, "*Not* that I have anything against the goyim, Sidney, she's a nice girl, but . . . ," he justifiably feels entitled to his past participle: "I'm assimilated," he declares.

Although he attributes his need for periodic retreats to an imaginary mountain top to a Jewish psyche "less discriminating than most," Brustein manifests distinctly Jewish traits. He loves life with the love of an idealist who prides himself on being true to his moral principles. An incurable optimist, at thirty-seven he refuses to be daunted by bad luck. For instance, the failure of his cabaret and his consequent indebtedness do not discourage him from investing in a small weekly newspaper. Even though he has sworn to put an end to his long career in the service of "every committee To Save, To Abolish, Prohibit, Preserve, Reserve and Conserve that ever was," Sidney is easily persuaded to support ward politician Wally O'Hara's campaign to clean up city government. Sidney is an incorrigible insurgent. "I

care!" he explains to his gay friend David who writes plays about meaninglessness and alienation, "I care about it all. It takes too much energy *not*
to care."

Ellen Schiff, *From Stereotype to Metaphor: The Jew in Contemporary Drama* (Albany:
State University of New York Press, 1982), pp. 156–57

ANNE CHENEY   Paul Robeson's influence on Lorraine Hansberry
is difficult to assess. They constantly crossed paths in her lifetime. She loved
his voice and the songs he sang. He was her first employer, at *Freedom.*
Indirectly she learned through him and *Freedom* of the dire condition in
which most blacks lived, and of the dangers of being an artist. He was an
inspiration and, to some extent, a warning.

Langston Hughes's influence is much more obvious. He did not allow
himself—especially in the McCarthy era—to become primarily involved in
the political struggle for racial equality. His poetry reflects the lives of black
people, frequently with humor, but he understates his sense of personal
frustration or anger, or of impending danger to those who do not understand
his poetry. Rather, he explains himself and others of his race. He did not
hate those who chose to misunderstand; rather, he found them absurd. Of
course, in "A Dream Deferred" Hughes does warn those who would thwart
the lives of others, but it is a detached warning, an offering from a wise
observer who is above all an artist.

Hansberry did not get her social consciousness primarily from Hughes.
What she got from him instead was a consciousness of the poetic possibilities
of her own race, an appreciation of the black American culture, and—
because of Hughes himself—an awareness that, in spite of all obstacles,
black people remain a dynamic, powerfully creative force in American
society whose achievements must be celebrated in art.

From W. E. B. Du Bois she gained an admiration for the black intellectual,
socialism, and black leadership. He spent most of his long life trying, with
mixed success, to get a hearing for racial equality in America. Ironically,
when the black population raised its collective voice and white people
began to show signs of listening at last, he moved to Ghana, where he
began to edit a multivolumed *Encyclopedia Africana.*

From Frederick Douglass, Hansberry learned about slavery and its psychology. This knowledge she would put to use in *The Drinking Gourd,* a play

too outspoken to be broadcast on commercial television. From Douglass, too, she learned the invaluable lesson that the sufferings of a people may be presented truthfully in ways that rise above propaganda to the level of art. This lesson, perhaps, was the key to the synthesis of action and language toward which, in her own very different kind of writing, she was working.

These four men, among many people, particularly influenced Hansberry. But they could not, finally, answer the question she asked herself. Du Bois—even though he founded *Phylon* and edited *Crisis* to promote black art—and Douglass were not as deeply devoted to art for its own sake as were Robeson and Hughes. Rather, Du Bois and Douglass used their considerable rhetorical skills to illuminate and investigate the black conditions. They left behind books now considered works of art, but the creation of art was not their primary intention. Robeson sacrificed his musical career to pursue justice for members of his race and to become a revolutionary. Hughes pursued his art and—when forced to choose—left the struggle to others.

One month after she questioned her commitment to revolutionary activity, Hansberry wrote in her journal: "Have the feeling I should throw myself back into the movement. . . . But that very impulse is immediately flushed with a thousand vacillations and forbidding images. . . . *comfort* has come to be its own corruption. . . . *Comfort.* Apparently I have sold my soul for it. I think when I get my health back I shall go into the South to find out what kind of revolutionary I am. . . ." Hansberry died six months after writing of her intention to go South, where militants were being murdered, and as a result never answered her question. She died with her dilemma unresolved.

Anne Cheney, *Lorraine Hansberry* (Boston: Twayne, 1984), pp. 53–54

AMIRI BARAKA   *Raisin* first appeared in 1959, in the earlier stages of the civil rights movement. As a document reflecting the essence of those struggles, *Raisin* is unexcelled. For many of us it was—and remains—the quintessential civil rights play. It is probably also the most widely appreciated black play (particularly by Afro-Americans).

But Hansberry has done more than *document*, which is the most limited form of realism. She is a "critical realist," the way that Langston Hughes, Richard Wright and Margaret Walker are. That is, she analyzes and assesses reality and shapes her statement as an esthetically powerful and politically advanced work of art.

George Thompson in *Poetry and Marxism* points out that drama is the most expressive artistic form to emerge from great social transformation. Shakespeare is the artist of the destruction of feudalism—and the emergence of capitalism. The mad Macbeths, bestial Richard IIIs and other feudal worthies are shown, like the whole class, as degenerating. This is why Shakespeare deals with race (*Othello*), anti-Semitism (*The Merchant of Venice*) and feminism (*The Taming of the Shrew*).

Hansberry's play, too, was political agitation. It dealt with the same issues of democratic rights and equality that were being aired in the streets, but it dealt with them realistically, not as political abstraction. ⟨. . .⟩

We thought Hansberry's play belonged to the "passive resistance" part of the movement, which ended the minute Malcolm's penetrating eyes and words began to charge through the media with deadly force. We thought her play "middle class" in that its focus seemed to be on "moving in white folks' neighborhoods," when most blacks were just trying to pay their rent in ghetto shacks.

We missed the essence of the work: that Hansberry had created a family engaged in the same class and ideological struggles as existed in the movement—and within individuals. What is most telling about our ignorance is that Hansberry's play remains overwhelmingly popular and evocative of black and white reality; and the masses of black people saw it was true.

The next two explosions in black drama, Baldwin's *Blues for Mr. Charlie* and my own *Dutchman* (both 1964), raise up the militance and self-defense clamor of the movement as it evolved into the Malcolm era. But neither play is as much a statement from the majority of blacks as is *Raisin*. For one thing, both (regardless of their "power") are too concerned with white people.

Lorraine Hansberry's play, though it seems "conservative" in form and content to the radical petite bourgeoisie, is the accurate telling and stunning vision of the real struggle. The concerns I once dismissed as "middle class"— of buying a house and moving into "white folks' neighborhood"—actually reflect the essence of black will to defeat segregation, discrimination and oppression. The Younger family is our common ghetto Fanny Lou Hammers, Malcolm X's and Angela Davises, etc. And their burden surely will be lifted or one day it certainly will explode.

Amiri Baraka, *"Raisin in the Sun*'s Enduring Passion," *Washington Post*, 16 November 1986, pp. F1, 3

STEVEN R. CARTER   Hansberry's extensive use of parallels to *Hamlet* in *Les Blancs* is highly creative and she gained many advantages by it. First, it permitted her to make an indirect but glowing tribute to one of the finest products of English and European culture, thus indicating her keen awareness that Europe has created far more than colonialism and that much of what Europe has done remains immensely valuable to the whole world, including Africa. This appreciation is even stated explicitly in the play by Tshembe: "Europe—in spite of all her crimes—has been a great and glorious star in the night. Other stars shone before it—and will again with it." Tshembe also attests to the continuing relevance of *Hamlet* and other great European works when, upon being summoned to a meeting of resistance fighters, he explains that "it's an old problem, really . . . Orestes . . . Hamlet . . . the rest of them . . . We've really got so many things we'd rather be doing."

Second, having praised the highest ideals and achievements of European civilization, Hansberry could—so easily—point to the multitude of ways in which the European colonial powers and their offshoot, the United States, were currently failing to adhere to them. When Charlie Morris, an American journalist who has been seeking a dialogue with Tshembe, exposes his failure to understand the African's reference to the fierce woman spirit summoning him to fight for his people, Tshembe reminds this representative of Western culture that "when you knew her you called her Joan of Arc! Queen Esther! La Passionara! And you did know her once, you did know her! But now you call her nothing, because she is dead for you! She does not exist for you!" As Tshembe rightly implies, one of the great tragic ironies of history is that so many of the countries that had fought hard, bloody battles to establish the principles of liberty, equality and fraternity within their own boundaries then fought hard, bloody battles to suppress these principles in other countries solely to satisfy their greed and lust for power. An African nationalist upholding these values may thus be judged a truer heir to the mantle of Hamlet than European colonizers of their American counterparts. However, as Hansberry knew full well, this mantle does not belong only to the more idealistic African revolutionaries but may be donned by anyone who finds the strength and commitment to wear it. At the end, Charlie Morris himself, after many mistakes and vacillations, seems prepared to defy established authority at home and abroad for what he now knows to be the truth about the fight against colonialism in Zatembe. On the other hand, as the speaker of the truth about Tshembe and the resistance movement, perhaps Charlie qualifies more as Horatio, but Horatio too deserves respect.

Third, by paralleling the European drama of Hamlet with the African fable of the thinking hyena, Hansberry affirms that wisdom and folly are not the exclusive properties of any culture and that African culture is one of the "stars that shone before" European culture "and will again with it." Margaret B. Wilkerson, in her introduction to the New American Library edition of *Lorraine Hansberry: The Collected Last Plays*, has argued that while "the parallels to Hamlet are obvious . . . Hansberry, instinctively recognizing the inappropriateness of relying only on a Western literary reference point, provides Tshembe with another metaphor—from African lore—Modingo, the wise hyena who lived between the lands of the elephants and the hyenas." While Wilkerson's point is in general well taken, it seems more likely that what Hansberry did was deliberate rather than instinctive. In an interview with Patricia Marks for Radio Station WNYC in New York, Hansberry suggested that "perhaps we must take a more respectful view of the fact that African leaders today say that with regard to Europe and European traditions in the world we will take the best of what Europe has produced and the best of what we have produced and try to create a superior civilization out of the synthesis. I agree with them and I think that it commands respect for what will be inherently African in that contribution." Hansberry's *Les Blancs* provides an excellent example of how such a synthesis might be formed.

Steven R. Carter, "Colonialism and Culture in Lorraine Hansberry's *Les Blancs*," *MELUS* 15, No. 1 (Spring 1988): 30–31

J. CHARLES WASHINGTON   Viewers of *A Raisin in the Sun* can be moved by a tragic hero who is elevated by his growth from ignorance to knowledge, and deeply affected by a realistic hero whose transcendence involves a tremendous sacrifice—at the play's end, Walter and his family are as poor and powerless as they were before. The new house provides a "pinch of dignity" that allows them a bit more breathing and living space, but their lives are essentially unchanged. Without the greater financial rewards the business could have produced, they must all continue working at the same menial jobs in order to survive and pay for the house. In fact, they may be even worse off, since the birth of Ruth's second child will mean an extra mouth to feed. Walter and Ruth have made no substantive economic progress; their current life is a modern version of the life of Lena and Big Walter. The principal hope that Ruth and Walter have is the one Lena and Big Walter had and which people everywhere have always had— that some day in the future their children will be able to make their parents' dreams come true.

Considering that this sobering reality should provide a cause for despair would involve a serious misunderstanding of the author's intention and a grievous contradiction of her faith in the perfectibility of humanity based on her conviction that humankind will "do what the apes never will— *impose* the reason for life on life." Moreover, this small but significant hope, as well as the characters who embody it, offers perhaps the best example of the universal materials the play abounds in, giving Hansberry's art its distinguishing mark and enduring value. Illustrating her ability to see synthesis where others could only see dichotomy, Hansberry discovered the basis of this universal hope, indeed of her faith in humanity, in the Black experience: ". . . if blackness brought pain, it was also a source of strength, renewal and inspiration, a window on the potentials of the human race. For if Negroes could survive America, then there was hope for the human race indeed."

J. Charles Washington, "A *Raisin in the Sun* Revisited," *Black American Literature Forum* 22, No. 1 (Spring 1988): 123–24

MARGARET B. WILKERSON   Lorraine Hansberry, despite her bourgeois upbringing, had seen the fruit of racism and segregation in the struggles of her neighbors who came from all classes, since all blacks were confined to the Black Metropolis, Bronzeville, of Chicago. She had seen the personal toll on her father, and herself had been the near-victim of a mob protesting her family's move into a white neighborhood. Exactly when and how her sexual radicalization developed is less clear at this point, but what is obvious is that the usual generalizations about the black middle class simply were not borne out by a study of her early life. She was attracted to the theatre as a laboratory for manipulating and interpreting human experience, especially as it related to race, class, and gender; theatre as a persuasive and visible art form that allowed her to comment on the contradictions within the human personality; and the drama as the most attractive medium for, as she said, talking to people and sharing her vision of human potential. She found confirmation in the progressive left of Harlem—which she immediately joined upon moving to New York City—because it gave theatre and other cultural activities high priority, including them as a necessary extension and expression of ideas. Part of Hansberry's achievement in *A Raisin in the Sun* was to embody progressive ideas in the life and struggle of a black family (without resorting to the jargon of the left), and to build that family into a metaphor that whites and blacks, liberals, radicals, and even some conservatives could affirm, *while* winning one of the most prized awards of the theatre establishment. She managed it so well that the two FBI agents who saw the Broadway production and reported on its political import to the Bureau saw no revolutionary danger in the play. They, of course, did not realize that Walter Lee's sons and Mama's daughters would stride the boards in the next two decades, changing for good the image of blacks in the theatre and creating the artistic arm of the black nationalist movement. The line of Hansberry's influence stretches into and beyond the 1960s, but it begins in the 1930s and 1940s as she grew up in the peculiar crucible of segregation known as Chicago.

> Margaret B. Wilkerson, "Excavating Our History: The Importance of Biographies of Women of Color," *Black American Literature Forum* 24, No. 1 (Spring 1990): 80–81

STEVEN R. CARTER   Hansberry's goal in all her work was realism—the truthful depiction, as she said, of "not only what is but what is possible . . . because that is part of reality too." A realism rooted, she hoped, in characters so truthfully and powerfully rendered that an audience could not but identify with them. But she did not think of realism as a specific form or genre, and strongly disagreed with those critics who saw it as limiting. As she told Studs Terkel, "I think that imagination has no bounds in realism—you can do anything which is permissible in terms of the truth of the characters. That's all you have to care about." She had a flair for significant, eye-and-mind-catching spectacle, as in Walter's imaginary spear-wielding table-top oratory and Iris Brustein's dance. *Les Blancs* in particular is filled with such spectacle, from the initial appearance of the woman warrior spirit with "cheeks painted for war," to Tshembe's elaborate ritual donning of ceremonial robes, to the gesture-filled oral storytelling of Peter/Ntali, to the explosion and gunshot-packed climax. Her use of spectacle, moreover, was almost always symbolic, as in Tshembe's construction of a wall of cloth between Charlie Morris and himself representing the spiritual wall between them at the moment. Her "realistic" drama in such instances differed little from expressionism or poetic fantasy; she always chose the best means to express the whole truth about her characters, no matter whether critics would have deemed it appropriate to her form or not.

As a politically and socially committed writer, Hansberry strove to present a host of unpleasant and challenging truths in her work, although often with such wit and dramatic force that they no longer seemed unpalatable but inevitable. She was unquestionably a Marxist but in the largest sense of this frequently narrowed and abused term, as unhindered by doctrine and as open to new ideas as was Marx himself, and as complicated, wide-ranging, open-minded, and even at times ambivalent in her approach to esthetics as Henri Arvon has shown Marx to be. Keeping faith with her myriad commitments never precluded the portrayal of the full complexity of life as Hansberry saw it. Few writers in any genre have delineated so completely and strikingly the social dilemmas of our time, and none have surpassed—or are likely to surpass—her ability to point out the heights toward which we should soar.

Steven R. Carter, *Hansberry's Drama: Commitment amid Complexity* (Urbana: University of Illinois Press, 1991), pp. 190–91

❖ Bibliography

A Raisin in the Sun. 1959.

The Movement: Documentary of a Struggle for Equality. 1964.

The Sign in Sidney Brustein's Window. 1965.

To Be Young, Gifted and Black: Lorraine Hansberry in Her Own Words. Adapted by Robert Nemiroff. 1969.

Les Blancs. Adapted by Robert Nemiroff. 1972.

Les Blancs: The Collected Last Plays of Lorraine Hansberry. Ed. Robert Nemiroff. 1972.

A Raisin in the Sun: The Unfilmed Original Screenplay. Ed. Robert Nemiroff. 1992.

✦ ✦ ✦

Robert Hayden
1913–1980

ROBERT EARL HAYDEN was born Asa Bundy Sheffey on August 4, 1913, in a poor neighborhood in Detroit, Michigan. When he was a young boy his mother, by then divorced, left him with foster parents, William and Sue Ellen Hayden (from whom he took his name) and left to seek work in Buffalo, New York; years later she returned and lived briefly with the Haydens, but conflicts with them forced her to move to a house next door. Hayden believed that his original name was Robert Sheffey; he did not learn his real name until he was forty.

After graduating from high school, Hayden was variously employed before entering Detroit City College (now Wayne State University) on a scholarship in 1932. He spent four years there but did not earn a degree. Between 1936 and 1940 he worked as a writer and researcher of black history and folklore on the WPA Federal Writers' Project in Detroit while studying part-time at the University of Michigan. In 1938 he won the university's Hopwood Minor Award for poetry, and after publishing a book of poems, *Heart-Shape in the Dust*, in 1940, he moved to Ann Arbor in 1941 to complete his education. After gaining his M.A. in 1944, he stayed on to teach for two years before joining the faculty of Fisk University in Nashville, Tennessee, in 1946. He had married Emma Morris in 1940; they had one child.

In 1948 Hayden established the Counterpoise Press at Fisk to encourage creative writing, particularly by black Americans. Although he wrote *The Lion and the Archer* in collaboration with Myron O'Higgins in 1948 and published a brief collection of poems, *Figure of Time*, in 1955, his heavy teaching load limited his production, and he found little recognition in America. However, his poems were translated widely, and his growing reputation abroad led to the publication in London of his second major book, *A Ballad of Remembrance* (1962), which won him the Grand Prize for Poetry at the First World Festival of Negro Arts in Dakar, Senegal, in 1966. That same year his *Selected Poems* appeared in New York, followed in 1970 by *Words in the Mourning Time* and in 1972 by *The Night-Blooming Cereus*.

During the 1960s Hayden was attacked by some black radicals for being an Uncle Tom because he refused to advocate a separate "Negro poetry" and for the occasional difficulty and obscurity of his work, which was considered elitist and inaccessible to the mass of black people. But Hayden countered that "there is no such thing as black literature. There's good literature, and there's bad. And that's all!"

Hayden retired from Fisk in 1969 and returned to the University of Michigan as professor of English, where he remained until his death; he was also much in demand as a visiting lecturer and poet. *Angle of Ascent: New and Selected Poems* appeared in 1975, the year in which he was elected a Fellow of the Academy of American Poets. In 1976 he became the first black American to serve as poetry consultant to the Library of Congress, and in his last years he received several honorary doctorates. His last collection of poems, *American Journal*, was published in 1978; an augmented edition appeared in 1982.

Hayden had converted to the Baha'i faith (a nineteenth-century Persian religion preaching universal tolerance) in 1942. He was poetry editor of the Baha'i quarterly journal *World Order* from 1967 until his death on February 25, 1980. His collected prose and collected poems were edited by Frederick Glaysher in 1984 and 1985, respectively.

▨ *Critical Extracts*

SELDEN RODMAN   It is possible that this modest pamphlet 〈*The Lion and the Archer*〉, containing thirteen short poems by two young Negro poets, may come to be regarded as the entering wedge in the "emancipation" of Negro poetry in America. Perhaps because writing poetry demands a greater degree of self-consciousness, perhaps because verse by Negroes has hitherto tended to lean heavily and uneasily on the inimitable folk-art of spirituals and blues, there has been nothing in this contemporary field to compare with, say, the painting of Horace Pippin or Jacob Lawrence. The recent books by Margaret Walker and Gwendolyn Brooks were steps in the direction of independence from a limited minstrel quaintness, but they lacked the experimental vigor of these poems.

> Selden Rodman, "Negro Poets," *New York Times Book Review*, 10 October 1948, p. 27

ROSEY POOL   In his "A Ballad of Remembrance," "Quadroon mermaids, afro angels, black saints balanced upon the switchblades of that air and sang." Every time I read the Ballad, when I read it just with my eyes, hearing the echo of the words singing inside me, or when I read it aloud to make it communicate with people, in an attempt to open their minds and ears to the voice of a true poet, whenever or wherever I make contact with that ballad of remembrance, I envy Mark Van Doren to whom Hayden addresses himself: "And therefore this is not only a ballad of remembrance . . . but also, Mark Van Doren, a poem of remembrance, a gift, a souvenir for you."

In that way every poet's poem is a gift, a souvenir to everyone who approaches it, and Robert Hayden is one of the Afro-American poets whose precious gifts have far too long lain unheeded.

Hayden is certainly not a "protest poet" in the usual sense of the word. He would refuse that label as he refuses to be pigeon-holed as a "Negro poet," or as one whose Negritude or race-identification features as a basic quality of his poetry. And still . . . he is all that. Not primarily, not deliberately, not in prepense, but naturally all that in him is "truly instinct, brain-matter, diastole, systole, reflex action," as he himself speaks of freedom and liberty as personified in the great Frederick Douglass.

At Dakar, as a member of the Grand Jury for the literature prizes, and before the Festival, in the pre-selection jury in Paris and London, my colleagues and I tried to recognize the qualities of true poetry: originality, creativeness, disciplined inspiration, craftsmanship in the handling of raw material, namely: the language . . . ability to communicate, the ability to sing via the printed word into the heart and mind of a reader.

On the great prize-giving night our jury-chairman, Langston Hughes, proudly announced that Robert E. Hayden of the United States was our Poet Laureate, and that the honorary mentions were given to Derek Walcott, of the West Indian island of St. Lucia, for his book *In a Green Night,* and to Christopher Okigbo, of Nigeria, for his collection of poetry, *Limits.* It had been a difficult choice. Still the jury thought that Hayden's work deserved the ultimate honor which could be awarded to "a book of poetry published between January 1962 and September 1965 which has not received any other prizes or distinctions."

Rosey Pool, "Robert Hayden: Poet Laureate," *Negro Digest* 15, No. 8 (June 1966): 41

DAVID GALLER   He oscillates from semi-dialect blues and corrupted ballads to Poundian notation; predictably, he resorts to the former for portraits of his childhood, family, and friends, and to the latter for "historical evidence" poems describing the white man's burden. Predictably, too, with a subject so fearfully basic and seemingly insoluble, Hayden is capable of high eclecticism when dealing with salvation (on the theological plane); witness his poems concerned with the Baha'i faith, a prominent nineteenth-century Persian sect whose leader was martyred. Might not the example of Jesus have sufficed? For the white man, probably.

Hayden is as gifted a poet as most we have; his problem is not one of talent but frame of reference. It is fascinating, moving, and finally devastating that the finest verse in his book ⟨*Selected Poems*⟩ (the speech on pages 69–70) is spoken by a Spanish sailor, a witness of the *Amistad* mutiny, who describes the slaughter of their captors by "murderous Africans". This speech the sailor delivers to American officials, saying at one point:

> . . . We find it paradoxical indeed
> that you whose wealth, whose tree of liberty
> are rooted in the labor of your slaves
> should suffer the august John Quincy Adams
> to speak with so much passion of the right
> of chattel slaves to kill their lawful masters . . .

Hayden is a superb ironist in this passage. The crime of it is he has not chosen his forte; it has chosen him.

David Galler, "Three Recent Volumes," *Poetry* 110, No. 4 (July 1967): 268–69

JULIUS LESTER   His images give the reader a new experience of the world. In his *Selected Poems* are found such lines as: "Graveblack vultures encircle afternoon"; "palmleaf knives of sunlight"; "autumn hills / in blazonry of farewell scarlet." And in *Words in the Mourning Time* these lines appear: "God brooms had swept / the mist away." He chooses words with the care of a sculptor chipping into marble and, in his poem "El-Hajj Malik El-Shabazz," from *Words in the Mourning Time*, a vivid historical portrait of Malcolm X is presented in six short lines:

> He X'd his name, became his people's anger,
> exhorted them to vengeance for their past;
> rebuked, admonished them,
> their scourger, who
> would shame them, drive them from
> lush ice gardens of their servitude.

Such a simple phrase—"He X'd his name"—but it sets up reverberations that extend back to August of 1619. ⟨. . .⟩

Robert Hayden refuses to be defined by anything other than the demands of his craft. He does not want to be restricted solely to the black experience or have his work judged on the basis of its relevance to the black political struggle. First and foremost, he is not a pawn in some kind of neo-medieval morality play. His task is, in his words, merely that which has always been the poet's task: "to reflect and illuminate the truth of human experience."

Julius Lester, [Review of *Words in the Mourning Time*], *New York Times Book Review*, 24 January 1971, pp. 5, 22

CHARLES T. DAVIS   History has haunted Robert Hayden from the beginning of his career as a poet. In 1941, when a graduate student at the University of Michigan, he worked on a series of poems dealing with slavery and the Civil War called *The Black Spear*, the manuscript which was to win for him a second Hopwood Award. This effort was no juvenile excursion, to be forgotten in the years of maturity. Though some of the poems have not been reprinted in *Selected Poems* (1966), *The Black Spear* survives in a severely altered form in Section Five of that volume. What remains is not simply "O Daedalus, Fly Away Home" and "Frederick Douglass," but a preoccupation with a continuing historical ambition. This was the desire to record accurately the yearnings, the frustrations, and the achievement of an enslaved but undestroyed people. "Middle Passage," "The Ballad of Nat Turner," and "Runagate, Runagate," all written later, share this concern. In these poems noble Blacks, Cinquez, Nat Turner, and Harriet Tubman, rise from oppression and obscurity.

An extended period of study and research, as well as correspondence in theme, links these later poems with *The Black Spear*. Hayden had intended "Middle Passage" to be the opening work of *The Black Spear*, but the poems in 1941 would not assume a shape that would satisfy a meticulous craftsman. "The Ballad of Nat Turner" and "Runagate, Runagate" come from poring over journals, notebooks, narratives, and histories dealing with the slave trade, plantation life, slave revolts, and the Underground Railroad, reading begun about 1940 and continued for perhaps a decade, judging from his recollection of the activity of composition.

A generation later Hayden displays an attachment somewhat less strong to historical themes. In 1966 "Frederick Douglass" closed Section Five of *Selected Poems* and the book, a sign of a surviving commitment. "El-Hajj Malik El-Shabazz (Malcolm X)" opens Section Three "Words in the Mourning Time" of Hayden's most recent book of poems, bearing the title of the section and published in 1970. Though the commitment to interpreting history is still present, the emphasis has changed. The poems of *The Black Spear* emerge from the suffering of Black people before Emancipation and record their assertion of manhood, more than the simple ability to survive, but those in "Words in the Mourning Time" describe the agony undergone by Malcolm and others to achieve spiritual liberation in our own day and the search for meaning in history upon which that liberation depends. What has endured through the years is the central importance of history in Hayden's poetry—not history as the poet would like it to be, but history as he has discovered it.

Charles T. Davis, "Robert Hayden's Use of History," *Modern Black Poets: A Collection of Critical Essays*, ed. Donald B. Gibson (Englewood Cliffs, NJ: Prentice-Hall, 1973), pp. 96–97

MICHAEL PAUL NOVAK   "Middle Passage" is Hayden's most ambitious poem and possibly his best. The title not only refers to the historical route of the slave ships but also to a middle passage in life, a place for a sea-change, a transformation. There are three historical speakers in the poem—the first a member of a crew troubled by the terrible treatment of the slaves, the second a tough slaver describing the purchase of the

Africans from "the nigger kings," and third, a self-righteous member of *The Amistad* recounting the revolt led by the slave Cinquez.

The poem is controlled, however, by a fourth voice, out of time, who through a series of refrain-like passages gives us the meaning of the poem. Alluding ironically to *The Tempest*, Hayden shows the economic significance of "black gold."

> Deep in the festering hold thy father lies,
> of his bones New England pews are made,
> those are altar lights that were his eyes.

But through this "Voyage through death, / voyage whose chartings are unlove" come other transformations, most significantly that of Cinquez, "the black prince." He becomes in his revolt a "deathless primaveral image / life that transfigures many lives." "Middle Passage" is a searing re-creation of the horrors of the slave trade, one that plunges into the darkest and deepest meanings of history—through the "Voyage through death / to life upon these shores."

In the 1970 volume *Words in the Mourning Time* Hayden attempts to portray recent history. There are poems about the life and death of Malcolm X, Vietnam, the assassinations of Robert Kennedy and Martin Luther King, but the events often seem to overwhelm his craft. There are effective poems in the book but none as memorable as the best poems in *Selected Poems*. They seem thinner, more hesitant than the earlier work as if the mourning has become too great for the words.

Michael Paul Novak, "Meditative, Ironic, Richly Human: The Poetry of Robert Hayden," *Midwest Quarterly* 15, No. 3 (April 1974): 283–84

CONSTANCE J. POST   The consideration of the way Hayden uses struggle in his poetry must finally rest upon his tragicomic view of life. In " 'Lear Is Gay' " Hayden, recalling Yeats' "Lapis Lazuli," praises that gaiety found in an old man who "can laugh sometimes as at a scarecrow whose hobo shoulders are a-twitch with crows." Dedicated to his friend Betsy Graves Reyneau, the poem expresses admiration for someone whose attitude towards irrevocable defeat is tempered with gaiety. The defeat may be the physical deterioration of the body as one is metamorphosed into a "tattered coat upon a stick," to draw a relevant image from Yeats. Or, generally speaking, it may be anything that is reduced to ineffectuality, which Hayden captures precisely in his image of the scarecrow that can no longer scare a crow.

For Hayden, to be able to laugh at the ravages of time is an achievement of the human spirit secure in the knowledge that everything alters even as we behold it. Thus as the jilted lover and the soul-weary people behold the singer in "Homage to the Empress of the Blues," their sorrow is transformed by the power of her song. She not only "flashed her golden smile," lustrous and radiant, but "shone that smile on us and sang." The light of the stars, their tension in delicate balance, is thereby reflected as she sings the blues. Her song thus embodies Hayden's imagery of the stars, his theme of struggle and his use of paradox, bearing eloquent testimony to Hayden's artistry as well as to her own.

> Constance J. Post, "Image and Idea in the Poetry of Robert Hayden," CLA Journal 20, No. 2 (December 1976): 174–75

WILLIAM LOGAN   Hayden exploits the classics and the contemporary, historical anecdote and personal encounter, to demonstrate that what grants history poignancy—that it cannot be altered—also gives pathos to the personal. His explorations of Black history appear in choice of subject matter and a slight widening of technique to include occasional swatches of song and dialect, rather than as impenetrable anger or voguish posture. He produces homages to both Mark Van Doren and Malcolm X; his poems conjure up a variety of lives caught in the desperation of poverty, or that of decadence. His most extreme emotions, and successes, reserved for that era that began with the arrival of slaves in America and ended with the Civil War and Reconstruction, produce a number of serious, haunted poems, including "The Dream," "The Ballad of Sue Ellen Westerfield," and the stunning "Middle Passage."

⟨. . .⟩ "Middle Passage" is the best contemporary poem I have read on slavery. It is a singular performance, one which Hayden's later poems have not matched, in part because it is a poem whose special construction does not invite imitation.

Hayden has not discovered other methods rich enough to encompass public or private history so well. The defects which mar his poetry include compositional tics (repetition, for example: "the name he never can he never can repeat") and, especially in the newer poems, occasional opaqueness. Some recent poems are contrived from feelings so momentary that only a fleeting satisfaction is achieved. At worst, in the new work the phrases break up, the words fly apart, and the associative structure holds no meaning. The poems may shatter into component images, individually attractive but fragmentary. There are few first-rate metaphors; the poems that remain in the mind persuade by narrative, not image. As one moves through the book ⟨Angle of Ascent⟩, it is disconcerting to find the older poems last. Such an ordering places the newer poems, whose methods are smaller, and which should be seen as the product of development, at a disadvantage; as the older poems drape themselves in description and narration, the newer work seems insubstantial.

William Logan, "Language against Fear," Poetry 130, No. 4 (July 1977): 227–28

HOWARD FAULKNER   Robert Hayden's recent assemblage of new and selected poetry, Angle of Ascent, suggests that he has found the theme he sought. Each of Hayden's poems can be reduced to a single pair of words from which the surface structure of the poem is generated. In this collection, these words number fewer than a dozen pairs. Below them, at the deepest level, is one word from which these pairs are generated and which embodies the theme Hayden has found: transformation. Hayden's world, like Richard Wilbur's, is one where the beautiful changes, and like Wilbur, Hayden is interested in describing those changes. But Hayden is a less hopeful poet, and the change is as likely as not to be a falling away from beauty. Unlike Wilbur's juggler-poet "who has won for once over the world's weight," Hayden holds out fainter, more shadowy hopes. At his most affirmative, sustained explicitly by the Bahai faith which is rarely overt in the poetry, Hayden contemplates the death of Martin Luther King and Robert Kennedy and concludes with the muted hope that

> the agonies of our deathbed childbed age
> are process, major means whereby,
> oh dreadfully, our humanness must be achieved.

And in "Theme and Variation" he writes:

> all things alter even as I behold
> all things alter, the stranger said.
> Alter, become a something more,
> a something less. Are the revelling shadows
> of a changing permanence.

Hayden has called himself a "realist who distrusts so-called reality." In describing what in "Theme and Variation" he calls "the striptease of reality," he finds a something less more often than a something more.

Transformation, the movement upward to or downward from beauty, is rarely depicted as a completed act; Hayden more frequently emphasizes the process, the working through. Two of his favorite devices, logically enough, are oxymoron and paradox, exemplified by the apparently obvious contradiction of "changing permanence" and by the more subtle tension of moods in "revelling shadows" and "steeps of flight," the latter also punning "steeps" with "steps." But whatever its nature, transformation is the source of the movement from the deep levels of Hayden's work to its surface, producing a poetic tension in three ways. First, there is the opposition of the paired words themselves, defining the terms of each poem. Second, given Hayden's ambivalent view of the possibilities of transformation, a dialectic arises from the poet's attention to change as the object of his descriptive allegiance and his balancing, rather wistful, attraction to permanence, suggested particularly by his uses of history, myth, and art. Third, the strain is manifested in Hayden's tendency to describe process in terms that move away from verbs to verbless structures, that is, away from a language drenched in time to one struggling to be freed from it.

Howard Faulkner, " 'Transformed by Steeps of Flight': The Poetry of Robert Hayden," *CLA Journal* 21, No. 2 (December 1977): 282–83

WILBURN WILLIAMS, JR.   Robert Hayden is a poet whose symbolistic imagination is intent on divining the shape of a transcendent order of spirit and grace that might redeem a world tragically bent on its own destruction. And his memory, assailed by the discontinuities created by its own fallibility, is equally determined to catch and preserve every shadow and echo of the actual human experience in which our terribleness stands revealed. In poem after poem Hayden balances the conflicting claims of the ideal and the actual. Spiritual enlightenment in his poetry is never the reward of evasion of material fact. The realities of imagination and the actualities of history are bound together in an intimate symbiotic alliance that makes neither thinkable without the other. Robert Hayden's poetry proposes that if it is in the higher order of spirit that the gross actualities of life find their true meaning, it is also true that the transcendent realm is meaningful to man only if it is visibly incarnate on the plane of human experience.

Now viewed as a theory of poetics Hayden's characteristic method of composition will hardly strike anyone as unique. His preoccupation with the relationship between natural and spiritual facts puts him squarely in the American literary tradition emanating from Emerson, and we are not at all amazed therefore when we find correspondences between his work and that of figures like Dickinson and Melville.

> Wilburn Williams, Jr., "Covenant of Timelessness & Time: Symbolism & History in Robert Hayden's *Angle of Ascent*," *Massachusetts Review* 18, No. 4 (Winter 1977): 731–32

JOHN S. WRIGHT   If Robert Earl Hayden had been a confessional poet, he would probably have made more capital out of a life rich with the dramatic tension he wanted his poems to have. He would have worked more pointedly the flamboyant ironies of a World War I era boyhood in the "Paradise Valley" section of Black Detroit. He would have exposed and explored how his work's almost ritual preoccupation with identity, with names, and with ambiguous realities reflected the bruising fact that "Robert Hayden" was his adoptive, not his legal name and that discovering what that "real" name was served as part of his initiation into fuller manhood. If the confessional mode had better fit him, he would have chronicled also the "burdens of consciousness" that his dual commitment to human freedom and artistic integrity made him bear; he would have logged the jagged confrontation with the Black Arts writers which ultimately turned his long tenure at Fisk University into a trial of words and which made him for a moment seem a naysayer to blackness and so become one of a younger generation's many scapegoat kings.

But Hayden was not a confessional poet like so many of his contemporaries because, as he acknowledged, he entered his own experiences so completely that he had no creative energy left afterward. He could admire the way that Anne Sexton, Robert Lowell, John Berryman, and Michael Harper made poems out of devastating personal experiences; but he countered, in his own defense, that "reticence has *its* aesthetic values *too*." And so, with words at least, he wore the mask, and won in wearing it the detached control and objectivity without which poetic marvels like his most widely acclaimed

poem, "Middle Passage," would not have been possible. From the apprentice
work of his earliest book, *Heart-Shape in the Dust* (1940), to the closing
lines of *American Journal*, he pushed toward the mastery of materials, outlook,
and technique that would enable him to strike through the masks reality
wore. And so he made himself, like the Malcolm X of his honorific poem
"El-Hajj Malik El-Shabazz," one of Ahab's Native Sons, though rejecting
Ahab.

The continuities in the progressive unmaskings, which Robert Hayden
described as his "slim offerings over four decades," are striking. His absorption
with the past, especially the black past, provided one axis of subject and
theme for him—an absorption that brooked no lost Edens, no nostalgia,
but which transformed archetype and artifact into a poetry of revelation.
At the same time, he was drawn more to the dramas of human personality
than to things or abstractions or philosophical ideas. In *American Journal*,
as in all his books, the places, landscapes, and localities he re-creates so
minutely live primarily through his heroic and what he called "baroque"
people—more often than not outsiders, pariahs, even losers. As he revealed
in an interview with John O'Brien, Hayden thought of himself as a "symbolist
of a kind," as a "realist who distrusts so-called reality," as a "romantic
realist." And he couched his symbolist explorations of human suffering and
transcendence in a world-view permeated by an omnipresent, though never
obtrusive, "God-consciousness." Poetry, indeed all art, he felt, was "ultimately religious in the broadest sense of the term"; if poets have any calling
beyond fulfilling the demands of their craft, he insisted, "it is to affirm the
humane, the universal, the potentially divine in the human creature."

> John S. Wright, "Homage to a Mystery Boy," *Georgia Review* 36, No. 4 (Winter
> 1982): 905–6

FRED M. FETROW   In his poetry, and in his conversations about
poetry, Robert Hayden frequently turned to one of his favorite themes—
the effort to distinguish appearance from reality, that search for truth,
whereby to illuminate and enrich human experience. One cannot read much
of Hayden's poetry without concluding that this ongoing pursuit of truth
was for him more than a favorite theme; it was perhaps closer to a "ruling
passion." The corpus of his work over the years—indeed, his career as a
poet—attests to the acute awareness with which he perceived reality. He

continued to marvel at life; he remained in the conviction that a higher reality resided beneath the surface reality, and that an artful expression of this higher reality would give an added dimension to the ordinary experience of his readers. This combination of faith and talent made him a truly marvelous poet.

Yet the literary critic who would trace the evolution of Hayden's poetic voice, who would analyze and explicate his over four decades of work, must begin by identifying with the speaker in "American Journal," as that otherworldly analyst expresses the frustration of trying to generalize about an ever-changing phenomenon:

> an organism that changes even as i
> examine it   fact and fantasy never twice the
> same   so many variables

Anyone trying to "capture" Robert Hayden has the same difficulty. Even in the fruition of his artistic goals, at the height of his poetic powers, Hayden did not content himself with self-satisfaction. Because he relentlessly pursued a constantly changing reality with untried themes and innovative poetic techniques, he scarcely could be expected to lie still under the critic's microscope. And yet it is precisely because Hayden continued throughout his career to be intrigued with life's "fact and fantasy" that his expressions of reality will continue to intrigue his readers and critics.

Fred M. Fetrow, *Robert Hayden* (Boston: Twayne, 1984), pp. 37–38

JOHN HATCHER   Most of the poems in *Heart-Shape in the Dust* are imitative, though the breadth of Hayden's sources implies a young poet who was continually experimenting, who was hardly dominated by interest in one poet or group of poets. The variety of styles and, more important, the consistent reliance on direct expression of abstraction and generalization, also demonstrate clearly a poet who is groping for his own voice. And at the same time, one finds in these experiments the concerns, the raw material which would form the basis for his later work. His Romantic poems, for example, may show his love of Keats, but they also show him looking for a technique which would allow the poet as persona, as character in his own poems, to use his own introspection to advantage. He would later utilize such modes in his intimate reflections on childhood and Paradise Valley. Similarly, in his call for a Negro poet, a 'dark singer' who can celebrate

Afro-American heroes, one senses the apprentice poet longing to undertake that task, which indeed he did successfully accomplish almost immediately in the early 1940s with his *Black Spear* sequence that won him the Hopwood award in 1942. Even his most blatant protest poems indicting racism, war and economic injustice foreshadow the themes he would later pursue, because he never lost sight, especially after his conversion to the Baha'i Faith, of his belief in the perfectibility of man and society.

Almost immediately, and seemingly mysteriously, his poetic voice would change and mature. He would synthesize and consolidate his gains and put aside imitation. He would arrive at a solid understanding of how a poem works. It is all here in this early collection in embryonic form, lurking behind the borrowed modes—his joy in language, his adept metrics and sense of line, the imaginative figurative image. *Heart-Shape in the Dust* anthologizes his beginnings, like a primeval soup into which the protean resources have been stirred, but as yet improperly blended. But to the careful eye, the voice is burgeoning, the dark singer about to unloose his song for the 'Inarticulate multitudes'.

John Hatcher, *From the Auroral Darkness: The Life and Poetry of Robert Hayden* (Oxford: George Ronald, 1984), pp. 104–5

PONTHEOLLA T. WILLIAMS   Robert Hayden ⟨. . .⟩ believed that poetry was a method by which men could momentarily come to live with chaos—out of what he called "ugliness." Like Yeats, he felt the poet "must lie down where the ladders start / In the rag-and-bone shop of the heart," and, like ⟨Dylan⟩ Thomas, he recognized the destructive capabilities of poetry. In a paper he prepared for his final presentation at the Library of Congress in 1978, he wrote: "Once I might have thought of my poetry as a release from tension, as catharsis, which it sometimes is. And once the writing of a poem might have provided me an escape from the ugliness I had to endure—but now I think of poetry as a way of discovery and definition." All of this is not to say, however, that the reader should be capable of relegating Hayden's poetic process to a mere vehicle of ideas and order. To do so would be to separate Hayden's poetic from his poetic meaning— something we cannot do if we are to allow Hayden or any poet his world. His best poems unfold not by design alone but by an internal network of words that are consciously aligned and methodically arranged in an organic fashion. These details appear in a calculated sequence, an order which defies any singular tranformation from one abstraction to another. He made a conscious effort to choose just the right word, the right image for his purpose. His best poems spring from his kaleidoscopic experiences and knowledge, his recollections and sensibilities. ⟨. . .⟩

Criticism must be a double-edged sword that seeks the truth. In Hayden's case it will acknowledge his early excesses of diction, substitutions of sentimental and hortatory rhetoric for ideas, a tendency toward obscurantism, a fondness for the exotic. Hayden took risks, including the risk of topicality. Like many of his virtues, his faults are expected in a poet whose aim was often to envision Utopian precepts and to create a noble race memory. But a poet is known for his successes, not for his failures. Hayden succeeded, whether his materials are statement, commentary, meditation, or celebration. He succeeded when his inspiration gave him subtlety in technique and the powers of imagination to make his "armature" serve his powers. He is one of the true poets of our century, one whom his audience will keep on reading as it keeps on listening to a Leontyne Price or Billie Holiday, or looking at a Jacob Laurence or Richard Hunt. His best poems are the work of a man fully human, who passionately cared about justice and who loved his fellow man—Eskimo, Indian, Vietnamese, European, American, white as well as black, and are both deeply and brightly intelligent. They treat existence with mastery and with sadness, or with delight and impassioned hope. An intellect of this quality, breadth, and delicacy of understanding is, indeed, a link betwween all of us and the past. This is true because he was, for us, the past made present, and he is our surest link with the future since it is that of us the future will know.

Pontheolla T. Williams, *Robert Hayden: A Critical Analysis of His Poetry* (Urbana: University of Illinois Press, 1987), pp. 178–79

MICHAEL G. COOKE   "The Night-Blooming Cereus," ⟨Hayden's⟩ most infallibly "mystical" work, is only obliquely "Baha'i." He chided Black Power advocates for trying to elide "realities," and was consistent enough in this regard not to let "a pharos [rising] like a temple" blind him to the "inward-falling slum" of Veracruz, Mexico. In short, whether dealing with Veracruz, with a diver's (or his own) mind, or with a boxing match off the Louisiana coast, Hayden may betray a preference but hardly a prejudice.

His way is to deal roundly with what is there, with all the clarity and justice that insight allows, with all the feeling that a great spirit affords, and with a fierce searching courage that would make truth not a pleasant but a possible and a necessary boon.

Such a thesis, however, has a troublesome corollary: if Hayden understood so much and was so gifted, why did he not put his gifts right out to serve the cause of his people? Why did he not at least show his people some way past suffering? Let us recall that in the very year of his triumph at Dakar both his university and his people in the form of outspoken radicals ostracized and denounced Robert Hayden. They were strong enough to drive him for a few years into silence and despair, but not enough to make him yield and revise his position. The question then arises: was Hayden just rigid, self-indulgent, and swallowed up in the vanity of his very gifts?

Michael G. Cooke, "Christopher Okigbo and Robert Hayden: From Mould to Stars,"
World Literature Written in English 30, No. 2 (Autumn 1990): 133

❖ *Bibliography*

Heart-Shape in the Dust. 1940.

The Lion and the Archer (with Myron O'Higgins). 1948.

Figure of Time. 1955.

Corrida de Toros. 1959.

A Ballad of Remembrance. 1962.

Gabriel: Hanged for Leading a Slave Revolt. 1966.

Selected Poems. 1966.

Kaleidoscope: Poems by American Negro Poets (editor). 1967.

Words in the Mourning Time. 1970.

Afro-American Literature: An Introduction (editor; with David J. Burrows and
    Frederick R. Lapides). 1971.

The Night-Blooming Cereus. 1972.

How I Write/1 (with Paul McCluskey). 1972.

The United States in Literature (editor; with James E. Miller and Robert O'Neal).
    1973.

American Models: A Collection of Modern Stories (editor; with James E. Miller
    and Robert O'Neal). 1973.

British Motifs: A Collection of Modern Stories (editor; with James E. Miller and
    Robert O'Neal). 1973.
The Lyric Pastoral: Arrangements and Techniques in Poetry (with James E. Miller
    and Robert O'Neal). 1974.
Angle of Ascent: New and Selected Poems. 1975.
American Journal. 1978, 1982.
Collected Prose. Ed. Frederick Glaysher. 1984.
Collected Poems. Ed. Frederick Glaysher. 1985.

⊠ ◈ ⊠

Melvin B. Tolson
1898–1966

MELVIN BEAUNORUS TOLSON was born on February 6, 1898, in Moberly, Missouri. Tolson's father, Alonzo, was a Methodist Episcopal preacher who was frequently reassigned to different churches in the Midwest, so that the family spent time in Missouri, Iowa, and elsewhere. Tolson began writing early, and at the age of fourteen his first poem was published in a local Iowa newspaper. He attended Fisk University in Nashville, Tennessee, and Lincoln University in Pennsylvania, where he received a B.A. in 1923. While at Lincoln, Tolson met Ruth Southall, whom he married in January of 1922. They had four children.

Tolson became an instructor of English at Wiley College in Marshall, Texas, in 1924. He taught literature courses and organized a debate team that enjoyed remarkable success under his leadership. While at Wiley, Tolson worked on fiction (including a novel, *Beyond the Zaretto,* whose manuscript was lost), but it was not until after he moved to Harlem in 1932 that he began writing the poetry that would win him critical recognition. He resumed his studies at Columbia University, where he earned a master's degree in 1940. He began assembling a volume of poetry, *A Gallery of Harlem Portraits,* a collection of portraits of Harlem personalities from all walks of life. The poems appeared separately in various periodicals and were published as a collection posthumously in 1979.

In 1937 Tolson was invited to write a weekly column, "Caviar and Cabbage," in the *Washington Tribune.* He wrote the column for seven years, commenting frequently on racial matters as well as promoting black writers and musicians. A selection of his columns was published in 1982.

Tolson's first published volume of poetry, *Rendezvous with America,* appeared in 1944. One poem in the collection, "Dark Symphony," had won first place in a poetry contest sponsored by the American Negro Exposition in Chicago. *Rendezvous with America* gives voice to some of Tolson's left-leaning political views in its attacks on capitalism, imperialism, and racism. The collection received generally favorable reviews.

In 1947 Tolson became a professor of English at Langston University in Oklahoma. In that year President William S. V. Tubman of Liberia bestowed upon Tolson the honor of being poet laureate of the African nation. To commemorate Liberia's forthcoming centennial in 1956, he wrote *Libretto for the Republic of Liberia* (1953). The long poem celebrates the democratic ideals of the nation but is written in a markedly modernist style, revealing the influence of T. S. Eliot, Ezra Pound, William Carlos Williams, and other experimental writers.

Meanwhile Tolson was involved in a variety of other activities. In 1952 he was elected mayor of the all-black community of Langston, serving for four terms. In 1952 his dramatic adaptation of Walter White's novel *The Fire in the Flint* premiered in Oklahoma City. Two years later Tolson was admitted to the Liberian Knighthood of the Order of the Star of Africa.

Tolson's last major work, *Harlem Gallery, Book I: The Curator* (1965), was intended to be the first volume of a five-book epic poem recording the history of blacks in America. It explores the role of art and the artist in the Harlem community. Tolson was, however, unable to finish the epic because of the increasing ill health of his final years. He underwent two operations for abdominal cancer in 1964 and three further operations in 1966; but he was unable to recover and died on August 29, 1966.

Critical Extracts

ARTHUR E. BURKE   Melvin Tolson's *Rendezvous with America*, just recently off the press, carries one back to Cullen's *Color* and Hughes's *Fine Clothes for the Jew*. No Negro poet save Sterling Brown, in his *Southern Road*, has published in one volume so much that is remarkable for its freshness, its poetic imagination, and, above all, its reflection of American life as it affects Negroes. The reader will not find here the same sort of color consciousness found in Cullen, the same rawness of life in Hughes, or the same satirical humor in Brown. All these elements are here, but in a mood peculiar to Tolson. ⟨. . .⟩

One of the most intriguing interests of *Rendezvous with America* is the variety of verse forms. "Rendezvous with America" and "Dark Symphony" are especially notable for their variations in rhythm, meter, tone color, and harmony. The one section which may disappoint is "Sonnets." Here Tolson does not achieve sufficient flexibility in the Shakespearean form to produce a truly lyrical quality. In form he is mechanical; in matter graphically succinct and never obscure. This suggests that his genius lies in the dramatic and lyrical veins, rather than in the delicately lyrical. But there is so much of real poetry in this first volume of his, so much of vital content too, that one hesitates to say he will not soar in song with his later poems.

Arthur E. Burke, "Lyrico-Dramatic," Crisis 52, No. 2 (February 1945): 61

GWENDOLYN BROOKS   Melvin Tolson is a member of the Academy. Many of his fellows do not concede his presence at their table, they do not look at him. But, like Silent Brother at other feasts, he is there—and honeying his bread with the handsomest of them.

Karl Shapiro (who writes "in Jew" to the extent that Tolson writes— quoting Shapiro—"in Negro") knows that this is the real circumstance, and registers it in his amazing introduction to *Harlem Gallery: Book I, The Curator*. Says Shapiro: "One of the rules of the poetic establishment is that Negroes are not admitted to the polite company of the anthology." Respected poets, including John Ciardi and the late Theodore Roethke, have praised Melvin Tolson and have tried, unsuccessfully, to impose him on the Upper Air.

Melvin Tolson offers this volume as preface to a comprehensive Harlem epic. Its roots are in the Twenties, but they extend to the present, and very strong here are the spirit and symbols of the African heritage the poet acknowledges and reverences. He is as skillful a language fancier as the ablest "Academician." But his language startles more, agitates more—because it is informed by the meanings of an inheritance both hellish and glorious.

You will find in this book a much embroidered concern with Art; many little scheduled and cleverly twisted echoes from known poetry ("with a wild surmise," "Xanthippe bereft of sonnets from the Portuguese," "a mute swan not at Coole," "a paltry thing with varicose veins," etc.); a reliance on clue-things, the thing-familiar; Harlemites of various "levels" and categories; humor and wit that effectively highlight the seriousness of his communiques.

Gwendolyn Brooks, "Books Noted," Negro Digest 14, No. 11 (September 1965): 51

MELVIN B. TOLSON   INTERVIEWER: The Negro has been the victim of ethnic stereotypes. Since you are a realist, may we assume that you take your characters from life?

TOLSON: If the house in which I was born had been located on the other side of town, I would not write about the characters I write about. Selah! In the *Harlem Gallery* I have a few characters from my life, who are designated by name: Louis Armstrong, for example, about whom Hideho Heights, a fictitious character, has composed a poem; however, I cannot vouch for the truth of Hideho's interpretation of Satchmo. The analysis of a real person's tridimensionality is never complete—his biology, his sociology, his psychology. A person may be, from day to day, from mood to mood, from situation to situation, a different jack-in-the-box. So one never knows what figure will be revealed when the lid is removed. This apocalypse of a personality on its Isle of Patmos often shakes the beholder with disbelief. In consternation one may say, sometimes even in terror, "After all these years, I thought I knew him!" To change the metaphor, a person in his lifetime may wear not one mask, but many, which are revelations of his complex nature and nurture. There is no such thing as a flat character in life—stereotypes notwithstanding. The candid camera of intimacy always reveals a personality in the round. People are the fruits—bitter or sweet— of the Heraclitean law of change. A work of art is an illusion of life—a world of make-believe. Its person, place or thing never existed except in the alchemy of the imagination. Yet, I dare say, we understand the people of that other world better than we understand the people of this world. My knowledge of Aeneas, Bloom, Prufrock, Captain Ahab, Othello, and Herzog is more comprehensive than my knowledge of my immediate friends and enemies. Each of these real persons is a multiple jack-in-the-box. Clyde Griffiths in *An American Tragedy* has a clearer identity than Lee Oswald, in spite of the voluminous *Report* of the Warren Commission. In fact, I think Robert Penn Warren could have done a better job in motivation than did Justice Earl Warren. The only Julius Caesar I know is the one Shakespeare created, although I read Julius Caesar's *Commentaries on the Gallic Wars* in the original Latin when I was a fledgling student.

INTERVIEWER: Do you mean that the only persons we can know totally are the characters in fiction—never people in everyday life?

TOLSON: Yes. The abysses of the unconscious are beyond the soundings of even a Freud. Yet, delineations of characters in the poem, the novel, the drama can give us a better understanding of people in a society. In order to get a comprehension of persons and classes, my old professor of sociology used to make his students read and analyze contemporary novels. It was only then that the cold theories and dead statistics came alive. Before that, they were like the valley of dry bones in the family Bible. By the way, Victor Hugo called the Book of Job the world's greatest tragedy. The aristocratic conception of tragedy comes alive under the black and white magic of Marcel Proust's *Rememberance of Things Past*.

> Melvin B. Tolson, "Melvin B. Tolson: An Interview: A Poet's Odyssey," *Anger, and Beyond: The Negro Writer in the United States*, ed. Herbert Hill (New York: Harper & Row, 1966), pp. 187–88

ROY FLASCH   *Rendezvous (with America)* contains a number of different types of poems with diversity of forms.

The poems in *Rendezvous* also reflect Tolson's interest both in art and in music. Just a few months before his death he confessed to an audience, "I'm frustrated twice. I'm a frustrated musician and a frustrated artist. But I went back to music and art in my poems." As a result of his interest in music and art, Tolson incorporated both art forms in the formula for writing poetry which he developed in the 1930's and which he called his "three S's of Parnassus"—sight, sound, and sense. *Sight* referred to the appearance of the poem on the page; *sound,* to the sound of the words (an element which he tested as he wrote by pacing the floor and reciting the lines loudly, regardless of the hour); *sense,* to the image, the appeal to the senses. He also relied on his knowledge of grammar and sentence construction in determining the varied line length as his poetry began to move away from conventional form.

Although the poems in *Rendezvous* are rooted in traditional style, Tolson often departs from restrictions which such form imposes; and, with the tools of sight, sound, and sense, he effects originality of style. He leans heavily on his "three S's of Parnassus" to bring forth originality out of metrical diversity. ⟨. . .⟩

Much of Tolson's poetry presents in unique forms the injustices suffered by the lower social classes, particularly the black man. Some of the poems in *Rendezvous* tend toward rhetoric, but in most of them his artistic control and technique prevent them from being propagandistic. The subject of race works its way into "A Song for Myself" in this stanza:

If hue
Of skin
Trademark
A sin,
Blame not
The *make*
For God's
Mistake.

Roy Flasch, *Melvin B. Tolson* (New York: Twayne, 1972), pp. 47–50

BLYDEN JACKSON   In the time of his birth Tolson belonged to the generation of the Harlem Renaissance. He went to the same college at almost the same time as Langston Hughes (Tolson's time was slightly earlier), and he and Hughes did join the same college fraternity. Tolson made his first pilgrimage to Harlem before the end of the Harlem Renaissance. At Columbia, he took, as the thirties began, an advanced degree in English, choosing for his thesis a topic which permitted him to concentrate on the writers of the Renaissance. He was then a poet unknown, an outsider looking in, living on the periphery of things both at Morningside Heights and in the literary circles of Harlem, a figure of little consequence to writers whom, in his prime, he would surpass.

Many years went by for Tolson before fame came his way. To Tolson, a man who loved enormously both people and the act of living, and a gadfly who was possessed of many talents, they were not idle years. The teaching alone that he did during them would have exhausted a lesser man. But Tolson was not a lesser man. He could become the teacher that he was, so vital and so captivating that his students constantly spoke of him as the greatest teacher they had ever had. He could crusade tirelessly in a thousand ways, privately and publicly, for human rights and defy both the South and the scared "administrators" of his profession in his efforts to ally himself with the Negro masses and lift those masses up. He could enjoy hugely his voracious appetite for comradeship with people, all people of every rank of life, talking interminably to all he met, an ancient mariner who never slept and never tired. He could play, indefatigably and sincerely, the role of good neighbor, participating in local politics, being mayor of an Oklahoma town, journeying widely throughout America to speak and to stimulate the speech of others, and raising his own family in a way that did him, and any father, proud. He could do all these things (as, indeed, he did) and still never forsake his passion, his first love, poetry.

If, then, like an autumn crocus, he, or at least his reputation, blossomed late, it was not because he neglected the muse. It may have been perhaps in part because his audience came to him late. But it was certainly also because, as a poet, he evolved. The later Tolson and the earlier one who worked largely in obscurity were not the same creature. The two were separated by a widening gulf of time and by a succession of styles, somewhat as in the case of Henry James, with the elder Tolson a decidedly more difficult creature to approach than the younger. For Tolson wanted not only to say everything, he also wanted to say it in every way. And in trying styles he became increasingly less easy to read. He had theories about poetry. He liked to talk about his theories. He spoke of the S-Trinity of Parnassus, the synchronization in a poem of sight and sound and sense. He felt that when that S-Trinity dealt with human beings it should be concerned with what he called the "tridimensionality" of a human being's "biology, psychology, . . . [and] sociology." He would say, a chuckle in his throat, that poetry required inspiration, expiration, and perspiration.

> Blyden Jackson, "From One 'New Negro' to Another, 1923–1972," *Black Poetry in America: Two Essays in Historical Interpretation* by Blyden Jackson and Louis D. Rubin, Jr. (Baton Rouge: Louisiana State University Press, 1974), pp. 70–72

MARIANN RUSSELL   In stressing again and again the diversity, the variety of Harlem life, Tolson referred to it as a *comédie larmoyante* ⟨tearful comedy⟩. "Harlem is a multiple jack-in-the-box. No Negro novelist has yet pictured Harlem in its diversity—not James Baldwin, not Ralph Ellison, not Richard Wright. It will take a black Balzac to do Harlem's *comédie larmoyante.*" This view of Harlem as a *comédie larmoyante* is obliquely related to the concept of ghetto laughter. In discussing the humor in *Harlem Gallery* ("devastating in its demolitions of hypocrisies, snobbishnesses, half-truths, sophistries"), Tolson equated "dark laughter," *lachen mit yastchekes,* and *"ghetto laughter."* He referred to Stanley Hyman's explanation of *Galgen-humor,* "gallows humor." In *The Tangled Bush,* Hyman pointed out that self-destructive humor is "characteristic of all oppressed peoples. Negro humor is so similar that the Negro poet Melvin Tolson characterizes it with the Yiddish phrase *lachen mit yastchekes,* 'laughing with needles stuck in

you.' " Such humor, a type of gallows humor, is, according to Hyman, "life-affirming, and greatness of soul consists in cracking a joke with the needles in you, or the noose around your neck, or life almost impossible to endure." Tolson thus related the tragicomic sense of his poetry and of black life to the affirmativeness of gallows humor. ⟨. . .⟩

From Tolson's Notebooks, one can see that dark laughter was stressed as a response to the strictures of the status quo. The ambivalent laughter of the ghetto not only embodies a personal response to pain but is linked to a communal defiance of the limitations that restrict the black man. Thus, "the ghetto's dark guffaws / that defy Manhattan's Bible Belt!" and the "dark dark laughter" of Harlem's "immemorial winter" are associated with the coming of the "new New / Order of things." This new order, an affirmative response springing from the confinement of ghetto living, either literally in Harlem or figuratively in black America, is captured in the penultimate stanza of the ode:

> In the black ghetto
> the white heather
> and the white almond grow.
> but the hyacinth
> and asphodel blow
> in the metropolis!

The tragicomic becomes a communal and an individual response that presages the race's ultimate role in the "Great White World."

Mariann Russell, *Melvin B. Tolson's* Harlem Gallery: A *Literary Analysis* (Columbia: University of Missouri Press, 1980), pp. 104–5.

KARL SHAPIRO   About the time I sent my book ⟨*Poems of a Jew*⟩ to Eliot I was publishing the black poet Melvin B. Tolson. My association and friendship with Tolson is the second most important event in my life as a critic, for here I came into contact with the new black cultural world, which was to reject me as it rejected Allen Tate.

Tolson's great poem *Libretto for the Republic of Liberia*, which was commissioned by that nation to celebrate its centennial, was published in 1953 with an introduction by Allen Tate. As far as I can tell, the poem is still only a succès d'estime even though, along with Tate and myself, Tolson's poetry was hailed by William Carlos Williams—who quotes a piece of it in *Paterson*—Theodore Roethke, Robert Frost, John Ciardi, and others. But Tate played a role in the final form of the *Libretto* which is not dissimilar to the role Pound had played in the formation of *The Waste Land*.

Tolson had sent an early version of the poem to Tate, with the request that he write a preface for it. After reading the manuscript, Tate returned it, saying that he was not interested in the propaganda of a Negro poet. Instead of taking offense, Tolson set about to correct this weakness, which he himself had criticized in the work of other black poets. A year later he submitted a new version to Tate, who wrote a remarkable preface. He praised the first-rate intelligence at work in the poem and observed, "For the first time, it seems to me, a Negro poet has assimilated completely the full poetic language of his time, and, by implication, the language of the Anglo-American poetic tradition." I was to question this statement when I wrote my introduction to Tolson's next book, *Harlem Gallery*. That was in 1965, before the use of the term "black" superseded "Negro," which is now as obsolete as "Israelite." When I said that Tolson wrote in Negro I was expessing an insight which was to be borne out before long by the adoption of "black." But Negroes were puzzled and even hurt by what I said.

     Karl Shapiro, "The Critic Outside," *American Scholar* 50, No. 2 (Spring 1981): 204–5

ROBERT M. FARNSWORTH   *Harlem Gallery* was to be the first volume of a five-volume poetic epic detailing the odyssey of the black American people. He began with the present, midtwentieth century, where his people had arrived. To measure how far they had come, what could be more appropiate than a gallery of their art? A people's place in history is determined in large part by their art, which is why Richard Wright's achievement was so important in 1938. *Harlem Gallery*, however, is narrated not from the perspective of the artist but from that of a gallery curator, a man who knows art and artists, but who also must mediate between the artists and the monied patrons of the gallery, patrons who if left to their own inclinations would destroy the very art they profess to be interested in. Tolson's poem dramatizes in considerable detail the Curator's friendships with artists while only sketchily implying his difficulties with "the bulls of Bashan" who provide the funds necessary for his gallery and for his job, but the reader is nevertheless constantly reminded of the compromises demanded of the Curator. ⟨. . .⟩

Harlem Gallery is divided into sections headed by the twenty-four letters of the Greek alphabet. Hideho Heights upon entering the Harlem Gallery challenges the precedence of the visual arts by ironically reminding his audience of the biblical injunction, "In the beginning was the Word . . . not the Brush!" The prophetic biblical tradition gives a special resonance to such Greek terms as *logos*, *alpha*, and *omega*, and the use of the Greek alphabet suggests both the comprehensiveness and the wholeness associated with moving from alpha to omega. Tolson intended a comprehensive epic representation of the event-filled odyssey of Afro-America, yet he also strongly believed that the midtwentieth century was a transition period in world history, which, though turbulent and threatening, nevertheless held promise that the fullest flowering of Afro-American culture and the fullest realization of world citizenship were still in the future.

> Robert M. Farnsworth, *Melvin B. Tolson 1898–1966: Plain Talk and Poetic Prophecy* (Columbia: University of Missouri Press, 1984), pp. 228–29

GARY SMITH   As Tolson's sonnets ably demonstrate, his best work is a fusion of art, philosophy, and socio-politics. Like the New Negro poets, he realized the value of art as an instrument for social change. His sonnets contain unmistakable racial consciousness, but his most persistent theme is the tyranny of social distance that blinds mankind to its essential oneness. This theme is found not only in his political fables but also in his social parables. In both, Tolson suggests that social democracy, when unfettered by race and class, is an attainable ideal. Yet, on a psychological level, as his personae grope toward an understanding of themselves, they almost invariably find their grief and frustrations reflected in the lives of others. Thus, the vitality of Tolson's poetry lies in the tension between an imagined, ideal world of social democracy and humanistic empathy and the real world of racial discrimination, political tyranny, and aberration. If Tolson's fables and parables describe mankind's inability to attain an ideal world, their morals are blueprints for change.

> Gary Smith, "A Hamlet Rives Us: The Sonnets of Melvin B. Tolson," *CLA Journal* 29, No. 3 (March 1986): 274–75

JON WOODSON   When Melvin B. Tolson arrived in Harlem in the fall of 1931 and was introduced to the Harlem Group of Negro writers, as he named them, what sort of a collection of men and women did he meet up with? This is a rather challenging and controversial question that perhaps cannot be answered. But Toomer was most closely associated with Bontemps, McKay, Aaron Douglas, Hughes, Cullen, Fauset, and Hurston, according to Benson and Dillard's account of Toomer's initial contacts with Harlem writers. Later some of these individuals dropped away, leaving Toomer's inner circle to consist of Douglas, Thurman, Jackman, Larsen, and Peterson. When Tolson arrived in Harlem in 1931, he met and later wrote his thesis on a number of Harlem writers, and that group included Wallace Thurman, one member of Jean Toomer's circle.

There are several indications that Wallace Thurman introduced Melvin Tolson to G. I. Gurdjieff's teachings during Tolson's stay in Harlem. The evidence that points in this direction appears in Tolson's poems, notes, and speeches. The poet hardly refers directly to his interest in Gurdjieff's teachings. The policy keeps with the secret nature of Gurdjieff's "work," as it is often called, for Gurdjieff's system was not taught outside of closed groups of committed students. Tolson's silence in this regard possibly indicates his dedication to the perpetuation of the esoteric system of thought and action. Throughout Tolson's poetry, and in most of the notes that remain from his lectures and classes, appear many of the penetrating ideas that Gurdjieff disseminated through Jean Toomer and Wallace Thurman. Far from playing a minor role, these truly esoteric ideas were pervasive, forming the essence of what may be called Tolson's philosophy; Tolson traveled throughout the South lecturing, and for a time wrote a newspaper column, all the while putting forth the ideas that were thought to have originated with him. What was meant by "inner observation," and what was the nature of the lessons that Jean Toomer brought with him from the Institute for the Harmonious Development of Man? What things did Gurdjieff's students know?

Darwin Turner summarizes the teachings:

> Gurdjieff professed to have the ability to help people fuse their fragmented selves into a new and perfect whole—a harmony of mind, body, and soul—through a system of mental and physical exercise emphasizing introspection, meditation, concentration, discipline, and self-liberation.

Turner's description sounds altogether uninspiring. The account is written so as to make readers wonder at the attractiveness of the methods. Yet

Toomer and many others werre powerfully attracted to Gurdjieff the teacher and equally to his teachings. Toomer was later to write that "with certain notable exceptions, every one of my main ideas has a Gurdjieff idea as a parent." This intellectual debt to Gurdjieff is also a feature of Melvin Tolson's thought, as it is for other followers of esoteric teachings, for Gurdjieff expressed ideas that were thought to be objective and were not to be perverted or altered according to the whim of subjective individuality. They were to be mastered in their pure form, and this feature of esoteric thought is pervasive. W. B. Yeats, the modernist poet and occultist, wrote that "Individuality is not as important as our age has imagined."

> Jon Woodson, "Melvin Tolson and the Art of Being Difficult," *Black American Poets Between Worlds, 1940–1960*, ed. R. Baxter Miller (Knoxville: University of Tennessee Press, 1986), pp. 26–28

MICHAEL BÉRUBÉ   ⟨. . .⟩ *Harlem Gallery* is not so much an artifact, a fossil, of modernist poetry as it is an enactment of the contradictory poetic and cultural claims of that poetry. On one hand, this amounts to saying that Tolson's "embrace" of modernism in *Harlem Gallery* goes far beyond the mere imitation of Eliot's and Pound's difficult techniques of allusion, compression, and ellipsis—that Tolson embraced not merely a technique but an entire ideology. On the other hand, it also suggests that, oddly enough, Tolson was right to think that "the modern idiom is here to stay"—but that it is here to stay in a way none of Tolson's critics have realized. The influence of Eliot and the New Critics has unquestionably waned as a force in the production of literature, giving way to, among other things, Beats and Black Aesthetics; nevertheless, the legacy of modernism—namely, an academy that fulfills the modernist impulse to create a literature to be studied rather than read—has changed irrevocably the practices of criticism, annotation, and explication on which Tolson's life-work self-consciously depends. ⟨. . .⟩ the institutionalization of criticism means that it can be described in terms of legitimation practices, demographics, and economics—and that neglect is therefore not a matter of anomaly or accident.

> Michael Bérubé, *Marginal Forces/Cultural Centers: Tolson, Pynchon, and the Politics of the Canon* (Ithaca, NY: Cornell University Press, 1992), pp. 64–65

ALDON L. NIELSON   Far from being an elitist, Tolson was a tireless propagandist among the people for his brand of modernism—as a teacher, a popular public speaker, a columnist, and a poet. Michael Bérubé has recently provided an apt appraisal of the type of populist aesthetic found in *Harlem Gallery*:

> On this count the poem is unambiguous. To do anything less than disseminate modernism to the masses is to give in to cultural forces which would patronize and condescend to "the people" by giving them the kind of art which, in Clement Greenberg's words, "predigests art for the spectator and spares him effort, provides him with a shortcut to the pleasure of art that detours what is necessarily difficult in genuine art."

In his regular columns in the *Washington Tribune*, which ran from 1937 through 1944, Tolson constantly suggested readings to his audience, generally couching these suggestions in the most contemporary terms: "If you want to get the lowdown on the ancient Greeks, read Sappho, the Minnie-the-Moocher of her day." He plugged Margaret Anderson's magazine *Common Ground*, giving the address for potential subscribers, and, in the tradition of Walt Whitman and Ezra Pound, he plugged his own poems as well:

> Of course, I want you to read "Rendezvous with America." ... I just received word that the *Atlantic Monthly* is bringing out my poem, "Babylon." Some of you read "Dark Symphony." Well, I hope you like this last piece. It has an interesting history.

It is true that Tolson quite consciously wrote more simply in his journalism than in his verse, but it is also true that he genuinely hoped that many of the people in his *Washington Tribune* audience would be among the readers of his verse. If some White writers and their works were alienated from their people, "The mouths of white books choke with dust," Tolson notes.

Aldon L. Nielson, "Melvin B. Tolson and the Deterritorialization of Modernism," *African American Review* 26, No. 2 (Summer 1992): 245–46

◼ *Bibliography*

Rendezvous with America. 1944.
Libretto for the Republic of Liberia. 1953.

Harlem Gallery, Book I: The Curator. 1965.

A Gallery of Harlem Portraits. Ed. Robert M. Farnsworth. 1979.

Caviar and Cabbage: Selected Columns from the Washington Tribune *1937–1944.* Ed. Robert M. Farnsworth. 1982.

Margaret Walker
b. 1915

MARGARET ABIGAIL WALKER was born on July 7, 1915, in Birmingham, Alabama. Her parents, Reverend Sigismund C. and Marion Dozier Walker, provided a culturally and academically rich environment for Margaret's upbringing. She was introduced not only to the Bible and to the standard English classics but also to black American literature and the folk mythology of the South.

Walker attended Northwestern University in Evanston, Illinois, where she became involved with the Works Progress Administration (WPA), working with troubled young women in Chicago's North Side. She began an unpublished novel, "Goose Island," about this community. After graduating from Northwestern Walker was hired as a junior writer for the WPA Writers' Project in Chicago, where she met such black literary figures as Willard Motley, Frank Yerby, Richard Wright, Arna Bontemps, and Sterling Brown. Walker and Wright became close friends and offered suggestions on the revision of each other's work. Her first poem had been published in the *Crisis* in 1934, and a few years later her poems were appearing in the prestigious *Poetry* and other magazines. Walker supplied considerable research for Wright's novel *Native Son* (1940), but in 1939 Wright abruptly broke off the friendship, wrongly believing that Walker had spread gossip about him.

Walker resumed her studies at the University of Iowa, securing an M.A. in 1940. Her thesis was a collection of poems published in 1942 under the title *For My People*, the first book by a black American woman to appear in the Yale Series of Younger Poets. The poems, written in long, cadenced stanzas reminiscent of biblical verse, utilize folk materials to illustrate the trials of blacks in America, but also stress the depth of Walker's attachment to her native South.

In 1941 Walker accepted a teaching position at Livingstone College in Salisbury, North Carolina. In June 1943 she married Firnist James Alexander, with whom she had four children. In 1949 she accepted a position at Jackson

152

State College in Jackson, Mississippi, where she would spend the next thirty years.

Walker's only novel, *Jubilee*, was submitted as her Ph.D. dissertation at the University of Iowa in 1965 and was published in 1966. This ambitious work—which Walker had conceived as early as the 1930s, and for which she received a Rosenwald Fellowship in 1944—traces the historical roots of Walker's family through the days before, during, and after the Civil War. The detailed re-creation of the daily life of a slave community reveals the exhaustive historical and linguistic research behind the work, but it met with mixed reviews.

During the writing of her novel, Walker did not abandon poetry. *Prophets for a New Day* (1970) and *October Journey* (1973) contain many poems addressing issues and personages of the civil rights movement, including elegies to Malcolm X and Martin Luther King, Jr. In 1973 Paula Giddings arranged for Walker and Nikki Giovanni to meet and discuss their views on poetry, art, and the black American community. *A Poetic Equation: Conversations Between Nikki Giovanni and Margaret Walker* was published in 1974.

Walker retired from Jackson State University in 1979. She has since devoted herself to writing and lecturing. A biography, *Richard Wright: Daemonic Genius*, appeared in 1988. *This Is My Century: New and Collected Poems* (1989) selects what the author believes to be her best poetic work, while *How I Wrote* Jubilee *and Other Essays on Life and Literature* (1990) gathers some of her essays and occasional prose writings.

◈ *Critical Extracts*

ARNA BONTEMPS   Miss Walker ⟨in *For My People*⟩ looks forward to the evolution of "The Great Society" in a "world that will hold all the people, all the races, all the Adams and Eves and their countless generations." She sees her people rebelling against hypocrisy—meaning, presumably, against the dissimulation by which the bitter, offended black man is often forced to live in some sections. She marks a struggle between pride and pain, the near-hopeless task of trying to maintain dignity under indignities. And she pins the blame for all the distress on the "money-hungry, glory-craving leeches." Simply put, her complaint is that her people are deceived and cheated.

The Negro's progress, so called, his quick achievement, his contribution to music, and all of that, leave Miss Walker quite cold. The question she asks is:

> How long have I been hated and hating?
> How long have I been living in hell for heaven?

The progress, if that is the word, has been made on the wrong fronts ("We have been believers believing in our burdens and our demigods too long"), and the result is a bitterness "flowing in our laughter," "cankerous mutiny eating through . . . our breasts." ⟨. . .⟩

One must agree with Stephen Vincent Benét, who introduced Miss Walker's work in *For My People*, that "this is part of our nation speaking."

Arna Bontemps, "Let My People Grow!," *New York Herald Tribune Books*, 3 January 1943, p. 3

ABRAHAM CHAPMAN   In its evocation of the folk experience and folk attitudes of Southern Negroes on the plantations when slavery seemed to be a permanent institution, during the Civil War and the Reconstruction years, this Houghton Mifflin Literary Fellowship Award novel ⟨*Jubilee*⟩ adds something distinctively different to the Civil War novel. Each of the fifty-eight chapters opens with lines from a spiritual or popular song of the day, and each chapter has its own title—devices which establish a broader framework and wider point of view than that of the novel's concealed, unidentified narrator. Some of the chapter headings suggest folk ways of thinking or folk wisdom: "Death is a mystery that only the squinch owl knows"; "This pot is boiling over and the fat is in the fire"; "Mister Lincoln is our Moses." Other headings suggest folk experiences: That for a chapter relating the efforts of a slave to escape to freedom is entitled "Put on men's clothes and a man's old cap"; others are headed "Seventy-five lashes on her naked back" and "They made us sing 'Dixie.' " ⟨. . .⟩

The author is so intent on presenting her historical data as accurately as possible, on correcting the distortions which have crept into so many Civil War novels, that at times she fails to transform her raw material into accomplished literary form. There are passages of very pedestrian prose. Fortunately, the colorful and musical speech of the Negro characters in the novel transcends the stilted prose of the narrator. The slave preacher, Brother Ezekiel, on his knees beside the bed of a dying slave in the slave cabin, prays: "Way down here in this here rain-washed world, kneelin here by this bed of affliction pain, your humble servant is a-knockin, and askin for your lovin mercy, and your tender love. This here sister is tired a-sufferin, Lord, and she wants to come on home."

> Abraham Chapman, "Negro Folksong," *Saturday Review*, 24 September 1966, pp. 43–44

STEPHEN E. HENDERSON   A generation ago, another beautiful black woman, Margaret Walker, focused all of that world of meaning that I have been trying to suggest in "For My People," probably the most comprehensively Soulful poem ever written. She tells it "like it is." Here is a section of that poem:

> For my playmates in the clay and dust and sand of Alabama
> backyards playing baptizing and preaching, and doctor and jail
> and soldier and school and mama and cooking and playhouse and
> concert and store and Miss Choomby and hair and company;
> For the cramped bewildered years we went to school to learn to
> know the reasons why and the answers to and the people who
> and the places where and the days when, in memory of the bitter
> hours when we discovered we were black and poor and small and
> different and nobody wondered and nobody understood;

Only a black American, I submit, can fully understand all of the tremendous emotional weight which that single word "hair" receives in this poem. It is almost as though the whole experience of blackness were there.

> Stephen E. Henderson, " 'Survival Motion': A Study of the Black Writer and the Black Revolution in America," *The Militant Black Writer in Africa and the United States* by Mercer Cook and Stephen E. Henderson (Madison: University of Wisconsin Press, 1969), pp. 101–2

PAULA GIDDINGS   Margaret Walker's philosophy of poetry fits into the structure of Christian eschatology: the preservation of the spirit beyond the flesh. But Christian explanations have never proved quite adequate for Blacks whose sensibilities are deeply rooted in the folk traditions. A case in point is the "Ballad of the Hoppy Toad" in *Prophets*, which is filled with the characters and imagery reminiscent of those in works by Zora Neale Hurston and Charles Chesnutt and has the nature of African proverbs. A simple tale on the surface, it raises some of the most fudamental questions of existence.

In "Ballad," we discover that the protagonist has found some goopher dust around her door. After prayer has failed to help, she asks Sis Avery, known for her own kind of JuJu, for advice. Suddenly, the storyteller sees a horse coming toward her, threatening to trample her to death. Sis Avery grabs the creature by the mane, holding it until it starts to "sweat and shrink," becomes a little horse and finally turns into a toad. Simultaneously, the goopher man, pictured running toward the whole scene, screams for Sis Avery not to kill the animal, for he dies at the same time it does.

It is an entertaining story, but if we examine it more closely, we can see some of its deeper meaning. The toad in Nigerian myth was responsible for man's reappearance after death on earth in another and inferior form. The horse symbolizes the power to infuse man with the spirit of god, evil or good, which can completely dominate the soul. In African mythology and belief, evil not only manifests itself in an actual embodiment, but that embodiment has a protean nature. This is a key to many African, and therefore African-American, attitudes and cultural expressions. More important, the poem speaks of the relationship between an imposed belief, in this case Christianity, and the traditional formulas for living. When Christian prayer failed, goopher hexes had to be used to counter goopher hexes. It was the implementation of traditional beliefs which maintained the moral order of the community, another important theme of Black life. It is reminiscent, for example, of the Haitians who practice Catholicism as their "official" religion, but use the images and rites of Vodun to regulate their daily lives.

This folk ballad in *Prophets* is an example of the poet's coming to another kind of resolution. In *For My People*, we are told of the fascinating feats of Big John Henry, Bad-Man Stagolee, Molly Means, Poppa Chicken and Kissie Lee; that is important because it preserves our folk history. But the strict rhyme scheme for these poems in many cases seem to control their content and depth, so that they become just portraitures. In "Hoppy Toad," however, content dominates form, not only creating interesting characters, but at the same time making important comments about our culture.

To say that there is room for Margaret Walker in this age of political poetry is an understatement. Her protest against white actions or Black inaction and, even more importantly, the manifestation of her love for Black people (which should not automatically be assumed in much of the contemporary poetry) are important keys in our struggle. She not only talks about the beauty of Black people, she is a distiller of our experiences—past, present and future. And these experiences are, as she says, "the truth of our living, and the meaning and beauty of our lives."

Paula Giddings, "Some Themes in the Poetry of Margaret Walker," *Black World* 21, No. 2 (December 1971): 24–25

BLYDEN JACKSON   A poet of the forties and fifties who did capitalize admirably on the racial aesthetic in an admirably racial way was Margaret Walker. In 1942 she published *For My People,* a collection of poems which had won a competition sponsored by the Yale University Younger Poets. Her title is racial, but in a good way—a simple, forthright restatement in three very ordinary words of the whole creed and program of the New Negro. Her poem, too, is racial, and also in some good ways. She had lived through the thirties and learned to think of the Negro in the highly sociological context in which everything associated with the thirties seemed to find a frame of reference. Her "people" are the kind who often were beginning (when she wrote *For My People*) to "have" case workers in the North and about whom in the South social scientists were then writing many monographs and books. In the title poem of *For My People* she does not idealize these people. She reproduces them sympathetically, but with great fidelity to fact. Her freeverse paragraphs, in the poem, tread upon each other's heels, full of their own case histories of the actual character of life in her Negro South and Negro North. In these case histories and in her expression of a millennial hope—"for my people . . . Let a new earth arise . . . another world be born"—she speaks in a secular vein, joining the wave of social activism that would lead on to school desegregation, Montgomery, the sit-ins, and *Soul on Ice,* as well as to a changing life style for the Negro masses.

In the matter of her style, Whitmanesque as her methods appear, and to some extent are, the precedent which she follows most, nevertheless, harks back to a folkway from the Negro past that is not secular, *i.e.,* to the mourners' bench of revival time in an "oldtime" Negro church when an "oldtime" Negro preacher called not only upon the mourners to mend their ways, but also upon his whole church to "rock," to join him in the singing, shouting, praying, and movements of the body that were all done in the rolling rhythms which control the rhythmic flow of *For My People*. It is not only the title poem of *For My People* which embraces the Negro's past, as well as his present and future; all of *For My People* is racial. Its prevading sense impressions of the oldtime Negro church especially at the height of its evangelical fervor are no accident. They are the Negro atmosphere for a complete review of a Negro world. What the Negro was, what he is and will be, are issues of concern in all of the poetry within this book. John Henry and Stagolee are in *For My People*, along with Molly Means and Yalluh Hammuh, as part of the Negro legend which the past provides. The northern ghetto is in *For My People* as a part of the Negro's present. Apparently, the northern ghetto will be a powerful factor in his future. And, thus, it is hardly the Negro past, folk or otherwise, which finally rules in *For My People*. Miss Walker's poetry addresses itself to the "gone" years only in the interest of the "now" years and the "maybe" years. Her world is an intensely racial universe (in spite of the fact that she sometimes writes a sonnet). Still, she does not look back to be turned into stone, a monument of monuments. Nor does she look forward to disown a bitter and unwanted heritage. It is a function of her poetry to call for a Negro who is whole, one who accepts what he has been at the same time that he dreams of what he may become. This function of hers clearly links her with her "people" and makes of her a racial poet. And yet her racialism seems not to interfere with her Americanism. Her New Negro is neither picturesque nor exotic. Neither his citizenship nor his race is equivocal. He belongs both to America and to himself. No African paganism subverts him; but, then, neither does any monomania to be white overwhelm him. He is a mourner, but a mourner who has not lost his hope of heaven.

Blyden Jackson, "From One 'New Negro' to Another, 1923–1972," *Black Poetry in America: Two Essays in Historical Interpretation* by Blyden Jackson and Louis D. Rubin, Jr. (Baton Rouge: Louisiana State University Press, 1974), pp. 67–69

R. BAXTER MILLER   "At the Lincoln Monument in Washington, August 28, 1963," presents analogues to Isaiah, Exodus, Genesis, and Deuteronomy. Written in two stanzas, the poem has forty-four lines. The speaker dramatizes chronicle through biblical myth, racial phenomenology, and Judaeo-Christian consciousness. She advances superbly with the participant to the interpreter, but even the latter speaks from within an aesthetic mask. The poetic vision authenticates the morality of her fable and the biblical analogue. The first stanza has twenty-eight lines, and the second has sixteen. As the speaker recalls the march on Washington, in which more than 250,000 people demonstrated for civil rights, she attributes to Martin Luther King, Jr., the leader of the movement, the same rhetorical art she now remembers him by. The analogue is Isaiah: "The grass withereth, the flower fadeth: but the word of our God shall stand for ever" (40:8). Two brothers, according to the fable, led the Israelites out of Egypt. Sentences of varied length complement the juxtaposition of cadences which rise and fall. The narrator names neither King as "Moses" nor King's youthful follower as "Aaron," yet she clarifies a richness of oration and implies the heroic spirit. King, before his death, said that he had been to the mountain top, and that he had seen the Promised Land. But the speaker literarily traces the paradigm of the life; she distills the love of the listeners who saw him and were inspired: "There they stand . . . / The old man with a dream he has lived to see come true."

Although the first eleven lines of the poem are descriptive, the twelfth combines chronicle and prefiguration. The speaker projects the social present into the mythical past. Her words come from a civil rights song, "We Woke Up One Morning with Our Minds Set on Freedom." The social activist wants the immediate and complete liberation which the rhetorician (speaker and writer) translates into literary symbol: "We woke up one morning in Egypt / And the river ran red with blood . . . / And the houses of death were afraid."

She remembers, too, the story of Jacob, who returns home with his two wives, Leah and Rachel (Genesis 30:25–43). Laban, the father-in-law, gave him speckled cattle, but now the narrator understands that Jacob's "*house* (Africa-America) has grown into a nation / The slaves break forth from bondage" (emphasis mine). In Old Testament fashion, she cautions against fatigue in the pursuit of liberty. Through heightened style, she becomes a prophet whose medium is eternal language. She has mastered alliteration, assonance, and resonance.

Write this word upon your hearts
And mark this message on the doors of your houses
See that you do not forget
How this day the Lord has set our faces toward freedom
Teach these words to your children
And see that they do not forget them.

R. Baxter Miller, "The 'Etched Flame' of Margaret Walker: Biblical and Literary Re-creation in Southern History," *Tennessee Studies in Literature* 26 (1981): 165–66

DELORES S. WILLIAMS   In the communal life-support model, the actions and life tasks of the major female characters sustain unity and community within social groups in both black and white society. In Margaret Walker's *Jubilee* the slave woman Vyry nurtures the slave master's family and her own black family. Similarly, Vyry's mother, Sis Hetta, by sleeping with Master Dutton (his wife refuses to do so), enables the Dutton family to remain intact. The consciousness and actions of both women are conditioned by the demands of the slavocracy and the slave community, and their personal needs are inextricably bound to community needs and goals.

These women undergo both positive and negative transformations. Hetta and Vyry experience the negative personal transformation that slavery inflicted upon black women, as Walker's description of the change in Hetta's body—and spirit—makes painfully clear. Hetta had once "looked like some African queen from the Congo. She had a long thin neck and she held her head high." But as the result of bearing children for the slavocracy, she was "no longer . . . slender and lovely."

> Her breasts were long and flabby; her belly always bloated,
> whether she was big in family way or not, and her legs and thighs
> were now covered with large broken blood vessels that made it
> painful when she stood long or walked far. . . . She was a sullen-
> looking woman . . . who rarely smiled.

Walker's whole plot is, in fact, structured around the central themes of bondage and freedom. Vyry's character unfolds in episodes dramatizing value conflicts between characters caught in various kinds of bondage. ⟨. . .⟩

Under the conditions of bondage, all aspects of her survival intelligence work together to help Vyry both endure and make the transformations needed for her family to survive the slave system. Although she emerged from her confrontation with Master Dutton feeling hopeless, Vyry experiences many positive transformations after emancipation. Once despondent about the meaninglessness of slave existence, she becomes hopeful. Once passive, she becomes assertive in her relationship with her husband, Innis Brown. She decides when and where they will build their second home. She establishes a relationship with the town's white people, who join forces to help Vyry and Innis build their house.

Vyry is transformed spiritually. During slavery she only prayed for the safety of black children and for black freedom. After emancipation she sees herself and her family connected to all people through their common condition of sinfulness. Therefore, she prays with a concern for all humankind. She acknowledges, "Lord, we ain't nothing but sinful human flesh. . . . We is evil peoples in a wicked world, but I'm asking you to let your forgiving love cover our sin, Lord."

Out of her experience of transformation from slave to free woman, Vyry emerges a resilient person participating in making a new history for black people.

> Delores S. Williams, "Black Women's Literature and the Task of Feminist Theology," *Immaculate and Powerful: The Female in Sacred Image and Social Reality*, ed. Clarissa W. Atkinson, Constance H. Buchanan, and Margaret R. Miles (Boston: Beacon Press, 1985), pp. 89, 91–92

LUCY M. FREIBERT   FREIBERT: When you write poetry, do you carry the poem around in your head first, or do you start right out putting things on paper?

WALKER: Regardless of the medium, whether you are a musician, a painter, a graphic artist, a plastic artist, or a sculptor, whether you are a writer or an architect, you begin the same way. Creative writing grows out of creative thinking, and nothing begins a work before the idea as a conceptualization; that is the beginning. All writers, all artists, all musicians, all people with creative talent begin with that creative thinking. They begin with conceptualization. You get an idea, and sometimes the whole process moves on mentally and unconsciously before it is given conscious artistic form, but the process begins with the idea.

Everything begins in the mind. You have an idea, and you may not know for a long time what form this idea is going to take or what you are going to say or how you are going to say it, but you have that first. For me it is intuitive. Some people are not intuitive. I'm intuitive. I in-tu-it. For me it begins with a concept, maybe before it is even an idea—a concept before it becomes thought or idea. It may begin with a picture. For the musician, I am sure it begins with a musical motif or a sound that the musician hears or senses. It is a process using the sensory perceptions, I guess you would say. You perceive or conceive. You perceive what is outside. You conceive what is inside. And you move from the perception of a concept or thought or idea to a figuration and a configuration.

The poet has nothing but words and language to be used as tools. And the poet—I think my father taught me this—the poet in my instance uses rhetorical devices. I have been told by some poets and even by some teachers that I am too rhetorical. I cannot conceive of writing poetry without metaphor and simile, synechdoche, metonymy, hyberbole. I grew up with that, and my work is rhetorical, but I think it is rhetorical in the best sense of the word. I had teachers who tried to break me of the habit. My father taught me my first lessons in rhetoric from an old English book that he had brought to this country. It gave all the rhetorical forms. I don't think a poet writes simply in grammatically correct language. I think all the greatest poets in the world were rhetoricians, and I believe in the rhetoric. Paul Engle has criticized me for it. He said, "Margaret was just too rhetorical." I laughed, because I am still rhetorical, and I always will be.

FREIBERT: That's what makes your voice so distinctive. What or who helped you find your voice?

WALKER: My father, really. I think Stephen Benét tells it in the introduction for *For My People*. It was not just that I heard the sermons my grandfather and my father preached, but it was that training my father gave me in the use of rhetoric. And I really didn't believe when I was a teenaged youngster growing up that you could write poetry without the use of simile and metaphor. I thought you had to use them. After I was older and had gained my own voice, I realized that I had read the Bible all my life and that the use of parallelism was what I had learned from the Bible: cataloguing and repetition and internal rhyme—not so much end rhyme, because that was what I had learned from ordinary poetry. I didn't think of the poetry in the Bible as ordinary, I thought it was extraordinary.

Lucy M. Freibert, "Southern Song: An Interview with Margaret Walker," *Frontiers* 9, No. 3 (1987), p. 32

ELEANOR W. TAYLOR   As the journey of memory, *This Is My Century: Black Synthesis of Time* reclaims the four matters of Afro-American poetry as *écriture*. Before the publication of "For My People" in 1937, these four matters had become traditional: the matter of Africa, the matter of America, the matter of the South, and the matter of the North. By 1773, the matter of Africa had been inscribed in the poetry of Phillis Wheatley, especially in the dedicatory "To Mycenaes." The African matter expands to embrace the Caribbean (Claude McKay), South America (Robert Hayden), and Europe (Langston Hughes). The matter of America begins with Lucy Terry's "Bars Fight" (*circa* 1746), not only the first extant poem by a person of African descent in the English colonies but one which establishes a distinctive sign of the Afro-American speaking mask in poetry: that of witness. Moreover, the matter of America expands to include the matter of the New World, adapting and metaphorically re-envisioning Caliban and Prospero in Shakespeare's *The Tempest*. And the matters of South and North configure regions in tropes and in linguistic particularities revealing, for one thing, how formal English is expanded and transmuted by black speech and music idioms. Along the axis of these matters, Margaret Walker's poetry references, mainly, the matter of America. It stands as a port of trade transacting the linguistic yield of what Richard Barksdale has called Southern Black Orature as that transforms the cadences of Southern and Midwestern American parole and formal English. Yet much of her prosody gains resonance from biblical cadence; her allusions range the mythical matter of the African discursive world.

   This Is My Century also reclaims the major themes of the pre- and post-industrial world which play about the matters of Negro poetry before 1937: colonialism, mercantilism, slavery, imperialism, racism, and gender chauvinism. And texturing the matters of Africa, America, North, and South before 1937, black poets weave the major ideas affecting the twentieth century which, in Margaret Walker's *Century* poem, become revolution, psychoanalysis, relativity, existentialism, and Pan-Africanism.

   Eleanor W. Taylor, " 'Bolder Measures Crashing Through': Margaret Walker's Poem of the Century," *Callaloo* 10, No. 4 (Fall 1987): 582

JOYCE PETTIS   The vital elements of Walker's work—its identity with the South, its historical perspective, folk tradition, and racial themes—

remain consistent in *Prophets for a New Day* as well as in the poems of *October Journey* (1973), a brief book (thirty-five pages) of mostly previously published poems. The title poem of the volume is notable for its thematic consistency with earlier ambivalent poems about the South. "October Journey," however, excels those earlier poems in its extravagant imagery of the physical appearance of the Southland in the fall, when the land is awash with warm autumnal colors. As in the earlier poems, landscape and memory change when reality intervenes and displaces the visual scene in the mind of the traveler.

The rigorous depiction of realism in the South and the demand for social, political, and economic changes for black Americans have been consistent characteristics of Walker's work. Her knowledge of tradition and history has constituted fecund sources from which she has extracted material for its transformation into art. Additionally, she has located her themes and insistence for change within a humanistic framework and within a tradition accessible to nonacademic as well as academic readers. But more than anything else, Walker has anchored her work in the love and experiences of her people.

Margaret Walker, Southern black woman poet and novelist, occupies a unique position in American literary history through her inclusion with two generations of writers. It is a well-earned position, however. Walker's work since the 1930s illustrates and confirms an unquestionable dedication to art, determination to survive as a writer, and refusal to be defeated by the "silences" that have often shut off women writers' voices. The second phase of her career, beginning with the appearance of *Jubilee,* affirms her commitment and perseverance. Since many of the pressures that have the potential for silencing have lessened during Walker's lifetime, readers can anticipate that her voice will continue to be raised strong and vibrantly among the current generation of Southern women writers.

Joyce Pettis, "Margaret Walker: Black Woman Writer of the South," *Southern Women Writers: The New Generation,* ed. Tonette Bond Inge (Tuscaloosa: University of Alabama Press, 1990), pp. 18–19

FLORENCE HOWE   *For My People:* More than any other poet I can think of, Margaret Walker's first poem in her first volume strikes the note that persists through her half-century of writing poems. Walker herself says she has selected ⟨for *This Is My Century: New and Collected Poems*⟩ 100 poems from 1000 she has written through this lifetime, but there are very few poems in this volume that one might call "personal." ⟨. . .⟩

When she says she "belong[s] to all the people I have met, / Am part of them, am molded by the throng," she is describing herself as a poet of history. For those who remember the sixties' civil rights movement, Walker's poems stir memories of the fearless children who ignored threats and attended Freedom Schools, of the sit-ins, of the demonstrations and of the deaths— Medgar Evers, the children of Birmingham, Andy Goodman, Michael Schwerner and James Chaney, Malcolm X, Martin Luther King. Much of this poetry is inspirational, often in elegies, the heroism of people who stood for human—not national or racial—dignity. It is not that Walker ignores race; the poems more often than not speak to "the color line." Rather, she speaks to it and beyond, perhaps because of that visionary quality her poetry has had from the first. Walker is the least sectarian Christian I can name. Steeped, she tells us, not only in the Bible, but in the "wisdom literature of the East," she values the lessons of the past, especially when they offer evidence of the human energy for spiritual as well as material survival.

Ultimately, then, as a poet of history, she is a poet of vision, of the flow of past not only into present, but of a reach into the future. The seven new poems called "Farish Street" that close the volume focus with camera-like intensity on the Southern street, its shops and people, and, at the same time, recall an ancestral African village, the "Root doctor, Hoodoo man" then and now. And in the series' final poem, "The Labyrinth of Life," Walker presents herself as "traveler," looking down the road "to the glory of the morning of all life." But the poems that precede this final group remind us of the terrible world still needing mending: "On Police Brutality," "Money, Honey, Money," "Power to the People," "They Have Put Us on Hold," "Inflation Blues"—the titles themselves a litany of troubles for all the have-nots, all the powerless who would have space to live.

Florence Howe, "Poet of History, Poet of Vision," *Women's Review of Books* 7, Nos. 10 & 11 (July 1990): 41–42

◈ Bibliography

For My People. 1942.
Jubilee. 1966.

The Ballad of the Free. 1966.

Prophets for a New Day. 1970.

How I Wrote Jubilee. 1972.

October Journey. 1973.

A Poetic Equation: Conversations between Nikki Giovanni and Margaret Walker (with Nikki Giovanni). 1974.

Richard Wright, Daemonic Genius: A Portrait of the Man, a Critical Look at His Work. 1988.

This Is My Century: New and Collected Poems. 1989.

How I Wrote Jubilee *and Other Essays on Life and Literature.* Ed. Maryemma Graham. 1990.

Jay Wright
b. 1935

JAY WRIGHT was born on May 25, 1935, in Albuquerque, New Mexico, the son of Leona Dailey and Mercer Murphy Wright. Wright attended high school in San Pedro, California, and, after graduation, served in the U.S. Army. In 1961 he received a B.A. from the University of California at Berkeley, briefly attended the Union Theological Seminary in New York, and attended postgraduate courses at Rutgers University, earning an M.A. in 1966.

Wright has chiefly received critical attention for his poetry. He draws on his formal education and knowledge of European literary traditions as well as the history of black Americans and anthropological studies of African and New World civilizations. Ritual and mythology also find a place in his poems.

Wright's first published volume was a small chapbook of poems, *Death as History* (1967); it received little attention, but many of the poems included in it were reprinted in *The Homecoming Singer* (1971), Wright's first major collection. The poems are greatly influenced by events in Wright's life, especially his artistic and spiritual development. Unlike other black American writers who draw on cultural connections to the agrarian South or the industrialized North, Wright uses the geography of the Southwest to relate, symbolically, the social alienation experienced by blacks in America.

Many of the themes found in *The Homecoming Singer* reappear in *Soothsayers and Omens* (1976) and *Dimensions of History* (1976). These volumes reflect Wright's travels in Mexico and in Scotland, where he stayed from 1971 to 1973 as a Fellow in Creative Writing at Dundee University. The poems in these two collections unite a quest for personal identity with an exploration of a mythological world view.

It was not until the publication of *The Double Invention of Komo* (1980), however, that Wright's ambitious themes were more successfully synthesized into a historical ritualized mythology. This long and complex poem utilizes a cosmogony conceived by the Komo, an all-male society that exists within the Bambara tribe and other tribes in Africa. A young man's initiation into this society serves as a symbol for the emotional maturation of the individual.

Several other collections of poetry have appeared in the last decade: *Explications/Interpretations* (1984), *Elaine's Book* (1988), and *Boleros* (1991), all continuing the search for metaphysical truth by means of ritual and myth derived from a wide array of Eastern and Western cultures. A *Selected Poems* appearing in 1987 cemented Wright's reputation as a major American poet, in spite of frequent criticisms of the difficulty and obscurity of much of his work.

As a dramatist Wright has also been successful, although to date only one of his plays, *Balloons* (1968), has been published in book form. Other, briefer plays have appeared in periodicals: *Love's Equator* (*Callaloo*, Fall 1983), *The Death and Return of Paul Batuata* (*Hambone*, Fall 1984), and *The Adoration of Fire* (*Southern Review*, Summer 1985). These plays, and other unpublished ones, develop the same mythological and religious themes as his poetry. Wright also wrote some plays for California radio stations in the 1960s.

Wright has been poet in residence at Tougaloo College and has taught at Talladega College and Yale University. He was the recipient of a Hodder Fellow in Playwriting at Princeton University in 1970–71. He currently resides in Piermont, New Hampshire.

◈ *Critical Extracts*

DAVID KALSTONE   Part of the point of Wright's title ⟨*The Home-coming Singer*⟩ is its tense. The homecoming singer is always approaching and never making the identifications he desires. His poems are about wishes to submerge himself, to recapture the affections of his old life or to be released into fiercer strength. His verse resembles prose; yet the lines pause at points where he branches out with participles and oddities of syntax to discover what energies are available in worlds he can't belong to. The rhythms—there are few full stops—deceive us into sharing others' dreams.

The book takes its most important turn when Wright comes to suspect his conjury and to see his freedom as thwarted vision:

You travel in cities
that travel in you,
lost in the ache
of knowing none.

Living in Mexico—the occasion for some of his best poems—chastens
and challenges him. Its foreignness heightens the pleasures and penalties
of living at a distance from his subjects. In the intense "Reflections Before
the Charity Hospital," he turns against his own vicarious impulses. After
some fierce attempts to imagine life inside the hospital walls, he sees his
own life as a kind of shrunken voyeurism:

It is not death
that I have felt within these walls.
It is the senseless, weightless,
time-denying feeling of not being here.

At this point *The Homecoming Singer* moves away from novelistic experience, the particulars of memory and description, to a technique more adven-
turous and visionary. The role of the youthful observer threatens to swallow
him; he turns to surrealistic landscapes of the mind.

David Kalstone, "Black Energies in a White Society," *New York Times Book Review,*
30 July 1972, pp. 4, 15

DUDLEY RANDALL   I was first struck by the length of the book
⟨*The Homecoming Singer*⟩. It has 95 pages of poetry. Then I was struck by
the length of the poems. There are no four-line or eight-line or even twelve-
or fourteen-line poems. One remembers how Catullus compressed a world
of excruciation into two lines, in *"odi et amo."* Most of these poems are a
page long. Some of them cover two or three pages, although I did read one
poem of 21 lines and another of 19.

But what has the length of a poem got to do with its quality? Doesn't a
poet have the right to make his poems as long as he wants to? Of course
he has. But it is also desirable to inspire the reader to turn the pages. There
must be some suspense in the action, some energy in the rhythm, some
power in the emotion, some surprise in the phrases, to motivate the reader
to turn the pages to see what is on the next one. I turned these pages very
slowly. That is why this review is so late.

But there were some poems that stimulated me to turn the pages rapidly.
"An Invitation to Madison County" has the same brooding sense of latent

terror that permeates Robert Hayden's "A Ballad of Remembrance" and
that a Black person feels in any Southern town.

> Fifteen minutes in the city,
> and nothing has happened.
> No one has asked me to move over
> for a small parade of pale women,
> or called me nigger, or asked me where I'm from.

Perhaps this was because of the shared Black experience. But "Jalapeña
Gypsies" was not about the Black experience, and I read it eagerly. And
the poems about Wright's father were moving.

Dudley Randall, [Review of *The Homecoming Singer*], *Black World* 22, No. 11 (September 1973): 90

HAROLD BLOOM   I have not read a contemporary black poet who
seems to me as important and permanent a writer as Jay Wright, whose
fourth book, *Soothsayers and Omens,* adds to a distinguished, difficult and
absurdly neglected body of work. Jay Wright is a learned, mythological poet,
whose difficulties rise not out of the initial strangeness of African mythology
but out of the intricate allegories of his interpretations.

Harold Bloom, "Harold Bloom on Poetry," *New Republic*, 26 November 1977, p. 26

DARRYL PINCKNEY   Much of what is widely admired in modern
poetry is difficult in one sense or another. But there is a kind of obscurity
that repels, one that has to do with deceit or delusion. Every poem has its
strategic laws, and unraveling them is part of the joy of reading. Then why
is it hard to care whether one can or cannot breathe the thin, piercing air
of Wright's lofty levels of meaning? The incredible monotony of this poem
⟨The Double Invention of Komo⟩ betrays the strain of the idea. It does not
have much convincing speculative force, and for all the intricacies of its
surface, the language of this poem does not speak to the ear with any
urgency, intimacy, or power.

This is a poem about escape, rebirth, consciousness, discovery, framed
by stages of an initiation right. It begins "This is the language of desire /
bana yiri kqrq . . ." and ends "You present me to sacred things. / I am reborn

into a new life. / My eyes open to Komo" in the same key, in the same tone, part of the aggressive complacency of enlightenment or religious feeling. Throughout, there is a discourse with history, both general and private, and about modes of perception, dulled by an utter opacity, which may be a form of shrewdness. The lack of drama slows the movement of the poem, though voices call out from a wood, from a village, from Paris, from Los Angeles, Berlin, Rome, Florence, Venice, Bad Nauheim, Albuquerque, Mexico City. Perhaps this is a poem about naming things, identifying with things, becoming things, the thingness of things, oneness, or "coming into the word"—large abstractions broken into steps that are meant to correspond to the process of acquiring knowledge. The initiate is a pilgrim, a *peregrinus*, insistent on what might pass for the classical mood. But what is discovered seems predetermined. This initiate has no need for humility, awe, or passion. He can, after all, follow Dante into exile—"Let sister Florence / truss herself in virtue"—and not contract malaria.

⟨. . .⟩ Page after page of the merely declarative, very prose-like, passage after passage of symbols mercilessly recapitulated, of lines that do not form true images. "As your initiate's agent on creation's knife / I open the membrane of my celebrant's voice." Or: "There is a tree that is divine. / Its scalar leaves reveal / a scapulary mother at its base." It might not be to the point to ask to understand the lines but the inner landscape Wright, apparently, is trying to open isn't very evocative or intriguing. Surrealism, if anything, has made it difficult for the surreal to move us.

Darryl Pinckney, "You're in the Army Now," *Parnassus: Poetry in Review* 9, No. 1 (Spring–Summer 1981): 307–8

CHARLES H. ROWELL   ROWELL: Most of your poems published after 1971 force me to rethink and re-evaluate my own concept of *the poem* or of *poetry*. What is a poem—or, what do you, a working poet, conceive poetry to be? And what are its functions? My questions seem strange, I'm certain, in 1984, but your poetry evokes them from me. The main of your poetry after *The Homecoming Singer* (1971; the poems in section two of *Soothsayers and Omens*, 1976, are, however, similar to those in *The Homecoming Singer*) is quite different as constructs, for example, from the contemporary poetry I have read.

WRIGHT: Theory is the angel in twentieth century intellectual life, but I'll risk a hip. I sometimes enjoy setting forth my paradigmatic relationship to the words *poetry* and *poem*. I almost said derivational, but that leads us into the tricky area of fixed laws, and any conception of fixed law introduces the troubling necessity of finding the origin of such a law. I suppose I shouldn't worry about that. So much of Anglo-American, and, unfortunately, black Afro-American, talk about poetry simply ignores that problem, and sets out a comfortable notion of poetry that accepts unspecified (and, when specified, contradictory) compositional rules. In developing my theory, I've begun by asking whether it is not true that poetry is what a particular literary community at a particular time says it is. The literary histories available to us suggest that this is so, up to a point. I haven't gone far, but you can see that I've already begun by acknowledging that no poet can be without the civilizing impress of history and tradition. Clapping that mathematical word, derivational, on the table wasn't as ingenuous as it may have seemed to you. Poetry, if I may rearrange some bones for a moment, does deduce one function from another. In recent years, I've been energized by Samuel Akpabot's statement that "the African lives in music and number." My reading of history impels me to think that music, speech and calculation (the measuring of time and event) have been the complex relationships in which human spirit, action, social and political relationships have been most gloriously exemplified. I realize that asserting this makes literary phenomena seem primary. You would expect a poet to insist upon literature's central position in human affairs. We hardly apologize for this insistence any longer. But I should stop here to say that I include in the speech community all those practitioners of verbal art who are not normally included: the griot, the old Testament prophet, the ritual chanter, the fabulist, the legist, the chronicler, the preacher, even the mathematician, among others. Quite a list, you say. What's left out? Why, nothing. Not even poetry. Among various speech communities, poetry finds its voice, and its unique functions, which, nevertheless, are like those of other disciplines—the discovery, explication, interpretation, exploration and transformation of experience. I've now come to the point where I can set down the basic elements of my theory, the one by which I'm guided in writing poetry. Poetry is a concentrated, polysemous, literary act which undertakes the discovery, explication, interpretation, exploration and transformation of experience. It differs from some other forms of speech (such as that used by the legist, the chronicler, the mathematician) in that it handles its "facts" with more disdain, if I might put it that way, insisting upon spiritual resonance. It differs from some other forms of speech (such as that used by the preacher, the ritual chanter, the fabulist) in that it handles its spiritual domain with slightly more critical detachment than they do. The paradox of the extreme manipulative consciousness of the two domains—spiritual and material—indeed, their association to produce what is at least a third and unique domain—is what distinguishes poetry from the other forms of speech. I was almost going to say that I assume that we can recognize the formal differences between a poem and a statute, or a mathematical formula, or a sermon, but I would have left the field too soon. A poem distinguishes itself by rhythmic balance, accent and imaginative dissolution and reconstruction of its materials. It has a rhetoric we recognize as something peculiar to what we call a poem, irrespective of its line count, its imagery or lack of it, its rhyme or lack of it, its metaphor or absence of it, its adherence to any accepted paradigm. What the new poem tries to do is to establish itself as a member of that class of things to create the third domain. This ought to be an unremarkable statement. ⟨. . .⟩ What should be remarkable is that I consider poetry to have a functional value equivalent to all other forms of speech in a social and historical community. Putting things this way means that I consider poetry to have social and historical responsibilities. The poet cannot escape these. These responsibilities manifest themselves in the act of writing poetry and in the act of the poem.

Charles H. Rowell, " 'The Unraveling of the Egg': An Interview with Jay Wright," *Callaloo* 6, No. 3 (Fall 1983): 3–4

JOHN HOLLANDER   Jay Wright's poetry is some of the most original and powerful that is being written in America. He shares with Geoffrey Hill a secularized religious power that keeps him questing among the chapels of ruined tropes, but unlike Hill he contends not with English poetic history, but with a peculiarly American body of fate. It involves a totally unique vision of an imaginative heritage which is institutionally and politically designated as Afro-American: Jay Wright makes the phrase mean more than it ever has. His vision is more truly and deeply responsible to the conceptual realms on each side of the hyphen partly because it reinterprets the significance of each of them. Or, to put it another way, by being a true poet and not a writer of modern journalistic jingle or editorial, or stand-up seriocomic or diarist in verse, he gives to the hyphenation itself a unique relational profundity which makes us feel that he had invented its meaning and use for the first time. Learned, intellectual in the deepest sense, a musician, a studious recluse, Wright has explored a terrain disputed by the powers of anthropology and philosophy. His poems are often strong spiritual exercises and thought-experiments troped as tribal rites, whether West African or Mexican Indian. ⟨. . .⟩

Wright's narrative structures (I should rather say, formats) in his larger poems derive from Pound to some degree, but his language—and this is more important—grew out of a love of Rilke and Hart Crane, the American poet he is in some ways closest to. His new book, *Expectations/Interpretations* (Callaloo Poetry Series, University of Kentucky, 1984), moves beyond the framework of rituals and fables of the Dogon people of West Africa to generate some of its own ad hoc songs and epistemological dances. ⟨. . .⟩ His absorption in the relation of bodies and places stems from a philosophical initiation into the seriousness of certain kinds of questions which daily life might have to hold to be frivolous. But the initiates and public singers in so many of his poems are not chanting primal charms below what Stevens called "the tension of the lyre." Rather they are part of a remarkable poet's tracking down of what the idea of "one's world" might mean, and the stakes are so high, the poet's mind so complex, the realm of knowledge through which he moves so dense and varied in terrain, that it is understandable why he has not so far commanded the kind of popularity that other writers of his generation—anecdotal, narcissistic, polemical, ironically smarmy— elicit. What is a readership taught to absorb easily and piously the literal litanies and versified vignettes of most Afro- and non-Afro-American poetry to make, for example, of Wright's explorations of the tropes of bodily members in his "Twenty-Two Tremblings of the Postulant"?—or, even more, of the post-Poundian colloquy of voices and texts in which David Hume, Hugh McDiarmid (as sort of prototypical forger of a feigned Scottish language for a true poetry), and a Scots colonial administrator in West Africa all surround the poet in his struggle with scepticism ("There may be more light / in David's perpetual twilight / than in our hidden hope for light," he says at one point) in a fine poem called "MacIntyre, the Captain and the Saints"? Wright requires passionate and intelligent readers who can understand the ways in which the imagination can transform the materials of learning.

So much discourse in America today about ethnic origins and searches for meaning in genealogical lineage has degenerated into sleazy cant and travesties of treks toward inner freedom that when an important and enduring poet like Wright takes up the great romantic matter of the quest for true spiritual—as opposed to merely biological—ancestry it will go unnoticed at first. The beasts of detraction (Wright's phrase, "a derry of jackals," is applicable here) can only approach such an artistic quest with a deafened and deafening clamor.

John Hollander, "Poetry in Review," *Yale Review* 74, No. 1 (November 1984): xvi–xix

---

VERA M. KUTZINSKI   ⟨. . .⟩ there is one thing we can be certain about: Wright's poetry is obsessed with history and with the history of the New World in particular. To be more precise, it is motivated by the desire, and in fact the need, to comprehend the complex relations between history, myth, and literature as different forms of self-knowledge. Wright's poet's journeys are set in motion by the search for a language that accommodates both myth and history, that plays off one against the other without submitting to the constraints of either. This interplay of myth and history also offers a key to Wright's use of ritual. *The Double Invention of Komo*, for instance, is explicitly described as a poem that "risks ritual's arrogance." At the same time, it is important for us to understand that poetry, as Wright insists elsewhere, is not ritual. Yet ritual ⟨. . .⟩ can be used in poetry, Wright and ⟨Wilson⟩ Harris would agree, "not as something in which we situate ourselves absolutely, but an unravelling of self-deception within self-revelation as we see through the various dogmatic proprietors of the globe within a play of contrasting structures and anti-structures." It is this play of contrasting structures and antistructures (that is, of myth and history) that Wright's poetry seeks to articulate through linguistic and formal rigor. The results are spectacular: Wright is one of the poets is our recent literary history who, to use ⟨William Carlos⟩ Williams's words, is "making the mass in which some later Eliot will dig." In neglecting his poetry, the criticism of Afro-American (and American) literature(s) has deprived itself of one of the most fascinating and fertile resources for a true critical revisionism. ⟨. . .⟩

Wright's work offers one of the most remarkable examples of an Afro-American poet maintaining a very active dialogue with a variety of traditions while at the same time confronting the problems posed by the idea of writing within the specific context of Afro-American culture. Wright is a most skillful weaver of poetic textures that well deserve to be called mythological in that they embrace both the timelessness of mythical discourse and the radical and inevitable historicity induced by the act of writing itself. There is no doubt that Wright is creating a mythology of Afro-American writing, but he is also constantly reminding himself and his readers of the precariousness of such an endeavor. His best poetry emerges from a confrontation—or what Ralph Ellison would call an "antagonistic cooperation"—between history and myth, in which myth is rendered historical and history mythical.

> Vera M. Kutzinski, "The Black Limbo: Jay Wright's Mythology of Writing," *Against the American Grain: Myth and History in William Carlos Williams, Jay Wright, and Nicolás Guillén* (Baltimore: Johns Hopkins University Press, 1987), pp. 50–51, 55

ROBERT B. STEPTO   For Wright as for Ellison—and others, too, including William Carlos Williams—the weave of community, history, and space is "already woven," and it is the poet's task to "uncover the weave." But what distinguishes Wright from these authors, and from many of his contemporaries as well, is that the weave he seeks to unveil or possibly reenact is from a loom of much larger scale. Whereas Ellison pursues the weave of a pluralized vernacular America ("America" meaning the United States), and speaks continually of the "fate" of that national geography, Wright unveils the strands and textures of the various transatlantic traditions of culture and consciousness.

Over the years, Wright has become more explicitly attentive to the tangle of black traditions binding the Americas to West Africa. One is therefore tempted to argue that from the view of literary history the poem behind Wright's art is Robert Hayden's "Middle Passage." It is worth suggesting that Wright's poetic act unlocks a Hayden line such as "Shuttles in the rocking loom of history." But claims of this sort for Wright's art are too culturally provincial and based upon too narrow a notion of what may constitute a precursory text. Wright has been "energized," as he likes to say, by texts and discourses as various as Dante's *Commedia*, Willard Van Orman Quine's work in logic, Benjamin Banneker's letters to Thomas Jefferson, J. B. Danquah's *Akan Doctrine of God*, and the jazz discourses of Albert Ayler and John Coltrane. In his art Wright is perhaps most obviously for New World readers an heir or sibling of Banneker, Hayden, Wilson Harris,

Alejo Carpentier, Eliot, Hart Crane, and Nicolás Guillén. But Augustine, Goethe, Rilke, and unnumbered, anonymous griots, singers, musicians, and the like also figure in his ancestral community. To argue, as Wright has argued, that poetic discourse is that which handles its facts with more disdain than that of, say, the mathematician or chronicler is to argue as well a rather specific definition of who the poets are or have been. This suggests the sweep and shape, as well as the discipline and drive, of Wright's aesthetic eclecticism. It suggests as well why he is now gaining the audience he has long deserved: Wright invites us to roam the cultures of the transatlantic world, to speak and know many tongues, to partake of the rituals through which we may be initiated into modes of individual and communal enhancement. In yet another age of great uncertainty, Wright enables us to imagine that breaking the vessels of the past is more an act of uncovering than sheer destruction, and that we need not necessarily choose between an intellectual and a spiritual life, for both can still be had.

Robert B. Stepto, "Introduction," *Selected Poems of Jay Wright* (Princeton: Princeton University Press, 1987), x–xi

---

HAROLD BLOOM   In Wright's powerful book, *Soothsayers and Omens*, the final chant, "The Dead," gives the central statement of his poetics, at least as I comprehend his vision. After admonishing his readers that our learning alone cannot suffice, since "it is not enough / to sip the knowledge / of our failings," the poet chants an intricate rhapsody of the self's return from its own achieved emptiness:

> The masks dance
> on this small point, and lead
> this soul, these souls,
> into the rhythm
> of the eye stripped of sight,
> the hand stripped of touch,
> the heart stripped of love,
> the body stripped of its own beginning,
> into the rhythm
> of emptiness and return,
> into the self
> moving against itself,
> into the self
> moving into itself,
> the word, and the first design.

The *askesis* here is Wright's characteristic apotropaic gesture toward tradition, toward all his traditions. As an immensely learned poet, Wright tries to defend himself against incessant allusiveness by stripping his diction, sometimes to an astonishing sparseness. The same movement in W. S. Merwin has damaged the art of one of our strongest contemporary poets, but Wright's minimalism is fortunately not nearly so prevalent. His most characteristic art returns always to that commodious lyricism I associate with American poetry at its most celebratory, in Whitman, in Stevens, in Crane, in Ashbery. ⟨. . .⟩

It is not to be believed, by me, that a verbal art this absolute will continue to suffer neglect. A Pindaric sublimity that allies Hölderlin, Rilke, and Hart Crane with Jay Wright is not now much in fashion, but that mode of high song always returns to us again. As an authentic poet of the Sublime, Wright labors to make us forsake easier pleasures for more difficult pleasures. Wright's reader is taught by him what Hölderlin and Rilke wished us to learn, which is that poetry compels us to answer the fearful triple question: more? equal to? or less than? Self is set against self, or an earlier version of the self against a later one, or culture against culture, or poem against poem. Jay Wright is a permanent American poet because he induces us to enter that agon—with past strength, our own or others'; with the desolations of culture; with the sorrows of history—and because he persuades us also that "it is not enough / to sip the knowledge / of our failings."

Harold Bloom, "Afterword," *Selected Poems of Jay Wright* (Princeton: Princeton University Press, 1987), pp. 195–97

ROBERT B. SHAW   Jay Wright is a difficult poet who makes few concessions to readers uneducated in the sources upon which his work has increasingly relied. These sources are anthropological. Wright's extensive knowledge of West African and Latin American cultures informs the structures and imbues the substance of many of his more elaborate pieces. As a black American born in New Mexico, Wright is well situated to explore cultural diversity, and as a poet he is equipped as well with a wide array of rhetorical skills. He seems in many ways a belated High Modernist; certainly his appropriation of myth and some of his particular kinds of stylistic density put one in mind of Eliot or, even more, Hart Crane, as the critics in this volume ⟨*Selected Poems of Jay Wright*⟩ both note.

I have found in this book some poems I was moved by, a great many more I was intrigued by, but not many that I am certain I understand. It is typically Wright's earlier poems which I accept (and enjoy) with fewer questions. These include some mordant descriptions of Mexican scenes, and some subtle, incisive attempts at self-definition. In these latter pieces Wright adds something of his own to the strong tradition of American poets seeking, questioning, and embracing their vocation. ⟨. . .⟩

In the later work, roughly the second half of the book, the content is frequently more esoteric and the rigor of the style does not relax to provide a helpful context in which references might be understood. ⟨. . .⟩ My distrust of the oracular increases year by year, and yet I do not wish to dismiss these poems. I would like to suggest that judgments of their value will be hard to form without the benefit of more commentary.

Robert B. Shaw, [Review of *Selected Poems of Jay Wright*], *Poetry* 152, No. 1 (April 1988): 45–46

ISIDORE OKPEWHO   We have seen journeys in Wright's earlier volumes of poetry, especially *The Homecoming Singer* and *Dimensions of History*; the journeys in *The Double Invention of Komo* are of a piece with those others in stressing what Wright conceives as the peregrine imperative in the emergent African-American personality. The journeys in this book, however, are more than a random sample of the cultures and nationalities that ultimately define the American cultural landscape. What Wright has done here is to identify what may be considered the best advertised or perhaps the most representative element in the places he visits, and to let his initiate's spirit engage with it in a dialectic that will determine the acceptability or otherwise of that element or trait within the character that the signs have set up for the initiate.

In Albuquerque, a black man's social rage and a hurt sense of pride almost get the better of his paternal duty, but good sense prevails in the end to let "the ritual fire of the moon / illuminate the dark hand / of the man's love for his son." In Bad Nauheim, the initiate's spirit is still contending with the Hitlerian complex and still rejects it:

> But I am not that boy,
> perpetrator of a strange act.
> My art is in sponging
> those who can be saved
> into wholeness.

In the end, however, the spirit learns to accommodate the "Germanic gabble" and seek its redemptive potential ("Let the new water subject me / to the danger of forgiving your injury"). Berlin presents an outlook of cold militarism ("barbed wire / and the shine / of silver in snow"), increasing noncompromise ("this city / of sealing sutures"), and isolationism ("the bottomless and shapeless / tankard of self-love"), and it would appear that here again—as in Germany generally—the spirit is a little ill at ease. In Florence (93–95), a Dantesque survey of the city's turbulent civil history yields an accommodating sense of fellowship and a heightened feeling of regeneration:

> Fellowship asserts the spirit's freedom,
> the seal of divinity . . .
> You have entered the wood;
> you turn, out of the holy waves,
> born again,
> even as trees renewed,
> pure and ready to mount to the stars.

Venice's architectural history reveals an ugliness that nevertheless turns to beauty (*"Formosa deformitas"*) in the eyes of the beholder, who opts to "cultivate open arms / to receive the blue water" threading through the city. The soul's excursions finally bring it homeward, to Mexico City and Consolapa (a little village in Mexico). At this point we are drawing towards the end of the initiation ceremony; the initiate has learned to "elevate the trinity of races in my blood"—the African, the European, and the Native American—and a romantic encounter with a woman whose "voice and body / have been turning above the name of my house" gradually reunites him with his double, so that he is ready to wake up from his ritual death.

Isidore Okpewho, "From a Goat Path in Africa: An Approach to the Poetry of Jay Wright," *Callaloo* 14, No. 3 (Summer 1991): 715–16

RON WELBURN   In the two later collections, *Elaine's Book* and *Boleros*, one realizes that Wright's quest for metaphysically derived properties of truth have indeed been assimilated, so that their subtle incorporation into individual poems and shorter poem-sequences betrays nothing of pretense. *Elaine's Book* contains the thematically engaging "Zapata and the Egungun Mask," its longest poem, in which the famed Mexican revolutionary who was a campesino addresses the Yoruba ritual mask that represents the intermediation between forces living and non-living. We are apt to find language in these two collections that is richer in metaphor than Wright's earlier poems, if that seems possible! He freely personifies inanimate objects and physical sensations: "No ruffled lace guitars clutch at the darkened windows" ("Madrid"); or the women who, knowing the autumnal flight of geese, "tell us that, if you listen, you can hear / their dove's voices ridge the air." Indeed, two of the book's short sequences, "Desire's Persistence"—whose "Winter" section contains the last example—and "The Anatomy of Resonance," are concerned with aural and visual perceptions. Several of the thirty-nine poems in *Boleros* lack titles outright, Wright preferring numbers to identify them instead. Spanish phrases, some idiomatically obscure, characterize many. Again, history, reality and myth blend without clear demarcations. Saints' days, the Muses, New England, and a Moorish-Iberian point of reference that stimulates thoughts about the cultures of the Americas are its themes. Wright's use of color is not as vivid as Wallace Stevens's, for example, but he responds to a symbolist's influence on the intellect and the senses without any lack of discipline in how he selects his images. The cover design of *Boleros* makes obvious Jay Wright's ideals of fusion and the kind of intellectual and metaphysical terrain he is willing to risk: a *bolero* is a Spanish dance at slow tempo; the figures depicted on the cover are a man and a woman in an African carving and they are playing a *balafon*, a precursor to the xylophone. Together constituting an image and impression on the senses, they demand that artist and public depend on an interactive freedom in order to attain a spiritual unity.

Ron Welburn, "Jay Wright's Poetics: An Appreciation," *MELUS* 18, No. 3 (Fall 1993): 68

◈ *Bibliography*

Death as History. 1967.
Balloons. 1968.
The Homecoming Singer. 1971.
Soothsayers and Omens. 1976.
The Albuquerque Graveyard. 1976.
Dimensions of History. 1976.

The Double Invention of Komo. 1980.
Explications/Interpretations. 1984.
Selected Poems. 1987.
Elaine's Book. 1988.
Boleros. 1991.